ARMISTIC AT YPRES 2018

Written, Compiled and Researched by
Andrew Thornton

ISBN-13: 978-1729654941

ISBN-10: 1729654940

First Published November 2018

Contents

Preface

This book has been compiled as part of my preparation as a guide for a tour to Ypres on the centenary of the Armistice, which came into effect at 11.00 o'clock on the morning of 11 November 1918 and marked the point at which hostilities ceased on the Western Front.

It is not intended to be a detailed guide of the events that took place in the Ypres Salient during the Great War, but is instead a collection of cameos of some of those who served there; individuals who are buried or commemorated in some of the cemeteries and memorials visited during the course of the tour; and also some impressions written by pilgrims who returned to the former battlefields in the years preceding the outbreak of a Second World War.

Andrew Thornton

Birmingham
November 2018

The Ramparts at Ypres, 11 November 1994

Crowds near the Ypres (Menin Gate) Memorial on 11 November 1993 on the 75th anniversary of the Armistice.

The British Forces contingent and the combined Bands of the 1st Battalion, The Devonshire and Dorset Regiment and 1st Battalion, The Cheshire Regiment at Ypres on 11 November 1993.

"To re-visit the battlefields of Belgium and France is the wish of every ex-Service man and this year I made my second pilgrimage to many a spot where I held a rifle. My first visit was when the scars of war were still fresh and unhealed on the countryside, now they are healed and man and nature have covered up that which was broken or destroyed. It is possible to mark the area in which one soldiered; the writer could make out the line of country along which he trudged from St Jean to Passchaendaele over duck-board tracks above shell holes whose lips touched in seemingly endless succession. But the country is now like that of England, sheaves of corn are stacked where twenty years ago was a sea of mud."[1]

Charles Preston – August 1937
Formerly 241276 Private C. W. Preston
1ˢᵗ Battalion, The Queen's (Royal West Surrey Regiment)

---

[1] Surrey Mirror, 27 August 1937.

The Immortal Salient

BRITISH TROOPS AT YPRES
13 OCTOBER 1914.

The first troops of the British Expeditionary Force to arrive at Ypres in 1914 were the 1/1st Northumberland Yeomanry (Hussars) (Territorial Force), who were the Divisional Cavalry to 7th Division. The remainder of 7th Division and 3rd Cavalry Division, under the command of IV Corps, arrived in the city the following day, before moving out to the east to engage the Germans advancing towards them.

They were by no means the first British soldiers to visit Ypres. In 1383 the city had been besieged by English and rebel Flemish troops from Ghent, led by Henry le Despenser, the Bishop of Norwich. The city however held out and the siege was broken as a French relief force approached.

In 1793 British troops under the command of The Duke of York marched through Ypres. Corporal Robert Brown, who served with the 1st Battalion, Coldstream Guards, made an entry in his journal for 20 August:

"Marched about five o'clock this morning, and in our route passed through the small, but strong town of Ypres and encamped near a small village called Boesinghe. The brigade of Guards lay in an orchard very pleasantly situated."[2]

During the final stages of the Napoleonic Wars Ypres was again garrisoned by British troops, in 1814 and again during the Waterloo Campaign of June 1815. The defensive fortifications around the city that had originally been constructed by Vauban following the French occupation of Ypres following the Treaty of Nimegen in 1678 were hastily reinforced under the supervision of Colonel Carmichael-Smyth of the Royal Engineers.

In 1914 German cavalrymen of the 3. Reiter-Division had briefly entered Ypres prior to the arrival of the British but left as they approached, but not before holding the Burgomaster to ransom and levying 75,000 Belgian francs from the inhabitants.

The story of the fighting around Ypres during the five years of the Great War is complex. As well as the five key "battles" fought between 1914 and 1918, which were in reality a series of large-scale operations, there were countless smaller localised engagements that took place.

The principle operations were:

- **First Battle of Ypres (19 October – 22 November 1914) – when the "salient" was formed as German forces surrounded the British and French troops on three sides.**
- **Second Battle of Ypres (22 April – 25 May 1915) – the Germans first used Chlorine gas against French and French Colonial troops on the opening day of their offensive.**

---

[2] A labourer from Libberton, near Biggar in Lanarkshire, Robert served in the Army for twenty years, five of which were spent with the 2nd Battalion of the 1st (Royal) Regiment of Foot before transferring to the Coldstream. Brown was a Corporal when he embarked for Flanders on active service in 1893 and chronicled his experiences fighting against the forces of Revolutionary France in an book which he had published on his return two years later, entitled "An Impartial Journal of a Detachment From the Brigade of Foot Guards, Commencing 20th February 1793 and ending 9th May 1795." Brown was discharged as a consequence of suffering from rheumatism, aged 40, on 27 March 1798 having attained the rank of Serjeant, and was admitted to receive a pension from the Royal Hospital at Chelsea. His book was republished in 2008 as "Corporal Brown's Campaign in the Low Countries: Recollections of a Coldstream Guards in the Early Campaigns against Revolutionary France 1793-1795" by Leonaur Ltd.

A German photograph of the battlefield towards Ypres covered in snow, c. 1917.

- Third Battle of Ypres (31 July – 10 November 1917) – often erroneously referred to as "Passchendaele." There were also local operations at Passchendaele and on the Polderhoek Spur in December 1917.
- The actions fought in the Ypres Salient during the German Lys Offensives between 10 and 29 April, which saw the British Second Army withdraw from the Passchendaele Ridge to defensive lines a short distance outside Ypres.
- The Fourth Battle of Ypres[3] (28 September – 2 October 1918) – The British Second Army, the Belgian Army and three French Corps, under the overall command of Albert I, King of the Belgians, swept across the former battlefields and advanced deep into Flanders.

On 14 October 1918 the last German long-range artillery shell landed in Ypres, four years almost to the day on which British troops first arrived in the city. As a gesture acknowledging the sacrifice of Ypres, the British Government conferred the Military Cross on the city, while the French awarded the Croix de Guerre.

---

[3] Sometimes referred to by some historians as the "fifth" battle.

Ypres – October 1914

L/393 Lance-Corporal Ernest Blackwell, a Reservist of the 17th (Duke of Cambridge's) Lancers attached to the 2nd Life Guards, wrote a cheerful letter to friends in Birmingham and was able to post it in Ypres:

"We have had some good times, rough times, and lots of excitement, but don't worry, I know how to look after myself, and the men I am in charge of are all experienced men. Our troop officer is great; he can speak the language and fears nothing. All of us would follow him anywhere and come out O.K. Our troops are inspiring confidence here. No matter what has happened in some of the towns we have passed through, first sight of a khaki uniform has made the inhabitants quite happy again. The Germans won't face us if they can get out of it. We have been chasing them all over the show. Only fifteen of our troop surprised fifty or more Uhlans on Tuesday, and they galloped away. We could not chase them at the time as we were dismounted and drinking coffee in a small village when they galloped up the street. Stokes and me were the first to get a shot in, but we were surprised to see them gallop away. One of our corporals yesterday dismounted to attend to a wounded German, and the brute turned over and shot him dead, so that has taught us another lesson. All the prisoners we have captured are fed up with the war. A lot of us think it will be practically over by Christmas. Of course, we don't get much news about the Navy.

17TH LANCERS

C.
W.
C.

CORPORAL
COX J.
ROBINSON F.
WILLIAMS W.

LANCE CORPORAL
BLACKWELL E.
HAMBLY B.
NIELD W.
PAYNE H. A.

PRIVATE
ADAMS W. S.
ALLISON C.
ARCHER O. J.
BRANDRAM W.
CHAPMAN G.
CLARK J.
COOK T.
DAVIES T. W.
DOCKERAY R.

PRIVATE
GOODCHILD A.
SERVED AS
SMITH A.
HEWITT A.
HUGHES B.
JONES A.
KINGSWELL A. H.
LEA G. E.
LLOYD T. C.
LYNCH O.
McLAREN D.
MASON G.
MUDD S. G.
PETTIGREW J. A.
PRATT J. B.
RAFFERTY P.
SAINSBURY F.
SAVILLE J.
SPENCER J. H.
WAGSTAFFE F.

COI
COX R
MORRI

LANC
DIGGI
GAMI
HERI
HOL
POW
SHE
TH
WA

My word! I am enjoying myself. We have the lot retreating where we are. Let them all know that I am O.K. and buck up. Don't forget that "feed" when I come home, and if you have a chance of helping a Belgian who is hard up, do it. They have been wonderfully good to us, among other things, (and) have kept us going with cigarettes."[4]

Born at St John's in Worcester, Blackwell had joined the 17th Lancers at Birmingham in 1907 and, on being transferred to the Reserve, was employed at the Moseley Road Depot of the Birmingham Corporation Tramways Department at the outbreak of the war. He was posted to the 2nd Life Guards at Ludgershall before they embarked for the front.

Lance-Corporal Blackwell was killed on 31 October 1914 at Verbrandenmolen and is commemorated on Panel 5 of the Ypres (Menin Gate) Memorial with other members of the 17th Lancers.

---

[4] Birmingham Daily Gazette, 4 November 1914.

Klein Zillebeke – November 1914

"It was dead of night when we first went to earth. All the time I was there it was warm! The shower of shells from the German artillery, which we could never see, was ceaseless. Day and night they screamed and burst overhead, but one gets used to them, and these showers, if you are under cover, of course, are treated as lightly as you might treat showers of rain. Shrapnel isn't so bad even if you are in the open, for you can judge where they will burst, and as they scatter forward and outward like an inflated paper bag which bursts at the sides, there is some chance of calculating where the fragments will strike, but the "Jack Johnsons," they're devil's eggs, and no mistake. With the enemy's foremost trench often within less than 150 yards of the first British trench, the need of watchful outposts is obvious. Every man is often his own outpost. It may be in the day-time that every eighth man will act as look-out, but at night it is always every other man, and sometimes more than that. It is a strange, mysterious game this battle at Ypres - absolutely an artillery duel, with here and there a game of hide and seek in the forests and woods of the neighbourhood. Cavalry are having nothing to do, and, in fact, many of our mounted men are in the trenches, with their horses away back at the base."[5]

3/8305 Private Arthur Twigg
"D" Company, 2nd Battalion, The Oxfordshire and Buckinghamshire Light Infantry

Born on 9 October 1879, Private Twigg was a Special Reservist and came from New Bradwell in Buckinghamshire. His family home being at 64 Spencer Street and he was employed as a railway labourer. Twigg was drafted to the 2nd Battalion as a reinforcement on 11 September 1914 and was wounded on 1 November when he was shot in the hand.

Twigg later transferred to the 1st Garrison Battalion, The Royal Warwickshire Regiment and was issued with the clasp and roses for his 1914 Star on 9 February 1938, his home address being 17 High Street in New Bradwell. Arthur Twigg was at that time employed as a gas fitters' mate at the London, Midland and Scottish Railway Works at Wolverton. He died in June 1956, aged 76.

---

[5] Wolverton Express, 4 December 1914.

South of Gheluvelt – November 1914

"On Nov. 9 we were in the firing line – hell on earth – when the Germans broke through the left of our line, so we formed up, fixed bayonets, and charged them back again. We lost a lot of our brave fellows, but they lost more. We captured 32 of them and two maxim guns. They were pleased to be captured. They gave us cigarettes, and even their watches to some of our fellows.

Next day my trench was blown up, and three of us were buried. We were got out somehow, and when it was dark we scrambled back through the woods to the hospital. This is the second time I have been buried, and I hope the last. I've got a bullet through my hat, one through the handle of my entrenching tool, one through the side of my bayonet, one through the leg of my trousers – and then they couldn't hit me. Rotten shots.

I shan't forget going into hospital. It was like going into heaven. Some hot tea, a clean shirt, and a bath, and above all a spring bed with white sheets, and we couldn't hear the 'Jack Johnsons.'"[6]

7550 Private William Kirk
1ˢᵗ Battalion, The Bedfordshire Regiment

Born at Marylebone on 23 November 1885, William Kirk was aged eighteen years and six months when he attested at London for The Bedfordshire Regiment on 18 May 1903. He was living with his parents at 20 Preston Street in Kentish Town and was employed as a glass engraver at the time of his enlistment. Kirk arrived at the Regimental Depot at Kempston Barracks the day following his attestation, and on completing his training was posted to the 2ⁿᵈ Battalion at Colchester on 21 August. Appointed a Lance-Corporal on 15 March 1904, Kirk was awarded his first Good Conduct badge on 18 May 1905, but was deprived of his stripe on 12 September. While stationed with the 2ⁿᵈ Battalion at Bordon he also qualified as a Mounted Infantryman at the Mounted Infantry School in Longmoor, and passed his 3ʳᵈ Class Certificate in Education on 4 July 1905. After completing three years with the Colours, he was transferred to the Class A Army Reserve on 17 May 1906.

Employed as a house painter and decorator, William married Ethel Lydia Waite at St Pancras Register Office on 9 April 1910, and they had four

---

[6] The People, 29 November 1914.

children together, their son John Robert being born on 4 September 1914 while his father was on active service. In 1914 William and his family lived at 21 Milton Grove in Tufnell Park.

Mobilised following the declaration of war, Kirk reported at Kempston Barracks on 5 August 1914 and was posted to the 3rd (Special Reserve) Battalion two days later. Later that month he was drafted to the 1st Battalion from the 3rd Bedfords at Felixstowe, and landed in France on 21 August. Private Kirk was wounded on 10 November while in positions south of Gheluvelt, and on being admitted to the Royal Victoria Hospital at Netley was posted onto the strength of the Regimental Depot on 16 November. He was discharged from hospital on 21 November and, after a period of leave, joined the 3rd Battalion at Felixstowe on 7 December. On 20 January 1915 Kirk was awarded ten days' confinement to barracks for improper conduct.

Posted to the Provisional Battalion forming at Denham in Buckinghamshire on 20 July 1915, that unit became the 1st Garrison Battalion of The Essex Regiment the following day and Private Kirk was transferred to that regiment on 31 July, being issued with the regimental number 22412. On 24 August the battalion embarked at Southampton for service on Mudros, arriving on the island on 3 September. Kirk went on to serve at Gallipoli and in Egypt before being invalided home, suffering from debility following an operation. Admitted to the Welsh Metropolitan War Hospital at Whitchurch on 4 April 1916, he was posted to the Regimental Depot at Warley Barracks on 5 April 1916. Kirk was discharged from hospital on 18 April and was transferred to the 1st (Reserve) Garrison Battalion, The Suffolk Regiment at Gravesend on 28 April. On 17 May he was discharged on the termination of his period of engagement.

William was sent the clasp and roses for his 1914 Star on 17 March 1920 and in 1939 is recorded as working as a builder's foreman, painter and decorator, residing with his wife Ethel and two sons at 4 Retcar Street in St Pancras.

William Kirk died in 1973, aged 87.

Ypres – November 1914

The Lichfield Mercury published an anonymous account of a soldiers' experiences during the Great War, in weekly parts between June and October 1934, under the collective title: ""War in the Trenches - As Seen Down a Local Tommy's Gunsights." The author of the memoir was **Reg Evans D.C.M.**, who lived at Armitage in Staffordshire and ran a newsagents' shop in the village.

In November 1914, he was serving as a Lance-Corporal in "F" Company of the 1/1ˢᵗ Battalion, The Hertfordshire Regiment (Territorial Force), and described his journey to France and his first experience of war near Ypres:

"We were up very early on the morning of November 5ᵗʰ, greatly to the annoyance of our host, who told us plainly that he wasn't going to have his house upset at that time of the morning, orders or no orders. We cheekily told him he needn't bother, as we were off to France to keep the Huns away from him; and Charley said bluntly that he hoped if they did land, some of them would be billetted on him for a change. We had to do a certain amount of hanging about once we had reported in the market square, and didn't finally leave Bury station until half-past eleven.[7] How we pushed out our chests and roared "Tipperary" as we passed through the town – what a scramble for pieces of chalk to mark "To Berlin" on the carriages – and then the train steamed out amid a roar of cheers, and we were started off on the great adventure.

It was night when we reached Southampton and proceeded straight on board an old cattle ship, "City of Chester," and shortly after midnight, accompanied by warships, we set sail. It was beautifully moonlight, and Charley and I wandered about the boat. To find ourselves actually on board a ship was a new experience to us both, and there was lots to interest us, especially the number of other vessels which, under cover of night, were travelling in both directions. Besides, there was a great want of room for sleeping accommodation. Early in the morning biscuits and tea were served out, and we finally disembarked about two p.m. at Le Havre, where we had a good uphill march along a rotten road till we reached the rest camp.[8] Here we were packed in, sixteen men to a tent, and in spite of the cold only one blanket per man was issued. Reveille was at seven, and though there was a rotten fog we were turned out for P.T. and later a route march and an

---

[7] Bury St Edmunds.
[8] No. 2 Rest Camp.

inspection. I was lucky enough afterwards to get a pass to Le Havre, and went down on a tram to have a look round and air my French.[9]

The sight of a sovereign acted as a talisman to the keeper of an estaminet or beer-house, and he proceeded to supply me with what seemed unlimited drinks and 27 francs in change. When I got back to the camp I found it all in disorder, orders having been received to stand by ready to move at once, but we managed to get a little sleep amongst the baggage. The sounding of the alarm about two o'clock set everybody stirring, and we were soon off to the station, where we had breakfast in the yard, whilst a long line of horse boxes, painted "8 chevaux, 40 hommes" (8 horses or 40 men) were coupled up to form our train. In these, all that day and the following night, in the most cramped positions imaginable, we crawled on through the country, knowing nothing of our destination until we found ourselves at St Omer. Whilst we were detraining rumours flew around that this was G.H.Q. and we were to be General French's bodyguard, but we were soon disillusioned, and found ourselves once more on the road, where at a dirty little village called Tatenheim (sic), or some such name, we were distributed to find billets in the various cowsheds.[10]

Next morning we were out about seven to receive instruction on the new rifle we had been issued with, as they were very different from those we had used in England. In the afternoon, in pouring rain, we had an inspection by Sir J. French and his staff. The men swore that the Commander-in-Chief hadn't turned up; and when we got back to the billets the news that we should probably stay where we were for at least a fortnight confirmed the pessimists, who insisted that our sole job would be to furnish guards for G.H.Q.[11]

Next morning we were out in the filthy blackness of a November morning at 5.30, full marching order, to dig trenches the other side of St Omer. About 11 o'clock up dashed an orderly asking for the officer in charge. Back to our billets at once. Off we set, full speed, sweating and swearing. We were to join

---

[9] The 1/1st Herts suffered their first loss on active service when 2682 Private Charles Castle, a painter from Ware who had attested at Hertford on 5 September, died while at No. 2 Rest Camp on 7 November, aged 35. He was the son of Francis and Elizabeth Castle and is buried at Ste. Marie Cemetery: Division 14, Row D, Grave 3. His widow, Emily, is recorded as living at 21 West Street in Ware after the war.

[10] The 1/1st Herts arrived at St Omer at 7 o'clock on the morning of 9 November, after travelling through the night. They then marched to billets at Tatinghem, where they remained until 11 November.

[11] Field Marshal Sir John French had in fact inspected only one company of the Battalion.

17

the 4th Brigade of Guards at Ypres.[12] Only about three-quarters of an hour to spare to get dinner, emergency rations and water, then all aboard a fleet of motor 'buses.

As we started we could hear the distant mutter of guns, but we had not the slightest idea what had taken place to cause our being sent forward so urgently. Our only official stop was at Cassel, where we all got out for a few minutes to stretch our legs, and some were lucky enough to get hold of a bottle or two of wine. Soon after we resumed our journey it started to rain in torrents. Those on the outside came crowding down for shelter, and before long, such was our state, equipment, rifles and men all crowded in an indescribable heap, I was glad to escape outside to avoid suffocation.

The bad condition of the road caused frequent stoppages to our convoy, and once we had to turn out and help haul one of the 'buses out of the mud in which it was stuck; but we finally arrived at Poperinghe amid a terrific hail and snowstorm, wet to the skin. Here, after a considerable delay, we were served out with rum and a day's rations, and then, falling in by companies and sections, we started about midnight our first march to the trenches. By the time we reached Ypres the rain had ceased, and the moon shining brightly showed us our first sight of war. Here and there houses lay in battered heaps across the road, blocking our path, and we occasionally saw a dead body amongst the ruins.[13]

I was too tired to look in the wood for one of the dug-outs which we were told were there, so another man and I, wet through as we were, curled up together in some undergrowth and had a couple of hours' sleep. When we awoke we managed, after great difficulty, to make a Dixie of tea, and, scrounging round with Gilbert, found a large dug-out just outside the wood which was unoccupied. With the captain's permission we took our kit over, and we were just making ourselves comfortable when orders came to move. We passed no end of artillery, and at last found ourselves in another wood, where we had to dig ourselves in on account of the shelling which was taking place. It rained incessantly all day, and just as it got dark we had to turn out again and go back to our morning quarters. Gilbert was whacked to the wide, but between us we got him along somehow, and eventually about half a

---

[12] The 1/1st Herts were not formally attached to 4th (Guards) Brigade until 20 November at Meteren.
[13] As the 1/1st Herts marched through Ypres, the Battalion came under artillery fire. One Officer and one Other Rank were hit by shell fragments, but were only slightly injured and only the Other Rank required any medical attention.

dozen of us shot packs and rifles and equipment into the top of the dug-out in the pouring rain and crawled inside, where we lay in a heap till morning.

When I woke up I was half perished with cold and damp, and had scarcely any feeling in my legs. The rain had been soaking into the dug-out all night, and our equipment and rifles outside were in an awful condition. We made some tea, and fags and bacca were issued, as well as two biscuits per man.

Looking round we could see two or three farms burning, and as we watched a calf wandering near our shelter was killed. Lord! the very earth seemed to stink of death, so fought over has this ground been, and we felt anything but happy over our immediate prospects. Next day we made a set at the unlucky calf and it was not long before it was hacked up and being cooked, but alarms of aeroplanes overhead caused a sudden dousing of fires and a posting of sentries to keep a look out for these unwelcome visitors. Cold bacon was issued, and we were told to eat our emergency rations as there was nothing else come up for us, and about four o'clock Captain Smeatham[14] came round and warned us to be ready to move again at a moment's notice. Aeroplanes had been seen dropping lights over the wood, and shortly afterwards there was a terrific noise and three or four large shells exploded near us.

This seemed the commencement of heavy firing which shook the earth with the shock. The noise was like a rushing wind, branches came crashing down from the trees, and in the gathering darkness the scene seemed indescribable. We were glad to get on the move again, heavy "coal-boxes" bursting all round us, and the mud on the road, being now knee-deep, made the feeling of desolation complete. Every now and then somebody would disappear with a splash into a shell-hole, but we draggled on, finally landing in what we were told was the reserve line of the wood. Another nightmare night, and feeling pretty rotten in the morning, sought out the M.O.'s cart in the rear. Luckily I fell in with some men of the Worcestershire Regiment,[15] with whom I spent the afternoon, and had a good feed before I wandered back.

The wood was covered with equipment and ammunition of all sorts, British, French and German, and other signs of the severe fighting which had recently taken place there.[16] We moved off about 6.30 to the trenches, which were two or three feet deep in running water, so that rest was impossible. My

---

[14] Captain Lovel Francis Smeatham.
[15] Probably soldiers from the 2nd Battalion, which served with 5th Brigade of 2nd Division.
[16] Lichfield Mercury, 6 July 1934.

first turn of duty was from 10 till 12, and about one o'clock, and again later, word was passed along to open rapid fire, as the Germans were attacking. Our new rifles, the working of which we had got only the most elementary knowledge, were all jammed, bolts wouldn't act, and when they did, and we got a round off, away shot the bayonet over the parapet – and then there was a scramble. "If Jerry only knew," we told one another, and what with this and the cold we began to realise the true meaning of the saying "Fed up and far from home."[17]

As it got lighter again we could see heaps of dead just beyond our trench. In a smashed-up farm on our right we found the body of a Prussian Guardsman, and nearby a British Tommy with a gaping wound in his stomach. Just a short distance separated them in death, and all round were other signs of the terrific hand-to-hand fighting which had taken place. The swishing of shots overhead cut our explorations short and we scuttled back to our trench, and shortly afterwards we found ourselves back on the road again with the news that the French were taking over that part of the line.[18]

We met them as we went back, and their straggling column and ours intermingled, but flowing in opposite directions, added to the feeling of being right off the earth and in a strange sphere, the thunder of the artillery in an incessant roll sounding like the efforts of a gigantic blacksmith to hammer things straight.

We lay that night as best we could in our old dug-out, and the next day as well. We had been over a week without a wash or shave and were plastered with filth, and the news we received of the death of Lord Roberts seemed quite in keeping with the state of our feelings.[19]

After a day or two of this existence, short of water and rations, with no light of any kind, so that we were forced to stay in our dug-outs soon after 4 o'clock because of the darkness, we had orders to be ready to move at once. There was a sharp frost by now, and this made the roads a bit better, though they were still in an awful state, and our legs seemed almost unable to

[17] The 1/1st Herts had relieved the 2nd Battalion, The Oxfordshire and Buckinghamshire Light Infantry on the evening of 14 November in positions between Polygon Wood and Nonne-Bosschen. Three companies were deployed in the front line and five were in reserve. The fighting that Lance-Corporal Evans saw the evidence of had taken place on 11 November.

[18] 153e Régiment d'Infanterie de Ligne. The relief took place on 16 November.

[19] Field Marshall Frederick Roberts V.C., 1st Earl Roberts, was taken ill with pneumonia while on a visit to France to meet troops of the Indian Corps and died at St Omer on 14 November 1914, aged 82.

support us.[20] To our surprise we found ourselves once more passing through Ypres, but there was practically no shelling, and only the lights from the burning debris to guide us."[21]

***

The son of Frances Evans, Reginald Josiah Thomas Evans, who was also known as Jack, was born on 10 January 1888 and was baptised at St George's Church in Camberwell on 2 March of that year. Reginald spent most of his childhood in the Wanstead Infant Orphan Asylum before becoming an apprentice wood borer at G. B. Kent and Son Ltd., at the Gade Brush Factory at Apsley. He joined "F" Company of The Hertfordshire Regiment (Territorial Force) at Hemel Hempstead in 1913, being issued with the regimental number 2170. Reginald was also a member of the Junior Imperial League and had organised the raising of funds for the Ulster Volunteer Force, as well as volunteering to fight with the U.V.F. should Home Rule for Ireland be confirmed. This, as he later recorded in his memoirs, caused a serious conflict of interests as a serving Territorial.[22]

On the declaration of war Reginald was embodied for service, and was recorded as the first Territorial to report for duty at the Drill Hall in Hemel Hempstead.[23] After training at Bury St Edmunds, where he volunteered for "Imperial Service" overseas, he disembarked in France with "F" Company of the 1/1st Battalion, The Hertfordshire Regiment at Le Havre on 6 November 1914. The 1/1st Herts were soon in action near Ypres and were attached to 4th (Guards) Brigade of 2nd Division on 22 November. In January 1915, the battalion was reorganised as four companies, and Reginald joined No. 2 Company of the "Herts Guards", as the Territorials had now become affectionately known by their comrades of the Foot Guards battalions.

---

[20] The 1/1st Herts took over trenches from 6th Cavalry Brigade a mile south-east of Zillebeke on 17 November. 2270 Corporal Ernest Boardman and 2238 Private Frederick James Darlow were killed on 18 November, and 2504 Private William Butts, 2747 Private George Haslear Catlin, 2518 Private George Edward Ellis, 2426 Private Walter William Flanders, 2428 Private Joseph William Johnson, 1911 Private Frank Pulley, 2636 Private Phillip James Robinson and 2746 Private Henry West all died on 19 November. The Battalion was relieved by the 2nd Battalion, Coldstream Guards and marched via Ypres to billets at Meteren.
[21] Lichfield Mercury, 13 July 1934.
[22] Lichfield Mercury, 22 June 1934.
[23] Hertfordshire, Hemel Hempstead Gazette and West Herts Advertiser, 8 August 1914 and Lichfield Mercury, 22 June 1934.

Reginald was a Corporal when he was awarded the Distinguished Conduct Medal later in 1915 for his actions while serving in the front line at Cuinchy. The citation for the award was published in The London Gazette on 16 November:

"For conspicuous gallantry and ability at Cuinchy on 22nd September 1915, when he went out in bright moonlight 150 yards to see how far the wire had been cut by artillery fire. He made an exhaustive examination of it, remained out an hour and a half, and returned with a report which was most valuable. He knew that our machine-guns were ordered to open fire at 10 p.m. but in order to complete his reconnaissance thoroughly he did not return till 10.30 p.m. He has frequently volunteered for and carried out useful patrol work of this nature."

Evans was shot in the mouth and severely wounded in February 1916 and was evacuated to hospital in England, where he underwent reconstructive plastic surgery at the Cambridge Military Hospital in Aldershot. On his recovery he was transferred to The Royal Sussex Regiment and posted to the 11th (Service) Battalion, seeing more active service fighting the Bolsheviks in North Russia during 1918 and 1919. Reginald held the rank of Sergeant on his demobilisation.

He returned to Hemel Hempstead and was issued with the clasp and roses for his 1914 Star on 1 December 1921. Reginald later moved to Staffordshire, where he married Evelyn Minnie Walker in 1924. Together they had four children (one of whom died in infancy) and Reginald ran a newsagents in Armitage, near Rugeley.

Reginald Evans D.C.M. died at Farladys in Armitage on 11 February 1943 and an obituary was published in The Lichfield Mercury on 19 February:

"The village of Armitage has suffered another great loss in the passing of Mr Reginald Evans ("Reg") at his home at Farladys on Thursday last, after a long and painful illness, patiently borne. Truly it could be said of him "He loved his fellowmen," for his life was one of service for others. A devoted husband and father, much sympathy is felt for his widow and three children. One of the Old Contemptibles of the Great War, he joined up in August, 1914 (sic), was in France November, 1914, twice mentioned in despatches, and awarded the D.C.M. for conspicuous bravery on September 22, 1915. In February, 1916, he was grievously wounded, and for many months was in hospital, where twelve operations were performed. Failing to be passed again for service in France he volunteered for the Russian Expeditionary Force, and was in Russia when the Armistice was signed. Upon his return to England he settled in Armitage, and but for a short time in London has lived there ever since, taking a quiet pride in working for the good of the village, particularly amongst the ex-Servicemen, who knew him as their friend. Whilst acting as secretary of the British Legion Joint Benevolent Committee he fought for benefits for disabled ex-Servicemen where cases have seemed almost hopeless, and won them.

Apart from his activities connected with the British Legion, in which he held many important official appointments, he was Clerk to the Armitage-with-Handsacre Parish Council, a position which again enabled him to work for the welfare of the village.

At the outbreak of the present war he was already a member of the local Observer Corps, but later, upon its formation, joined the L.D.V., and became a Lieutenant in the Home Guard, doing his bit in this until ill health forced him to resign early last year. Most of his youth was spent in Hemel Hampsted (sic), where he was secretary of the Junior Imperial League.

It is worthy to note that his widow's family have been connected with the village of Armitage for over 100 years, and that her grandfather, William Wood, was the first headmaster of the Armitage National School when it was opened in 1839."

Reg Evans' funeral took place on 14 February and he was buried in the churchyard of St John the Baptist in the village.

The memorial plaque erected to all ranks of the 1/1st Hertfordshire Regiment who died while serving around Ypres that was erected inside St George's Memorial Church.

At 6 o'clock on the morning of 21 February 1915, the Germans detonated three mines under the trenches held by "D" Squadron of the 16th (The Queen's) Lancers at Groenenburg Farm near Zillebeke, and then made a quick assault to take the position. Fierce hand-to-hand fighting ensued as the surviving Lancers tried to hold back the attack. Reinforcements from "A" Squadron and a reserve Troop from "D" Squadron quickly moved up to hold the line, but the trench that had been mined was lost. A counter-attack was made three hours after the mines had been exploded but, despite a request for support, the French infantry neighbouring the Lancers initially would not join the attack unless ordered to do so by their commanding officer. Eventually, the French commander came up the line and the troops moved forward, but suffered heavy casualties. "A" Squadron of the 20th Hussars also joined the counter-attack, but was unable to retake the captured trench. The 16th Lancers lost seven Officers and 47 Other Ranks killed, wounded and missing during the action.

5009 Squadron Quartermaster-Sergeant Frank William Brill, of the 16th (The Queen's) Lancers wrote a detailed account of his regiment's tour in the trenches at Zillebeke to his father, who had also served with the 16th Lancers and lived in Cheltenham:

"I will tell you about our trip on trench duty.

We left our billets loaded up with all sorts of kit and boarded motor-'buses which took us about 16 miles, where we dismounted and proceeded to a large, empty reformatory, in which place we remained five days, as reserve for the other half of the brigade which were actually in the trenches. This place we stopped in is just in range of the German big guns, and every day they let us know it by bombarding us for about half an hour. As soon as it commenced we were directed to the cellars, where we were comparatively safe, although their heavy shells used to shake the building through and through. On one occasion I was in company with Mr ---------, and just after we retired to the cellars a shell passed straight through the building adjoining that one we had just left. Of course, you can guess it was very trying to the nerves, as one never had any warning until the shells actually arrived. At 3 a.m. on the 18th we left billets to go in support of the French, who were expecting an attack. Nothing occurred until we commenced to return by twos and threes over the open country, and some of our men were spotted, and the German artillery gave them some shrapnel, which, unfortunately, killed one and wounded four of our men. The same night we started for our five-mile walk to take up our duty in the trenches, and owing to the roads being shelled intermittently, we had to keep to the open country. The country here is awful, water lying about everywhere, and shell holes all over the place; not a building in this district but what has been made untenable by shell fire. This walk seemed interminable. Weighed down with kit necessary for our stay in the trenches and often over our knees in liquid mud, it was a most trying experience. Eventually we arrived and relieved the --------- Hussars, who, you may be sure, were pleased to get away. We immediately took up our duties, and at 3 a.m. I retired to try a sleep.

Now, to describe the trenches. Immediately opposite my front the enemy trenches were about 60 yards away, but it varied to the left and right; in some places they are as close as 15 yards. Between the trenches, which are situated in a pine wood, the ground is one tangle of fallen and splintered trees, barbed wire, etc., which makes a rapid advance by either side impossible. The bottoms of the trenches are more or less liquid mud everywhere, but the authorities have thoughtfully provided rubber boots for the men. The trenches have to be constantly drained, for which duty men are told off. At the rear of the trenches are what are called drainage trenches, which carry off the mud and water to the country behind, where we are finished with it. The difficulties of good drainage are great, to judge by one of my experiences. I found one of the drainage trenches blocked up, and in endeavouring to clear it we came across two dead men, evidently left there unburied during some previous fight – not a nice job to get on with.

The men off-duty sleep in what are known as dug-outs. These are little shelters burrowed out of the earth, about 2½ feet high and covered with branches and earth. When you can find a dry one it is fairly comfortable, but with so much rain falling that is a difficult matter. Warmth is provided by braziers at various parts of the trenches, and very comfortable they are; but when you know that every bit of coke and charcoal has to be carried up by hand you can guess there is not too much fuel left to burn. We did fairly well for grub; of course, no bread was issued, but with the aid of the brazier I got some hot drinks through the day and night, in the shape of tea, cocoa, coffee (tinned), and Oxo, which what is needed more than anything. It was extremely difficult to get a proper rest, as most of the day and night shells would be whizzing over our heads hurrying and shrieking on their journey of destruction. At night an intermittent rifle rifle was kept up on both sides, and occasionally someone would imagine an attack was about to take place, and then there would be a proper roar of musketry until it was found out to be a false alarm. During these attacks star-lights would be fired, and the whole line lit up almost like daylight. It was one of my duties to fire these. The German snipers were very clever and audacious, and one had to be careful all through the day not to show a bit of oneself. Of course, we had our snipers out also, and they did very well. One of my men sniping was armed with a sporting rifle with telescopic sights, which made his shooting very accurate. The particular sniper who worried my sector of the trench we nicknamed Otto, and I'm pleased to say, although he expended much ammunition, he did not get anyone.

Our first night in the trenches an unfortunate thing happened. One of the dug-outs fell in and suffocated and partially buried one of our men; poor chap, he was dead when he had been dug out. Our disasterous day was Sunday, the 21ˢ. About 5.45 a.m. we were all awakened by a terrific explosion, and everyone at one went to his post. Shortly afterwards word was passed down the line that a portion of D Squadron trenches had been mined and blown up by the Germans, who were rapidly occupying that part of our trenches. The position was critical, but our men rallied on a new line and held on like grim death, and some of our machine guns were also brought up. Two troops of my squadron were sent in support, and hard work they had, as some of the communication trenches had to be blocked to prevent the further advance of the Germans. The enemy now started to throw hand-bombs and to use their trench mortar, and we replied likewise. I assisted a sergeant of my squadron with the hand-bombs, and we got some good hits, every one of which raised a cheer from our boys, as the enemy were in some trenches only about 15 yards away.

After that I took up a rifle and spotted a German taking comfortable pot-shots at our fellows, so I waited on him and the fourth time he showed himself I got him right through the forehead, so he will fire no more. Just at this time an artillery officer arrived with a trench mortar, and I assisted him in firing it, and it was great sport, as the bombs they threw are terrific in explosion.

Just about this time I was talking to one of the officers, and all of a sudden something hit a tree immediately in front of us, and he rolled over. Poor chap, he was hit in the arm. I managed to bind him up, and he got away to the rear. It was eleven o'clock before I got a chance to look round, and I then had a drink of water and a bit of grub, and afterwards carried sandbags, ammunition, and cleaned rifles, which were in an awful state. Our officers and men were good, and there was no thought of further retirement, although our casualties were heavy. The French came up to help us, and in their advance lost 60 out of 82 men in the company. The following are our casualties: Major Campbell, slightly wounded, Major Neave, wounded and died; Capt. Nash, killed; Capt. Evans, wounded; Lieut. King, killed; Lieut. Beech, killed; Lieut. Cross, blown up and missing; Lieut. Ryan, blown up and missing; Lieut. Patrick, seriously wounded; Lieut. Thornton, wounded; Lieut. Allen, wounded; and the total regimental casualties are 80 killed, wounded and missing, including officers. Of course, a lot of the missing must have been killed in the explosion. Of course, after this everybody was on the qui vive for mining, and two men in my squadron pluckily volunteered to go out at night and endeavour to find out if the Germans were diggin towards us but they discovered nothing.

On Tuesday, the 23rd, we were relieved at 12 midnight, and after a long walk arrived at our motor-'buses. I was soon asleep, and did not wake up until we arrived at our billets. I then had breakfast and had a sleep; a bath and change at dinner-time, and then another sleep; and we started work on Thursday morning. On Friday we changed billets again, and are back in the same district as before, about 25 miles to the west."[24]

Frank Brill was commissioned in the field on 15 July 1915 and joined the 6th Dragoon Guards (Carabiniers). He attained the rank of Captain and continued to serve with the regiment after the Armistice, being issued with the clasp and roses for his 1914 Star on 1 July 1920.

---

[24] Gloucestershire Echo, 4 March 1915.

After leaving the Army, he lived at Box Tree Cottage at Badgeworth, and in later life resided at 2 Fairfield Park Road in Cheltenham. Frank Brill died at Cheltenham on 24 February 1962.

Two Lancers from "D" Squadron who took part in the fighting later wrote home describing their experiences. **L/3884 Lance-Corporal Thomas Copsey** gave an account of the action to his mother at Tunbridge Wells:

"No doubt you have seen in the papers what the 16th Lancers went through in the trenches. I was in the very trench that was blown up, and shall never forget it as long as I live. We are going to have another turn at them in a week or two's time, when we hope to have a good revenge. I must get even with them, as they have got my haversack with cigarettes, tobacco, razor, and every mortal thing that I possessed. Even my hat got blown off and buried. We are having a few days' rest, exercising our horses in the morning and learning to throw bombs and dig trenches in the afternoon."[25]

Another description was written by **L/2655 Lance-Sergeant Horace Harper** to his friend, Mr H. Allen, who lived at 29 Salisbury Street in Bedford:

"Just a line to let you know that I am quite well. We have been out of the trenches nearly a month now. Don't know when we are going up again. The last time we were in five days, leaving our horses in billets and going up in motor buses. It was the nearest I have been to the German trenches, only 20 yards away. All was quiet until Sunday morning, Mar. (sic – February) 21st, when at dawn the Germans blew our trench up and immediately clambered over the parapet on top of us. Well, we made a fight for it, which was fairly hot while it lasted. We were forced to yield some ground, entrenching ourselves 50 yards further back. A counter-attack was made with the assistance of the French. We could not get at them with the bayonet, their fire was too murderous, so had to fall back. Our casualties were heavy. We had nearly all our officers put out of action, 6 killed and 4 wounded. In the ranks my squadron suffered most, having just half killed and wounded. Our Chaplain took a snapshot of us who were left."[26]

Corporal Harper had landed in France on 17 August 1914 and was later promoted to the rank of Sergeant. He was transferred to the Section A Army Reserve on 13 March 1919 issued with the clasp and roses for his 1914 Star on 4 February 1922.

---

[25] Kent and Sussex Courier, 2 April 1915. Lance-Corporal Copsey died on 25 May 1915 near Hooge and is commemorated on the Ypres (Menin Gate) Memorial.
[26] Bedfordshire Times and Independent, 16 April 1915.

BURIED WHILST HELPING OUR ALLIES.

5402 Lance-Sergeant Gilbert Percy Liggins was one of eleven 16th Lancers who were reported as missing following the explosion of the mines under "D" Squadron's trench on 21 February 1915. His fate was still uncertain when news was published in The Leamington Spa Courier on 5 March 1915:

SGT. GILBERT LIGGINS MISSING.

"Official notice was received by the wife of Sgt. Gilbert Liggins (16[th]Lancers) on Monday last that her husband had been missing since the 21st February. Sgt. Liggins went to France on the 17th August, and up to the 21st ult. had been in the thick of the fighting. He had been promoted from Corporal during the war. He is one of the finest horsemen in his regiment, and was amongst those who rode at Olympia. Trooper (sic) J. Carter, of the 9th Lancers, who was invalided home three weeks ago, reported that his regiment had relieved the 16th Lancers after their trenches were blown in, and that he feared that Sergeant Liggins was amongst the missing. Sergeant H. Satchwell also sent home word to the same effect, so that there seems little room for hoping that he will rejoin, although there is a strong probability that he had been taken prisoner by the Germans. The news comes at a bad time, as his mother is slowly recovering from many months' illness. Curiously enough, the particular trench in question seemed to be the meeting-place for Kenilworth men, for Corporal Fred Nixon (R.E.) was in the same trench only two days previous to its being blown up."

Another appeal for information regarding Lance-Sergeant Liggins was made in The Coventry Herald on 9 July 1915:

"News is still sought by Mrs Liggins, of Llanross, Southbank Road, and Mrs Liggins, of Windy Arbour, about their son and husband respectively, Corpl. Gilbert Liggins, who was buried in a mined trench on the French front some months ago. Neither the British War Office nor the German Concentration Camps have any news of him, although it is hoped that some friend at the front might be able to send a message of hope. Corpl. Liggins was a regular, attached to the 16th Lancers, who, in the early days of the Yser (sic – Ypres) operations, proceeded with other cavalry regiments to the French lines. No sooner, however, had they got in the trenches than they blew up, burying almost all the occupants. The hope is entertained that the gallant corporal has been rescued and is suffering from temporary loss of memory."

Lance-Sergeant Gilbert Percy Liggins was eventually presumed to have been killed and is commemorated on Panel 5 of the Ypres (Menin Gate) Memorial.

Ypres – April 1915

Zuavenstellung bei Langemark.

A German photograph showing dead French Colonial troops who had been killed
during the attack launched on 22 April 1915

"We have been at it ever since the night of the 22nd April when the enemy
broke through our line to the left. Our battalion was out of the trenches at
the time, we came in handy. We were told that the Germans held a piece of
wood and that we had to clear them out. They had entrenched themselves
strongly in front of the wood.

With the 16th Battalion as supports we made a surprise night attack, about
midnight, and got quite a reception with machine guns and rifle fire, but we
sent them back all right. We lost heavily, especially in officers, and if it
hadn't been a dark night we should have been worse.

Along with the 16th, we held the trench all the next day and night under very
heavy shell fire. After daybreak next morning, the 10th Battalion was sent to
reinforce the 8th. We landed with a bunch of the 13th who were holding a
short line of reserve trenches. The German artillery fire was something
awful. Between "Jack Johnsons," "Willie Chaser," shrapnel, and the
poisonous gas fumes they sent over, it was pretty hot. I don't know how
many of the enemy were in front of us; the place seemed to be alive with
them.

When they attacked we stayed until they had got within three or four hundred yards, then we were forced to fall back a piece to where reinforcements were coming up fast; then we began to hold them. It hasn't gone off yet, but we are having it a little easier. A fellow don't get much sleep at this game, and you have to dig yourself in all the time.

I could tell you a whole lot more, but it will have to wait till some other time when things are not so busy. I am writing this in a hole in the ground, under shell fire."[27]

20042 Private Alexander Francis Kennedy
10ᵗʰ Battalion (Canadians), Canadian Expeditionary Force

Kennedy wrote his letter to his father at Pitlochry, in which he described his experiences of the counter-attack, which was launched just before midnight of 22 April, and the subsequent fighting at Kitchener's Wood.

Alexander Kennedy was born on 3 June 1889 and was working as a carpenter when he attested for the C.E.F. at Valcartier on 24 September 1914. At the time of his enlistment he was a member Active Militia, serving with the 103ʳᵈ Regiment (Calgary Rifles).

Private Kennedy was killed on 5 February 1916 and is commemorated on Panel 24 of the Ypres (Menin Gate) Memorial.

---

[27] Perthshire Advertiser, 12 May 1915.

Ypres – July 1915

"With other men of my regiment we passed through a town somewhere in Belgium, and oh, what a place, deserted except for two or three military police, who are far back from the firing line. There isn't a house in the whole town which has not been hit by the German shells or otherwise, "Jack Johnsons." Some are down to the ground, others with roofs off, in fact all have had shell fever, here and there buildings are still smouldering. One or two houses which I saw just reminded me of when I used to get up in the morning with cups and saucers on the tables, half-full of coffee, and as I expect the inhabitants have had to clear out of it. Further on we marched till we came to a large square and shells were coming over our heads. One of my chums yelled out, 'get your gags on lads,' and, by Jove, we didn't half want them on, too, as the smell was cruel. Looking around we noticed two dead horses, which had been partly blown away by shells. The next thing we came to was a hole commonly called a "J.J." and I can assure you it is 50ft. by 20ft. deep, which had penetrated the sewerage, and it smelled awful."[28]

3/6063 Private Edgar Bollington
1ˢᵗ Battalion, The East Yorkshire Regiment

Born on 12 February 1895, Edgar Bollington was a Special Reservist and attested for the 3ʳᵈ (Special Reserve) Battalion, The East Yorkshire Regiment at Sheffield on 26 August 1912, aged 17 years and six months. Edgar was employed as a labourer at a cutlery works. Mobilised at the outbreak of the war, he was drafted to the 1ˢᵗ Battalion in France on 23 October 1914 and served with the Machine Gun Section.

Private Bollington was sent home on 22 June 1916 and was discharged as being unfit for further war service on 13 August 1916 and was issued with a Silver War Badge.

Edgar returned to work as a labourer and died at Sheffield in September 1944, aged 49.

---

[28] Sheffield Evening Telegraph, 29 July 1915.

Dugouts in Armagh Wood – July 1915

"The dugout has become an integral part in the everyday life of the trenches. No trench is complete without one, from the point of view of comfort. When a company has finished its turn in the trenches, two or three days as the case may be, it returns to the dugouts for generally a like period. These reserved dugouts are usually larger than the trench ones, and are, if possible, under trees or on a railway or other bank or under a hedge in order that they may not be observed by aeroplanes. Those in a wood are the best, they have good roofs of poles and earth which the tenants fondly imagine to be watertight, basing this theory on a light shower or two.

One night, however, it comes on to rain, and continues to rain, with the result that the occupants wake up to find pools of water on the floor and a steady stream dripping into the ration bag. This is followed by a hasty collection of oil sheets and a spade, the oil sheet for the roof, the spade to dig a trench in the vain endeavour to keep the water from draining in through the door. That finished, the next endeavour is to try and scrape together enough dry wood for a fire, and an hour will probably find two men crouched over a small biscuit tin, pierced with holes, trying to persuade a very smoky fire to cheer up a bit. Having reached a stage described as nearly boiling, finally a compromise is effected, and cocoa is used instead of tea; probably while it is still too hot to drink, the occupants are informed that they are wanted for fatigue. The messenger departs hurriedly, probably wishing he could draw a carbonised sheet over the doorway to tone down a few of the following remarks.

The first communication trench it was my pleasure to proceed along upset all my theories of trenches; it was two feet wide and three deep. One foot was water, with a good proportion of mud at the bottom; also at the bottom were floorboards about six feet along, with cross pieces, just like ladders.
Unfortunately people have a habit of taking off the cross pieces and using them for firewood, the resulting holes being embarrassing; and in that first trench between every other plank was a hole. We did 100 yards of this, and I had just decided that the guide ought to be shot, when the trench shallowed suddenly, and word was passed down to keep low. All very well I thought to walk double with a valise and a bundle of sacks on your back and a rifle in the other hand. We carried on for a matter of twenty yards, and then halted, as a message came down that the rear guide was wanted.

Twenty minutes later the rear guide passed up; ten minutes later he passed down, and the word came, about-turn. We had taken the wrong turn, and the blessings heaped on the front guide should have withered him. An hour later we found the fire trench, and it seemed like heaven.

One of the most chief and interesting topics of the trenches is relief. In many trenches a battalion is told it will be up for so many days, generally about eight. The first two days are confined to mild, mere speculation as to who the relieving force will be. That night a horrible rumour comes up the line. The C.O. has offered to stay a bit longer. "How much longer – a week?" "No, three days." "Why?" "Oh, the Fifth are wanted down the line." Four days later and rumour says that the -------- have been cut up, have relieved another division, have gone blitey (sic) (i.e., home), and the latest says they will be up to-morrow. Two days later the battalion still holds the trenches and has centred its hopes on the Tail-twisters.[29] The Adjutant's servants report that the Adjutant saw the transport officer, and that the transport is some miles farther back – our relief tomorrow is certain.

Twenty-four days later finds a small part of tired men waiting for their two days, as usual. Some of them have worked hard for two days building quite a luxurious dug-out at the back of the trench, with the full expectation of occupying it for many comparatively peaceful days. The relief draws near along the trench. The man who proud of his eyesight says: "Who are those? Say, you chaps, here's the relief." "What relief?" "The relief – the Tail-twisters, I suppose." "Just our luck," says the pessimist; "build a dug-out and move. We should have done it sooner." "Coming, cert," says the corporal. "Good-bye Twisters; you'll find water just along the trench. Carry on there in front."[30]

1227 Corporal John Gunning Fazakerley
1/6th (Rifle) Battalion, The King's (Liverpool Regiment) (Territorial Force)

John Fazakerley was born on 28 October 1893[31] was an apprentice bookbinder, working at his father's business at 28 Sandhurst Street when he attested for the 6th Kings –The Liverpool Rifles – on 16 October 1911. Embodied at the outbreak of the war he disembarked at Le Havre on 25 February 1915.

---

[29] "Tail-Twisters" or "Twisters" was a nickname sometimes used to describe the two Staffordshire Regiments (South and North), referring to the Stafford Knot worn on their cap badge.
[30] Liverpool Daily Post, 27 August 1915.
[31] Some records give his birthdate as 28 October 1894.

The view towards Square Wood and Armagh Wood, taken from Hill 60 in July 1929 by a former soldier from Spalding who had served in the area with 46th (North Midland) Division in 1915.

Fazakerley was wounded on 9 August 1916 during his battalion's attack on Guillemont. He was later recommended for a commission and after successfully completing his training at an Officer Cadet Battalion became a Temporary Second-Lieutenant in The King's (Liverpool Regiment) on 30 May 1917. Posted to the 12th (Service) Battalion, he was wounded again on 20 November 1917 during the Battle of Cambrai, when he suffered perforated eardrums, caused by a tank firing its 6 pdr gun behind him at close quarters.[32]

After the war, Fazakerley lived at 28 Albert Square in Kennington and by 1939 he was residing at 8 Bourne Avenue in Salisbury, employed as a clerk by the Ministry of Agriculture, Fisheries and Food.

John Gunning Fazakerley died in Berkshire in 1975, aged 81.

---

[32] WO 339/90640.

Trenches near Hooge - July 1915

"We have been in the trenches this time for ten days and were very glad to get relieved. I expect we shall be out now for about eight days. We were placed in the ramparts at ---- (Ypres) for the first five days, but were up at the trenches every night. We were in the second line of trenches, and it was our duty to carry the rations to our other companions who were in the firing line. This is very hard work carrying very heavy loads up through narrow trenches and dodging shells every now and then. During the day-time we were pretty safe, as we were under cover from their fire, living in an underground tunnel, but we had to go out occasionally through the day on to go out occasionally through the day on fatigue, and when we did we could always look out for heavy shelling. One day we were going out about mid-day on fatigue, and got so far up the road when the Germans had us spotted, and didn't half send over some of their shells. They were exploding in the fields on either side of us, and a few burst on the road. It was a case of going on a few yards and then dropping flat on our faces in a ditch. We can hear the shells coming; the sound is something like two express trains passing each other. In the case of shrapnel it bursts up a height, and you can hear the pieces of metal, etc., dropping to the ground like a huge hammer. Some pieces are quite small, and look very much like a burnt cinder.

One night we were under very heavy shell fire when on our way to the trenches with rations, but only two of our men were hit. The Germans, I hear, are very much afraid of the French 75 gun, which makes a huge report, and can fire, I think 28 rounds per minute. Our artillery seem to be using many more shells than they were a few months back. The five days in the trenches meant five days of hard work on fatigues, etc., but we didn't suffer much loss of men like the two of our Companies who were holding the first line' they lost something like 100 men (killed and wounded).

One thing I saw of interest – one of the German aircraft brought to earth by one of our own. A German Taube had been seen circling around our trenches for some time, and our artillery were shelling it, but one of our own airmen, who was in pursuit of the Taube, managed to nicely drop a bomb upon the enemy. The Taube caught fire, but for a few moments looked as though it was going to get back to its own lines before descending. The pilot was unable to control his machine, however, and, after a bit of a struggle, had to descend to our lines.

I believe the men on the Taube were burnt to death before our fellows got to the machine; at least that is what the Engineers told me. As soon as the machine dropped into our lines you should have heard the cheering that our fellows set up."[33]

12150 Corporal Owen Greenslade
"D" Company, 10th (Service) Battalion, The Durham Light Infantry

Owen Greenslade came from Barnstaple and had written his letter to his parents, John and Elizabeth Greenslade, who lived at 8 Allen Bank in the Newport district of the town.

The German aircraft that he had witnessed crashing on 25 July had been shot down by Captain Lanoe George Hawker, who would later be awarded the Victoria Cross for his action. The pilot. Oberleutnant Uebelacker, and the observer, Hauptmann Roser, were both killed.

Corporal Greenslade was killed on 19 August 1915, aged 21, and is commemorated on the Ypres (Menin Gate) Memorial.

---

[33] Exeter and Plymouth Gazette, 13 August 1915.

Positions in the woods around the Chateau at St Jean - 20 August

"Somewhere in France (sic)"

"It would be interesting to know what impression the average civilian forms of life in the firing line. No doubt the general impression is that of a lot of Tommies on the one side blazing away all day at the Boches, similarly entrenched, shells falling thick and fast, and vague visions of aerial torpedoes, and other forms of German frightfulness. Probably little thought is given to how Tommy manages to get there, and the miles of communication trenches to be traversed before the actual firing line is reached; how the food, ammunition, and other supplies are conveyed to the trenches – no light task under fair conditions and fraught with great danger and difficulties when the approaches of the supply wagons are heavily bombarded, or in wet weather, when the trenches are a foot deep in mud, and it is impossible to gain a proper foothold.

What a ration fatigue after heavy rain is like is now my intention to describe. We are waiting about two miles behind the firing line for the wagons to come up. It has been raining heavily all day, but has stopped just before nightfall. The night is pitch dark, and the flares that are being thrown from line to line show up with a brilliant clearness, and appear to be very much nearer than they really are. There is an incessant crack of rifles, and an occasional bullet whizzes past and flattens itself against a wall somewhere at our back. Comparatively speaking, things are quiet in the actual firing line, but overhead huge 15in. shells are screaming with monotonous regularity, bursting at no very great distance in the rear. The noise of the large calibre shells moving through the air is not unlike that of an express train, and as one of these shells is bursting a wit asks if anyone wants to catch the last train home.

The shells are bursting about a mile away and in the vicinity of the road which forms the only means of approach for the transport in the "dumping ground." The battalion S-M. is apparently very worried, and moves from place to place giving orders and making final arrangements. A rifleman walks up and asks him if he has the candles for the major, which causes that worried warrant officer to rap out very sharply that he is not a walking William Whiteley, but after a few enquiries the articles in question are found.

A distant rumble is heard, and with it comes a general relaxation of the nervous tension which has unconsciously got hold of everyone. The rumble gradually gets louder too loud in fact, which proves it to be the approach of an ammunition column coming along at full gallop, much in the manner of the old horse fire engines. The roads are bad, and it is wonderful that the column is able to move at such a pace. A little later another rumble is heard, and this proves to be the convoy for which we are waiting. The limbers are quickly and systematically unloaded under the supervision of the different company quarter-master sergeants, and then taken over by the carrying parties. The rations are first put up in canvas bags before being loaded, these bags being tied together at the top for slinging over the shoulder. The men who do not carry rations take water which is put up in two-gallon petrol tins. Of course, the eagerly-looked-for mail is not forgotten.

It must not be forgotten that the night is very dark, and a lot of rain had fallen during the day. The men proceed in single file, keeping close touch until the communication trench is reached.

Just a word about the communication trench. It is, perhaps, a mile and a half, as the crow flies, to the firing line, which means between two and three miles through the trench, owing to its zigzag construction. Perhaps half the trench is boarded, the remainder is churned at the bottom into a thick, yellow, clayey mud, from six inches to three feet deep, while water accumulates in holes anything up to waist deep. As regards the boarded portions, many of the boards are broken, some have staves removed, and there is often a rise or fall of about a foot between two adjoining boards.

Parts of the trench have been blown in by shells, parts are so narrow that it requires a great effort to squeeze through. There are bridges to go under that nexessitate considerable cramping, and last, but not least, there are the telephone wires which have broken loose, and have a nasty knock of tripping one up. The rations are delivered in due course, however, and Tommy is contentedly smoking his cigarette ten minutes later.

Just a word about Kitchener's men before I close – I speak of course from my knowledge of the men in our brigade. Not from the first have they shown fear, when they entered the trenches some months ago. They have been right along the line since then, and have experienced every kind of German frightfulness. They have charged the German line in face of murderous fire, and met death smilingly. The Germans must have some commission from hell if they are to devise a frightfulness which will destroy the moral(e) of these troops."[34]

A/556 Rifleman William Whitmore
Machine-Gun Section, 8th (Service) Battalion, The King's Royal Rifle Corps

Whitmore had arrived in France on 19 May 1915. Later appointed Acting Corporal, he was commissioned as a Second-Lieutenant of The Rifle Brigade on 30 January 1918.

---

[34] Birmingham Daily Mail, 1 October 1915.

The Bluff – 27 January 1916

"Fifty yards from the Huns,
Somewhere in France (sic).

... This is the Kaiser's birthday and to show that we indulge in no 'Hymns of Hate' we have been sending a few birthday presents to our friends over the way. But they didn't seem to like them, and started to return them. However, we beat them easily in generosity, and consequently are now able to get a much nearer view of the inside of their support trenches. We started at 11.30 and stopped at 1.30. Unfortunately, one of the return presents landed just opposite my little dug-out in a support trench, filling the place with a foot of mud, and covering all my shaving tackle, etc. Although I had been there an hour before, I was at the time in the firing-line observing our fire through a periscope. Strange to say, it is by far the safest place on such occasions, as neither side wish to shell the front trenches, owing to the close proximity (30 yards in some places). I like this observing, and never feel so elated as when I see one of our big 9.2's burst plump on the top of their parapet, and the sandbags and stuff all goes flying sky high.

On Tuesday I had to take over command of a new trench we are making on the edge of a crater. The only way to it is to creep over the ridge by night, and come back the following night. We worked hard all the night with sandbags. One poor fellow was hit in the back, and fell just at my feet. Having expected something might happen, I had previously provided myself with a flask of brandy and some iodine. Having given him some of the former, I put on a field dressing. We then got him away to a safer place, and wrapped him up till the stretcher-bearers came and took him away... At 8.45 another 100 men of the ---------- came up, and then the Huns sent over six high explosive shrapnel, which burst about 30 yards to our right. However, it was close enough, unfortunately, to kill one man and wound one officer and four men of this party. One was hit quite close to me... and I busied myself with bandaging up one man's leg, another's shoulder and another with two broken fingers... My iodine again came in useful, but it much have made their wounds smart like anything, yet never a word of complaint or murmur... When the stretcher-bearers had got the wounded away we went back to our work again, and although four more shells came over, I'm glad to say we had no further casualties... What was most striking was the cheerful endurance of the wounded."[85]

---

[85] Kent and Sussex Courier, 11 February 1916.

Second-Lieutenant Charles Cecil Field
The Queen's Own (Royal West Kent Regiment) attached 2nd Battalion, The Suffolk Regiment

Charles Field was born at Ranskill in Nottinghamshire on 20 May 1895 and had been educated at the Abbey School at Beckenham, where his father, the Reverend Walter St John Field M.A., was the vicar at the parish church of St George's, and at the King's School in Canterbury. Due to start at Keeble College in Oxford, Charles instead attested for the 19th (Service) Battalion, The Royal Fusiliers (2nd Public Schools) on 15 September 1914. He was commissioned as a Temporary Second-Lieutenant on 15 January 1915 and posted to the 9th (Reserve) Battalion, The Queen's Own (Royal West Kent Regiment), transferring to the 8th Battalion in July. Field was drafted to France on 7 October 1915 and posted to "Y" Company of the 2nd Suffolks.

Charles was killed on 30 March 1916 while making a bombing attack on German positions at St Eloi and is buried at Voormezeele Enclosures No. 1 and No. 2: Plot I, Row D, Grave 3.

St Eloi – 26 March 1916

"We had patches on our backs to distinguish us from other battalions. I carried wire cutters, and when he had our shrapnel helmets on we looked like a lot of Chinese. Well, on Sunday, March 26th, we left for St Eloi, everybody in good spirits. We had some Belgian beer at dinner and we all thought it might be the last we should ever have, which it was for a lot of my pals. I told them (all I knew) I was coming back all right. I was not afraid of that myself. We were kept shivering with cold and wet feet in the trenches all night waiting for the order to attack. At 4 a.m. we went over the top and lay down in front of the German trenches.The signal to attack was the blowing up of the "Mound of Death," so called because of the many lives lost there. I was just dozing off when "Bang!" The very ground where we were jumped and rocked like a boat. Tons of earth went in the air, and the hole it made would hold the Wesleyan chapel at Porthleven. I was bruised by the fallen debris, but did not notice it much at the time. Then came the order to charge, and we went over the obstacles like cats. I knew the sooner I got to the German trenches the safer I should be. I passed the first line all right though the shots were thick as hail. In getting through some barbed wire I felt a sharp blow on my left ankle. I looked expecting to see my boot gone, but it was still there – but it left a nasty bruise next day. Something seemed to say to me "Get on!" And as I moved a chap got in my place, only to be shot dead the next moment (another narrow squeak). It was like a gale of wind with the shells flying. A Corporal shouted to me to hurry the men up, and we made another dash. Just as I got to the second trench I felt a "plonk" in my leg. "Oh!" I said, "I got it." I looked down and saw a hole in my leg, and bleeding badly; so I thought, "this is no place for me – I'm off." Very funny but I was as cool as I am now. The getting away was the worst. I felt my strength going, so I knew I must be quick, and as I could not walk I started crawling and rolling, and was plastered from head to foot with mud. A poor fellow shouted to me, "Which is the way out?" I said, "Follow me." I could not help him, as I could hardly help myself. The action started at 4.15 a.m. I was wounded about 6 a.m., and at 7.30 I was in safety."[36]

G/18198 Private Gilbert Campbell Blight
4th Battalion, The Royal Fusiliers (City of London Regiment)

---

[36] Private Blight wrote his letter to his father, Amos, who lived at Porthleven, describing his experiences during the attack mounted by his battalion and the 1st Battalion, The Northumberland Fusiliers against German positions at St Eloi on 27 March 1916. Private Blight's letter was printed in The West Briton and Cornwall Advertiser on 17 April 1916.

Born in 1884 at Kensington, Gilbert Blight was employed as an assistant at a grocer's shop (he described himself as a "provisions merchant") in Porthleven when he was attested at Cambourne on 2 July 1915. Private Blight was posted to the the 6th (Extra Reserve) Battalion, The Royal Fusiliers and was drafted to the France on 2 January 1916. After being wounded at St Eloi, Blight was evacuated to hospital in England, being placed on the strength of the Regimental Depot. On his recovery, he returned to the 6th Battalion at Dover on 14 August 1916. Blight was drafted to France again on 16 March 1917 and posted to the 22nd (Service) Battalion (Kensington). He was wounded for a second time on 22 June. Blight was transferred to the Army Service Corps on 26 November 1917 and underwent training as a Driver at No. 1 Reserve Mechanical Transport Depot at Grove Park. He was transferred to the Class Z Army Reserve on demobilisation at No. 1 Dispersal Unit in Fovant on 11 March 1919.

Gilbert Blight died on 1 December 1949.

A German photograph of the ruins of the Church of Our Lady at Zonnebeke, taken in 1916.

14649 Drummer William Dimmelow
1st Battalion, The North Staffordshire Regiment

William Dimmelow was born on 8 October 1896 at Fenton, the son of Ephraim and Jane Dimmelow. He lived with his family at 45 Best Street and worked as a potter's attendant before being employed as a collier. William was diminutive, only five feet, two inches tall, and had grey eyes, dark brown hair and a sallow complexion. He attested for The North Staffordshire Regiment at Stoke-on-Trent on 31 August 1914 and was sent to the Regimental Depot at Whittington Barracks before being posted to the 4th (Extra Reserve) Battalion on 3 September. Private Dimmelow was sent to Jersey with the 4th North Staffords and on 28 November was drafted to the 11th Battalion, which moved to Alderney in February 1915. While stationed on the island, Dimmelow was awarded three days' Field Punishment No. 1. Private Dimmelow was transferred back to the 4th Battalion on Guernsey on 21 September and appointed as a Drummer on 7 October, before reverting back to Private at the end of the month. On 4 November, he was placed on a draft to France and was posted to the 8th (Service) Battalion, before being transferred instead to the 1st North Staffords on 23 November.

Dimmelow was re-appointed as a Drummer and on 31 July 1917, he was selected to perform a specific task during the 1st Battalion's attack on Groenenburg Farm, Image Crescent and Jehovah Trench. During the days preceding the assault, one Drummer from each of the four companies was picked by the Sergeant-Drummer to sound the "Charge" on their bugles as the 1st North Staffords went "over the top."

Bernard Martin, an junior officer with the 1st North Staffords who was wounded on 31 July 1917, later recalled the drummers practicing the call in his memoirs, "Poor Bloody Infantry," which were published in 1987, but believed the plan to be a great folly and the idea of an officer that he described as an old grey-haired "dug-out." However, Martin's recollections were incorrect, written so long after the events he described, was far from being a "dug-out," the 1st North Staffords were at this time commanded by Vyvyan Vavasour Pope, who was aged twenty-five. Pope would remain in command of the 1st North Staffords until he was wounded on 21 March 1918, the injury resulting in him having to have his right arm amputated. He transferred to the Tank Corps in 1920 and rose steadily through the ranks until he died, in an air crash in Egypt on 5 October 1941, having attained the rank of Lieutenant-General, on his way to assume command of XXX Corps.

German troops photographed amidst the ruins of Groenenberg Farm, c.1916.

At "Zero Hour," 3.50 a.m. on 31 July, the drummers of the 1st North Staffords sounded the charge and the battalion commenced their attack. The battalion secured the remains of Groenenberg Farm, before moving forward towards to take Image Crescent and Jehova Trench. Coming under enfilade fire from Bulgar Wood on the left and a German position known as Lower Star Post on their right flank, the North Staffords retired to Bodmin Copse. The 1st Battalion suffered 45 killed and a further 21 missing at the end of the day. Drummer Dimmelow was the only drummer left unscathed as the assault continued, and received a gunshot wound to his right thigh on 1 August. He kept his bugle with him, and his actions on 31 July were mentioned in the battalion history, which was published in 1932.

Drummer Dimmelow was evacuated home on 7 August and was posted onto the strength of the Northern Command Depot at Ripon on 19 September. On 16 January 1918, following his discharge from hospital, Dimmelow was posted to the 3rd (Special Reserve) Battalion, The North Staffordshire Regiment at Wallsend and was appointed a Drummer on 27 January. He was compulsorily transferred to The Leicestershire Regiment on 21 June 1918, and was transferred again to the Royal Army Medical Corps on 29 July, being posted to the 8th Training Battalion. Dimmelow was transferred to the Class P Army Reserve on 13 September 1918 before being finally discharged as surplus to military requirements on 11 February 1919. William lived at 13 Crown Street in Shelton following his discharge and received his Silver War Badge on 5 February 1920. He died in 1976, and the bugle that Drummer Dimmelow used to sound the "Charge" on during the assault on 31 July 1917 is preserved in The Staffordshire Regiment Museum.

Another member of the same battalion who distinguished himself during the attack on 31 July 1917 was **7658 Lance-Corporal Charles Ernest Smith D.C.M.**

Charles Smith came from Kingsbury and worked as a miner at Kingsbury Colliery. His father, Joseph, was an old soldier and had served in Afghanistan during the Second Afghan War between 1878 and 1880. Mobilised from the Reserve at the outbreak of the war, Smith was drafted to France on 9 December 1914 and joined the 1st Battalion at Rue du Bois.

On 31 July 1917, Lance-Corporal Smith was acting as a stretcher-bearer during the 1st Battalion's attack on Groenenburg Farm, Image Crescent and Jehovah Trench. The 1st North Staffords' History, published in 1932, detailed the part played by Lance-Corporal Smith during the attack:

"After the attack had been held up, any movement between Image Crescent and Jehova trench became very difficult, as apart from the bad going over the torn and cratered ground, the German artillery sniped any movement about the former, while their machine guns in Bulgar Wood engaged any available target about the latter. (It was) in these circumstances that a stretcher-bearer, Lance-Corporal Smith, displayed such devotion to duty in constantly evacuating wounded from Jehova trench to Image Crescent, that he was recommended the Victoria Cross. The recommendation was unsuccessful, but he received the D.C.M. as an immediate award."

Charles Smith was wounded on 31 July 1917, suffering shrapnel wounds to the right thigh. The citation for his Distinguished Conduct Medal was published in the London Gazette on 26 January 1918:

"For conspicuous gallantry and devotion to duty when a stretcher-bearer. After the advance had been held up by hostile machine-gun fire, he walked from shell-hole to shell-hole in our most advanced positions under heavy fire, searching for, dressing, and bringing in the wounded for some three hours until he was at last wounded in fetching a stretcher for a wounded man. He displayed the utmost indifference to personal danger, and set a magnificent example by his coolness and courage under heavy fire."

Posted to the 3rd (Special Reserve) Battalion at Wallsend on being discharged from hospital, Lance-Corporal Smith was decorated with his Distinguished Conduct Medal at a ceremony held at Newcastle-upon-Tyne on 19 December 1917 and on Christmas Eve a special presentation was made to him when he returned home on furlough:

7658 Lance-Corporal Charles Ernest Smith D.C.M.

KINGSBURY SOLDIER HONOURED.

"At a smoking concert at Kingsbury Working-men's Club, on December 24, L.-Corpl. C. E. Smith received from the inhabitants of Kingsbury and Piccadilly presents in recognition of his gaining the Military Medal,[37] also the D.C.M. The Rev. E. B. R. de Jersey presented L.-Corpl. Smith with a silver watch and chain, a silver cruet, and a silver rose bowl. Sergt.-Major Barlow, Mr W. Wright, Mr J. Maddox, and Mr D. Wright gave songs during the evening. L. Corpl. Smith received his medals at Newcastle-on-Tyne on December 19."[38]

Ernie, who had five brothers who served during the war, recovered from his wound and was transferred to the Class Z Army Reserve on 21 January 1919 on being demobilised, and married Nora Millicent Thompson at Kingsbury Parish Church on 8 June 1919.

Following his demobilisation, Ernie left Kingsbury for Doncaster to look for work at the pits there, as there were no jobs then on offer at the local collieries. He found employment at Bentley Main Colliery, but later returned to Kingsbury, residing with his wife and children at 37 Ralph Crescent, and he worked at Kingsbury Colliery.

Charles Ernest Smith D.C.M. died in 1968.

---

[37] This reference is incorrect, as Lance-Corporal Smith was awarded the Distinguished Conduct Medal only.
[38] Tamworth Herald, 5 January 1918.

Lieutenant James Bull M.C.
56th Battalion, Australian Imperial Force

Born at Norton Canes, near Cannock in Staffordshire, in 1890, James Bull was living on Norton East Road and working at No. 11 Pit of the Conduit Colliery as a miner when he attested for 2nd North Midland Field Company, Royal Engineers (Territorial Force) at Norton Hall on 1 June 1908. Giving his age at his enlistment as seventeen years and three months, he was posted to the Mounted Section of the Company as a Driver and issued with the regimental number 1084. Driver Bull was examined for his Certificate in Trade Efficiency on 27 July by George Wardle, and his skills were assessed as "good." He went to the Annual Camp held at Towyn on 2 August, and attended the subsequent camps at Towyn (1909) and at Hindlow Camp, near Buxton (1910). While serving with the Company, James fell foul of the law when he was spotted cycling at 10.25 p.m. on 3 April 1909 on the Walsall Road in Rushall without a light, for which he was fined 6s.[39] In January 1911, at the annual prize-giving held at Norton Hall, Driver Bull was awarded first place for the best driving skill and all-round efficiency, for which he received a crowned crossed whips and spur badge, to be worn on his uniform, and 15s. prize money.[40]

Driver Bull was discharged, at his own request, from 2nd North Midland Company on 7 February 1911, by which time he had already sailed from Southampton, on board the S.S. Otway, for a new life in Australia. James went to work as a farmer at Trangie in New South Wales.

On 15 January 1915, together with Josiah Cooper Birch, who had also emigrated to Australia from Norton Canes, he attested for the Australian Imperial Force at Liverpool in New South Wales. Both he and Birch were posted to the 4th Battalion, Bull being issued with the service number 1713, while Josiah Birch was given the number 1721. They both embarked on the H.M.A.T. A9 Shropshire, with the Fourth Reinforcement for the 4th Battalion, on 17 March, destined for Egypt. No doubt due to his previous military experience, Private Bull was appointed Lance-Corporal on 30 March.

Bull served with the 4th Battalion on the Gallipoli Peninsula from 31 May 1915 and took part in the Battle of Lone Pine between 6 and 10 August. The 4th Battalion was withdrawn to Lemnos on 13 September to refit, and while on the island Bull was again appointed a Lance-Corporal on 11 October. He returned to Gallipoli with the 4th Battalion on 30 October, and was appointed a Temporary Corporal on 2 November, being promoted to Corporal on 29 November. The Battalion was evacuated from Anzac Cove on 19 December and Corporal Bull and his comrades of the 4th Battalion landed at Alexandria on New Years' Eve, and proceeded to a camp at Mustaphi, before moving to Tel-el-Kebir on 2 January 1916. On 20 January, Bull was appointed a Temporary Sergeant.

On 16 February, the 56th Battalion was formed from a cadre provided by the 4th Battalion, under the command of Major Alan Humphrey Scott, and Bull was transferred to the new battalion. He was appointed an acting Company

---

[39] Walsall Advertiser, 24 April 1909.
[40] Lichfield Mercury, 13 January 1911.

Sergeant-Major on 29 February, before reverting to Temporary Sergeant and being promoted to the rank of Sergeant on 7 March. Bull received further promotion on 30 May, when he was appointed Company Sergeant-Major, with the rank of Warrant Officer, Class II, but was admitted to No. 1 Australian General Hospital at Ismalia the following day suffering from tonscilitis. He was released a few days later and sailed with the 56th Battalion for France, disembarking at Marseilles on 30 June.

C.S.M. Bull was serving with the 56th Battalion during the failed attack at Fromelles on 19 July, where the battalion was fortunately deployed in reserve, and on 30 August was commissioned in the field as a Second-Lieutenant. News of his promotion was printed in The Birmingham Evening Despatch on 6 October:

A NORTON CANES ANZAC.

"In February, 1911, James Bull, aged 25, nephew of Mr George Bull, of Norton Canes, went out to Australia and found employment in the farming industry. About 12 months ago he enlisted in a battalion of the Australian Imperial Force, and his uncle has just received news that he has been made a second-lieutenant.

Prior to leaving Norton Canes he was a driver in the 2nd North Midland Field Co., R.E. (T.F.), and was employed at No. 11 pit of the Conduit Colliery."

The story was also published by The Walsall Observer on 7 October:

"**Commission for Former Resident.** – Mr James Bull, of the Australian Forces, has been promoted to Second Lieutenant. He is a nephew of Mr George Bull, of Norton Canes, and in February, 1911, went out to Australia, where he took up farming. He joined the 56th Battalion of the Australian Force, and took part in heavy fighting at Gallipoli, including that at Suvla Bay; and though he was unwounded, he afterwards had an illness and was for a time in hospital in Egypt. Later, with his regiment, he went to another theatre of war. He is 25 years of age, and prior to leaving Norton Canes was employed at the No. 11 Pit of the Conduit Colliery. He was also a driver in the 2nd North Midland Field Company of the Royal Engineers (T.F.)."

On 8 October, Second-Lieutenant Bull was sent on a Course of Instruction on the Lewis Gun, and returned to the 56th Battalion on 15 October, and attended a second course between 9 and 18 November. He was granted leave between 29 November and 13 December.

On 2 February 1917, Bull was wounded, receiving a gunshot wound to the buttock, and was admitted to 15th Field Ambulance before being sent to the South Midland Casualty Clearing Station, and was admitted to the 2nd Red Cross Hospital at Rouen on 7 February. He was then evacuated to England on board the H.M.H.S. St Patrick and admitted to the 3rd London General Hospital for treatment to his wound. Bull was discharged from hospital on 13 March. Posted to No. 1 Command Depot, A.I.F., at Perham Down, Second-Lieutenant Bull was passed fit for General Service by a Medical Board held on 30 March and was drafted back to France on 13 May, being posted to the 5th Division A.I.F. Base Depot at Etaples two days later. He rejoined the 56th Battalion on 20 May. Bull had also been promoted to Lieutenant on 6 March, and was appointed Lewis Gun Officer for the 56th Battalion on 29 July.

Lieutenant Bull distinguished himself during the fighting at Polygon Wood on 26 September, during which the 56th Battalion lost 255 killed, wounded and missing. The recommendation for the award of the Military Cross to Lieutenant James Bull, 56th Battalion, Australian Imperial Force, written by his Commanding Officer on 21 December:

"This officer is my Lewis Gun Officer and was attached to Battalion Headquarters during the operations in POLYGON WOOD.

He was responsible for the laying out of the tapes and the guides for the Battalion prior to the attack - a work which he carried out with conspicuous coolness, ability and success - although under fire at the time. When the final objective of the Battalion was reached he was invaluable in assisting the few remaining officers to site and use their Lewis Guns to the best advantage and owing to the heavy casualties in Officers, he remained in the front line and helped reorganise the troops there.

The late Lieut-Colonel Scott spoke very highly indeed of his coolness and soldierly qualities throughout the operation. Lieut. Bull has been with the Battalion for two years and has always proved a thoroughly reliable and efficient Officer.

I recommend him very highly.

This Officer has not previously been awarded any military decorations."

(Signed) A.F.G. Simpson, Lieut-Colonel
Commanding 56th Battalion, A.I.F.

Brigadier-General J. Hobkirk, commanding 14th Brigade, originally confirmed a recommendation for the award of a Mention in Despatches on 8 March 1918, for Lieutenant Bull's gallantry during the period between 26 September 1917 and 25 February 1918, but instead supported the recommendation that Bull should receive the Military Cross.

Lieutenant Bull's Military Cross was announced in The London Gazette on 3 June 1918 and in The Commonwealth of Australia Gazette on 9 November.

Lieutenant Bull was granted leave to England between 30 October and 18 November and on 25 November, Bull reported sick and was admitted to the 5th Division Rest Station for dental treatment, returning to the 56th Battalion on 16 December.

Lieutenant Bull was wounded for a second time on 18 April 1918 near Amiens, and was evacuated to No. 8 General Hospital suffering from gas poisoning. He was later sent back to England and admitted again to 3rd London General Hospital at Wandsworth. Lieutenant Bull's arrival was reported in The Lichfield Mercury on 3 May:

"Mr Geo. Bull, senior, Norton East Road, Norton Canes, has received news that his nephew, Lieut. James Bull, Australian Forces, has been badly gassed and is now in a London hospital. Lieut. Bull went out to Australia about four years before the outbreak of the war."

After being released from hospital and a period of covalesence, Lieutenant Bull returned to France on 12 August and rejoined the 56th Battalion on 22 August. He was posted to the Australian Corps School on 4 October and did not return to his unit, which had amalgamated with the 54th Battalion on 11 October to become the 54th/56th Battalion, until 11 November, the day that the Armistice came into effect. Lieutenant Bull was granted leave to Paris in December but was admitted to No. 39 General Hospital at Le Havre on 15 January 1919, before being transferred by hospital ship to England, and was admitted to 1st Australian Dermatological Hospital at Bulford for treatment. He was discharged from hospital on 16 March but was re-admitted the following day. He assumed duties as Assistant Adjutant at the A.I.F. Depot at Park House in Tidworth on 27 June, and served in the post until 1 August. Bull was posted to the Agricultural Depot at Sutton Veny on 30 August, before being admitted again to 1st Australian Dematological Hospital on 10 September, suffering from venereal disease. He was discharged from hospital on 23 October and returned to Sutton

Veny before sailing for Austrailia on 1 November on board the troop transport Nestor. He was demobilised on his return home and returned to farming, marrying Annie Beatrice Dyke, who also came from Norton Canes and had emigrated to Australia to join him, in 1921. James and Annie lived at Trangie and later moved to Dubbo, and together they had four children.

In 1967, James made an application for Anzac Commemorative Medallion, which had been instituted in that year, and his letter outlined his service:

"82 Blandford Street
Collaroy Plateau
N.S.W.

March 20th 1967

To,

Secretary of the Army.
Dear Sir,

I hereby wish to make application for the Gallipoli Medal (sic) now ready for issue. Details of Service as follows.

I joined the 4th Battalion as a reinforcement on Gallipoli in June 1915 & continued on Service with the 4th Batt. until the evacuation taking part in Lone Pine and all other actions after which we were evacuated back into Egypt where the 1st Brigade was split up & the 14th Brigade formed.

I was then posted to the 56th Batt. I went to France continuing to serve with the 56th Batt. until the armistice. I held various ranks & was commissioned on the Field. I was also awarded the Military Cross.

No. 1713 James Bull, Lieut. M.C.
4th & 56th Battallion (sic)
A.I.F."

James Bull M.C. died at Dubbo in New South Wales on 27 July 1974 and is buried at Dubbo General Cemetery. His name can also be found on the Roll of Honour of the former scholars of Norton Canes Boys' School, which is now located at Norton Canes Primary Academy.

Ypres: The Cloth Hall and "In Flanders Fields" Museum

The original Cloth Hall (Lakenhal/Lakenhalle in Flemish) was completed in 1304 and at that time was one of largest commercial buildings in Europe, emphasising the significance of Ypres and a centre for trading and importance of the manufacture of cloth and lace to the region.

When British troops first arrived in the city on 13 October 1914, the ground floor of the hall was used as stabling for horses, but the building soon began to sustain hits from German artillery which culminated with a massive bombardment on 22 November that set fire to the Cloth Hall and Belfry. Four more years of war reduced the building to a battered shell, with little of the external walls left standing.

Although it was initially proposed in some quarters, particularly in Britain, that Ypres would be left in a devastated state as a permanent memorial to the Great War the Belgians refused to allow this to happen and began to rebuild their shattered city.

The ruins of the Belfry and Cloth Hall, photographed c. 1922.

Reconstruction work began in 1928, under the direction of architects Jules Coomans and P. A. Pauwels using the original plans and, where possible, material salvaged from the original fabric of the building. By 1934 the western wing of the Cloth Hall and the Belfry had been completed. The outbreak of the Second World War interrupted the rebuilding of the remainder of the Cloth Hall and the work was not finally completed until 1967.

An interesting and often overlooked memorial on the wall of the Cloth Hall, close to the entrance to the "In Flanders Fields" Museum, commemorates the liberation of Ypres by the 1ˢᵗ Polish Armoured Division on 6 September 1944.

Photographs of Ypres taken by German servicemen during 1940.

The Cloth Hall and Belfry, photographed in 1961.

As early as 1919 a few intrepid visitors journeyed to Ypres in order to view the former battlefields or to try and find the graves of loved ones. The potential for tourism was quickly recognised by British ex-servicemen and Belgians and Ypres soon became a busy centre for pilgrims, with hotels and restaurants being opened and traders selling postcards and other souvenirs.

Lieutenant-Colonel (Retired) Arthur Wilmot Rickman D.S.O. and Bar, of The Northumberland Fusiliers returned to Ypres in 1920 and recounted his impressions of his visit:

"On arrival at Ypres one first encountered the tourist element and large char-a-bancs with megaphones describing the horrors of war. Ypres is busy; houses have arisen and reinforced concrete hotels and restaurants were in Ypres Square. The Cloth Hall and the Cathedral are to be left as a war memorial. I went along the Menin road, passing Hooge, as far as Sanctuary Wood. The ground is still littered with duds and shell cases, and one still found boxes of Mills' bombs, equipment, etc., and standing very vigorously out were large numbers of derelict tanks.

Turning back from Sanctuary Wood I went along the Paschendaele (sic) Road to Broseiende (sic), thence to Paschendaele Ridge. Practically nothing has been done in the devastated area East of Ypres and as far as the eye could see the whole country looks a mass of blackened ruin. Water was standing about in shell holes, but the trenches had either mostly fallen in or been blotted out of existence, but most noticeable in all areas traversed this day was the large number of pill boxes, which, though filled with water inside, were still in a good state of repair."[41]

Taxis waiting outside the Cloth Hall to take visitors on guided tours around the battlefield, c. 1930.

[41] Berwick Advertiser, 31 December 1920. Rickman had been the Commanding Officer of the 11th (Service) Battalion, The East Lancashire Regiment (Accrington) between 1 March 1915 and 22 October 1919.

British pilgrims eating their lunch in Ypres while on an organised tour of the battlefields during the late 1920s.

German pilgrims visiting Langemark and Ypres in 1937.

An early pioneer of battlefield tourism around Ypres, and the founder of the Ypres Salient War Museum, was **Leo Norbury Murphy**.

Born at Manchester in 1891, Murphy joined The Queen's (Royal West Surrey Regiment) in 1907, his regimental number being L/9094. He was serving as a Private with the 1st Battalion at the outbreak of the Great War and landed in France on 9 August 1914. Murphy was later transferred to the 10B Battalion, The Royal Fusiliers, which was employed on military intelligence tasks, and appointed an Acting Corporal. Murphy was awarded the Medaille Militaire and Croix de Guerre by the French Government for his part in assisting the evacuation of civilians from Bethune in April 1918.

Following his demobilisation in 1919 Leo returned to France, where he married and had a son. He moved to Vlamertinghe in 1921 and soon set up a business – the British Touring and Information Bureau – based in the Grand Place at Ypres providing guided tours around the battlefields of the Ypres Salient. Murphy also joined the Ypres Branch of the British Legion on its formation and served as President of the Ypres Branch of The Old Contemptibles' Association, and when the tourist season closed during the winter months worked as an electrician and sold applicances from his premises on the Grand Place, advertising his services in the local Flemish newspapers.

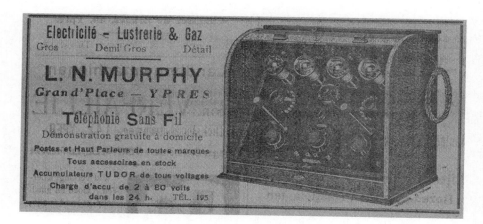

An advertisement, printed in Het Ypersche Weekblad of 15 January 1927, for "Electrical Lighting and Gas" and "Wireless Telephony" services offered by Leo Murphy. This business provided him with an alternative source of income during the winter months when battlefield tourists were not as prevailent in Ypres.

An advertisement placed in the October 1937 edition of "The Old Contemptible" – the official organ of The Old Contemptibles' Association, for battlefield package tours to Ypres offered by Leo Murphy.

Leo Murphy, photographed in conversation with Field Marshal Sir John French, 1ˢᵗ Earl of Ypres and Lieutenant-General Sir William Pulteney.

Murphy was a larger-than-life character not adverse to self-promotion, and contemporary press reports often refer to him as an officer (he was never commissioned) or as an "Irishman" on account of his surname. During the 1920s Murphy established the "Ypres Salient War Museum" and his collection was moved to the rebuilt western wing of the Cloth Hall in 1937.

Following the outbreak of the Second World War Murphy was advised by the Belgian authorities to evacuate his collection to Britain, and by 1940 it had been installed at Gloucester Place in Brighton, charging an admission of 1s. for adults, 6d. for children, and half-price entry to members of the armed forces.[42] Leo Murphy and his family returned to Belgium following the end of the Second World War and he died on 21 August 1951. He was buried at Ypres Town Cemetery.

The museum was re-established in the west wing of the Cloth Hall and over the many years has evolved as tastes and technology have changed. Retitled the Salient 1914-1918 War Museum, the displays were modernised in 1984 before being radically remodeled the following decade. The "In Flanders Fields" Museum was reopened in April 1998 and incorporated multimedia displays for the first time. The museum was again closed for refurbishment several years later and on 11 June 2012 was inaugurated in its current form.

---

[42] Sussex Agricultural Express, 8 March 1940.

St George's Memorial Church

Designed by Sir Reginald Blomfield, the church was built to serve the British community that arrived in Ypres in the years following the Great War, many of them ex-servicemen who were employed by the Imperial War Graves Commission. The church serves as a memorial to those who served and died in the Ypres Salient during the Great War and contains many memorials to individuals, regiments and divisions.

The building of the Church was first proposed by the Ypres League in 1924 and its President, Field Marshal Lord French, made an appeal for donations. The Ypres League was founded on 28 September 1920 by a Canadian, Colonel Beckels Wilson, and its membership was composed of those who had served in the Ypres salient during the Great War and the relatives of those who had died there. Regular acts of remembrance and pilgrimages to Ypres were organised by the League throughout the 1920s and 1930s.

The foundation stone for the church was laid by Field Marshal Lord Plumer on 24 July 1927. Building work continued for the next two years and on 29 March 1929 the church was dedicated by the Bishop of Fulham. A British School was also dedicated on the same day as the church and was funded by donations from Old Etonians, opening to its first pupils on 9 April.

Among the many memorials inside St George's Church is laid up the Standard of the Slough Branch of The Old Contemptibles' Association, which was presented and dedicated on 28 June 1931.[43]

---

[43] Uxbridge & West Drayton Gazette, 3 July 1931.

The idea of creating an association of those who had served with the British Expeditionary Force in 1914, and who were holders of the 1914 Star with clasp, was instigated by Captain John Patrick Danny, formerly of the Royal Artillery.[44] On 25 June 1925 he and six other "Old Contemptibles" met at the Hackney United Services Club, at the "Red House" on Powerscroft Road in Clapton, to discuss the formation of such a group. The first General Meeting of The Old Contemptibles Association took place on 28 July, and Captain Danny was elected as treasurer. Members of the new Association were to be known as "Chums," irrespective of their rank, and only those who were holders of the 1914 Star with the clasp – in reality a bar to be sewn onto the ribbon of the medal – that indicated that individuals had "served under fire or who had operated within range of enemy mobile artillery in France or Belgium during the period between 5 August and 22 November 1914" would be eligible to join.

By the time of the 1930 Annual Conference, held in Birmingham, it was reported that the Association had 8,000 Chums in 60 Branches and that three overseas branches; one at Vancouver, an Australian Branch at Melbourne and a Branch formed at Ypres from Old Contemptibles living and working in Belgium, had been raised.[45] On 3 February 1930 the General Committee of the Ypres League offered complimentary membership to each Branch of The Old Contemptibles' Association "as a token of comradeship with the remembrance of those of the old Army who, to save their country, gave their lives in the First Battle of Ypres, October 19th to November 22nd, 1914."[46] Five years later there were over 100 Branches, and a Branch was also formed at The Hague from nine Old Contemptibles resident in the Netherlands, and by October 1938 this number had increased to 187, with applications for membership being received from the United States and India, as well as a proposal to form a Branch in South Africa.[47]

---

[44] Captain Danny had in fact enlisted using an assumed name. Born Reszo Engel in Hungary in 1872, when he attested for the Royal Regiment of Artillery in London he stated that he had been born at Stepney in 1878. Danny was employed as a garage foreman when he was mobilised from the Reserve at the outbreak of the war, and as 82558 Sergeant J. P. Danny landed in France with XXXIII Brigade, Royal Field Artillery on 6 November 1914. He was commissioned on 1 November 1915 and was issued with his 1914 Star on 18 October 1919, the clasp and roses were forwarded to him on 18 May 1920. Captain Danny died at his home at 68 Gunton Road in Clapton on 20 May 1928, was buried with full military honours at Abney Park Cemetery in Stoke Newington on 25 May.
[45] Birmingham Daily Gazette, 10 February 1930.
[46] The Ypres Times, Volume 5, No. 3, July 1930, p. 23.
[47] Sunderland Daily Echo and Shipping Gazette, 23 August 1935, The Old Contemptible – The Official Organ of The Old Contemptibles' Association, No. 43, July 1937, pp. 4-5 and Western Morning News, 24 October 1938.

The size of the Association increased when Old Contemptibles of Wales, formed in 1932, formally merged with the Association in 1940 and The Old Contemptibles' Association of Northern Ireland, which had been inaugurated in 1935, amalgamated with the national body in 1946.[48] At its peak, between the end of the Second World War and the organisation's Silver Jubilee Year of 1950, The Old Contemptibles' Association had over 220 Branches in the United Kingdom and Northern Ireland, as well as in the Republic of Ireland (Dublin Central Branch, formed in October 1929), Canada, Australia, New Zealand, and two Branches in the United States.[49] The National Executive of the Association disbanded in 1976, but some branches continued to meet until the last group, the London and South East Area, finally closed in 1994.

There are also three Squadron Standards of the Household Cavalry laid up at St George's Church. The first Standard, which is positioned over the Main Door, was laid up at a ceremony held on 3rd July 1967 and had been presented to the 1st Life Guards in 1911 by King George V. Found at Combermere Barracks in 1950, the Standard had been given to Lieutenant-Colonel F. F. B. St George, C.V.O. formerly The Life Guards, whose brother Second-Lieutenant Howard Avenal Bligh St George was killed on 15 November 1914, aged 19. He was the second son of Howard Bligh St George and Florence Evelyn St George and is buried at Zillebeke Churchyard: Row A, Grave 2. After being held at his home in Gloucestershire for many years, Colonel St George had decided to place the Standard in the care of St George's, as stated in an article that he wrote for "The Blue:" The Regimental Journal of The Royal Horse Guards (The Blues):

"It seemed to me a worthy gift for perhaps two reasons. It is an old Household Cavalry Standard which will always be a reminder of what the three Regiments, the First Life Guards, the Second Life Guards, and the Blues suffered in defence of the city of Ypres. The second reason is that it is a Standard which was carried at the Coronation of King George V, the beloved Sovereign of those who in the First War gave their lives."[50]

---

[48] Western Mail, 4 March 1940 and Northern Whig & Belfast Post, 24 July 1947. At the point of the amalgamation with The Old Contempibles' Association of Northern Ireland, three Ulster Branches of The Old Contemptibles' Association were in existence: Belfast Branch, Ulster No. 1 Branch and the Londonderry Branch. The Ulster No. 1 Branch had received its dispensation in 1943 and at the time of its inauguration was the 222nd on the Roll of The Old Contemptibles' Association (Ballymena Observer, 24 December 1943).

[49] Northern Whig & Belfast Post, 8 April 1946 and The Old Contemptibles' Association Silver Jubilee Grand Re-Union Programme, p. 14.

[50] "The Blue:" The Regimental Journal of The Royal Horse Guards (The Blues) 1968, p. 61.

On 23 February 2016, The Life Guards and the Blues and Royals each laid up a Squadron Standard at St George's Church in Ieper, in memory of the Household Cavalrymen (and the 1ˢᵗ (Royal) Dragoons) who served at Ypres during the Great War. The ceremony took place in the presence of the Princess Royal, Colonel of the Blues and Royals. The Standards are laid up on either side of the window dedicated to all ranks of the Household Cavalry, Brigade of Guards and the Guards Division who served in the Salient during the Great War, which is positioned above the altar.

St George's Memorial Church, 8 August 2018.

The Ypres (Menin Gate) Memorial

More commonly known simply as the Menin Gate, the Ypres (Menin Gate) Memorial (the correct title) commemorates 54,394[51] soldiers of the British Expeditionary Force, as well as the Canadian, Australian, South African, Indian and West Indian forces, who for the most part died between October 1914 and midnight of 15 August 1917 and whose remains were not identified after the war.

Although the vast majority of those who are commemorated on the panels died while serving in the Ypres Salient, there are also included a few soldiers who died during the early battles fought by the British Expeditionary Force in 1914 – at Mons, Le Cateau and on the Aisne – as well as men who died while prisoners of war, either in France and Belgium as a result of wounds or in Germany while in captivity. Although the official cut-off date for commemorations on the memorial was set as 15 August 1917, soldiers who died after that date and have no known grave are commemorated on the Tyne Cot Memorial, there are a significant number of men whose names can be found on the panels who are recorded as having died after that date.

---

[51] The Commonwealth War Graves Commission website records 54,611 names as listed on the Ypres (Menin Gate) Memorial, but this includes the aliases that had been used by some of the soldiers recorded on the memorial.

The Menin Gate was known as the Hangoartpoort during the Middle Ages, and was at that time a narrow gateway on the eastern side of the city's defences, but when the Vauban fortifications were constructed during the 17th Century the gate was widened and the ramparts on either side were built. It was around this time that it was called the Menenpoort, denoting that the road that passed through it led to Menin.

When British troops first marched into Ypres in October 1914 two lions carved from limestone stood on plinths on either side of the Menin Gate. During the war the Lions were severely damaged by shellfire and fell from their positions, one lost its right foreleg and the other having part of its head missing. The lions were presented to Australian War Memorial at Canberra by the City of Ypres in 1936, and the Australians presented a bronze casting of C. Web Gilbert's "Digger" sculpture in return.

The lions were originally displayed at Canberra in their damaged wartime condition, but in 1985 it was decided to renovate them. The work was done by sculptor Kasimiers L. Zywuszko, but in such a way as the replacement parts could be removed if there was a need to revert the lions to their previous state. Zywuszko completed the work in 1987 and the lions were again displayed at the Australian War Memorial from 1991.

Between 2014 and 2015 the lions were loaned to the Canadian War Museum in Ottawa.

In 2017 they returned to Ieper for the centenary commemorations of the Third Battle of Ypres, mounted on brick plinths constructed by the Commonwealth War Graves Commission in front of the Ypres (Menin Gate) Memorial. The lions remained in positon until after Armistice Day and were then returned to Australia, but the Australian Government agreed to provide replicas to stand on the plinths. The new lions were placed in position in October 2018 and formally inaugurated at a special ceremony held on the evening of 5 November.

Officers of 1ˢᵗ Cavalry Division standing in front of one of the lions at the Menin Gate in February 1915.

The Memorial was designed by Sir Reginald Blomfield, with sculptures by Sir William Reid Dick, and was constructed between 1923 and 1927. It was unveiled by Field-Marshal Lord Plumer on 24 July 1927, and the ceremony was broadcast live on the wireless by the B.B.C. Since its inauguration, the Ypres (Menin Gate) Memorial has been the backdrop for numerous commemorations of significant anniversaries of the battles fought in the Ypres Salient, most recently on 31 July 2017 those held to mark the centenary of the commencement of the Third Battle of Ypres.

On 26 May 1940 the memorial formed part of the defensive line manned by troops of the 4th Battalion, The East Yorkshire Regiment, which formed part of 150th Infantry Brigade of 50th (Northumbrian) Infantry Division. The infantry were joined the following day at the gate by a section of 101st Army Troops Company, Royal Monmouthshire Royal Engineers, commanded by Second-Lieutenant David Arthur Smith. Smith and his sappers were attached to the 12th Royal Lancers and had carried out several demolitions during the previous days to hold up the advance of German forces. His party placed charges of the bridge across the moat in front of the memorial, and at around 4 o'clock on the afternoon of 27 May they were detonated. The memorial sustained damage from the explosion, some of which can still be seen on the eastern side, and the Commanding Officer of the 4th East Yorkshires had his car destroyed by falling masonry. The Germans quickly repaired the damage to the bridge and roadway, but work on repairing the memorial was not completed until after the Second World War.

A photograph taken by a German serviceman in 1940, showing the damage caused to the road passing beneath the Ypres (Menin Gate) Memorial caused by the demolition of the bridge in front of the memorial on 27 May.

At the unveiling of the Ypres (Menin Gate) Memorial in 1927, buglers of the 2nd Battalion, The Somerset Light Infantry sounded the Last Post. The following year the Superintendent of Police in Ypres, Pierre Vandenbraambussche, conceived the idea that the Last Post should be sounded every night at 8 o'clock beneath the memorial during the summer months. The ceremony stopped in October 1928, at the close of the main tourist season, but the following spring a Last Post Committee was formed. The Antwerp Branch of the British Legion presented four silver bugles to the Committee, and these were used by firemen of the Ypres Fire Brigade to sound the call when the ceremony resumed on 11 November 1929. The nightly observance was broken during the Second World War, between 20 May 1940 and 6 September 1944, and resumed on the night following the liberation of Ypres from German occupation by 1st Polish Armoured Division. After the Second World War two more silver bugles were donated to the Last Post Committee by the Blackpool and Fleetwood Branch of The Old Contemptibles Association, and two silver cavalry trumpets were given by Colonel I. Whitaker in 1959 in memory of former cavalrymen and gunners who had served in the Ypres Salient. The ceremony still takes place every night and over the past thirty years has expanded as interest in the Great War has grown and attendances at the memorial increased significantly.

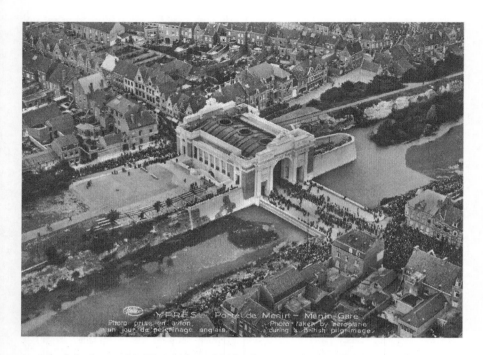

YPRES. Porte de Menin — Menin Gare
Photo prise en avion
un jour de pèlerinage anglais.
Photo taken by aeroplane
during a British pilgrimage.

At 11 o'clock on 11 November 2018, the Last Post will be sounded under the Ypres (Menin Gate) Memorial for the 31,221ˢᵗ time, in addition to the usual ceremony at 8 o'clock in the evening.

The names of the soldiers commemorated on the memorial are carved into stone panels that not only face the road inside the main hall, but also on the staircases and loggias that are on either side. Unlike the names carved on other Commonwealth War Graves Commission memorials, those on the Ypres (Menin Gate) Memorial appear as black text. This was achieved by sticking lining paper over the panels and using a blow-lamp to scorch away the paper over the inscribed lettering, leaving only that inside the carved spaces intact. Any excess paper was then brushed away and the lettering was spray-painted, with the panels being washed to leave only the blackened inscriptions visible.

Of the over 54,000 soldiers commemorated on the Ypres (Menin Gate) Memorial, and individual soldiers whose names were omitted from the original panel lists have their names inscribed on the Addenda Panels. Eight men awarded the Victoria Cross are also commemorated on the memorial.

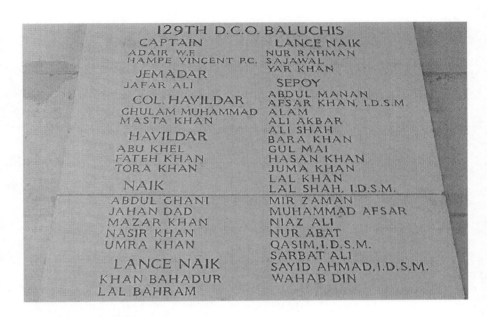

129TH D.C.O. BALUCHIS

CAPTAIN	**LANCE NAIK**
ADAIR W.F	NUR RAHMAN
HAMPE VINCENT P.C.	SAJAWAL
	YAR KHAN
JEMADAR	
JAFAR ALI	**SEPOY**
	ABDUL MANAN
COL. HAVILDAR	AFSAR KHAN, I.D.S.M.
GHULAM MUHAMMAD	ALAM
MASTA KHAN	ALI AKBAR
	ALI SHAH
HAVILDAR	BARA KHAN
ABU KHEL	GUL MAI
FATEH KHAN	HASAN KHAN
TORA KHAN	JUMA KHAN
	LAL KHAN
NAIK	LAL SHAH, I.D.S.M.
ABDUL GHANI	MIR ZAMAN
JAHAN DAD	MUHAMMAD AFSAR
MAZAR KHAN	NIAZ ALI
NASIR KHAN	NUR ABAT
UMRA KHAN	QASIM, I.D.S.M.
	SARBAT ALI
LANCE NAIK	SAYID AHMAD, I.D.S.M.
KHAN BAHADUR	WAHAB DIN
LAL BAHRAM	

3600 Sepoy Afsar Khan I.D.S.M.
129th (Duke of Connaught's Own) Baluchis

The son of Kabu Ali, who lived in the village of Polena near Gujar Khan in the Rawalpindi District of the Punjab (now in Pakistan), Sepoy Khan was stationed with his regiment at Ferozepore in the Punjab (now Firozpur in India) and embarked for France on the H.M.T. Ellinga, his regiment forming part of the Ferozepore Brigade of the 3rd (Lahore) Division. Khan was a member of the battalion's Machine Gun Section, which was equipped with two Maxim machine guns.

After stopping briefly at Aden, the 129th Baluchis arrived at Suez on 9 September before disembarking two days later and entraining at Port Tewfik for Cairo, where they encamped on the racecourse at Heliopolis and carried out training. The regiment embarked again on the H.M.T. Ellinga at Alexandria on 17 September and left the port two days later as part of a convoy sailing for France. The 129th Baluchis eventually reached Marseilles on 26 September and disembarked, moving to a camp at Orleans where further training was carried out.

The following month the 129th Baluchis were sent north by train towards Ypres, being conveyed by motor buses to St Eloi on 23 October before marching to Hollebeke where they deployed alongside dismounted cavalrymen of 3rd Cavalry Brigade of 2nd Cavalry Division.

On 31 October Sepoy Khan was serving his machine gun positioned at Jardine's Farm, to the south-west of Hollebeke, firing at the advancing Germans. After one of the machine guns was put out of action by a shell burst, Khan and the rest of his crew continued to fire on the enemy as they moved forward. He and four of his comrades were shot or bayoneted but 4050 Sepoy Khudadad Khan, though seriously wounded, kept the gun in action until the position was overrun. For his actions that day Khudadad Khan became the first Indian soldier to be awarded the Victoria Cross.

Sepoy Afsar Khan was posthumously awarded the Indian Distinguished Service Medal for his part in the fighting on 31 October 1914, the award being announced in The London Gazette on 18 February 1915. The Corps Commander of the Indian Corps, General Sir James Willcocks, also paid tribute to Afsar and his fallen comrades, stating in his account of the Indian Corps in France: "Engrave these names in letters of gold for all time."[52]

Sepoy Afsar Khan I.D.S.M. is commemorated on Panel 1 of the Ypres (Menin Gate) Memorial. The Commonwealth War Graves Commission records that he died on 30 October 1914.

The Indian Forces Memorial on the Ramparts at Ypres, located a short distance from the Ypres (Menin Gate) Memorial, commemorates the service of troops of the Indian Corps in Flanders during the Great War. It was unveiled on 12 March 2011.

Nearby is another memorial to the Gurkha Riflemen from Nepal who also served in the Ypres salient during 1915 as part of the 3rd (Lahore) Division.

---

[52] General Sir James Willcocks, *With the Indians in France* (London, Constable & Company Ltd, 1920), p. 43.

An Indian soldier photographed with men of the 1/6th Battalion, The South Staffordshire Regiment at their billets near Ouderdom in June 1915.
(Courtesy of the late Jake Whitehouse)

Just after midnight on 26 June 1915, the 1/5th Battalion, The South Staffordshire Regiment arrived at their new billets at "F" Huts, near Ouderdom, having completed three months in the front line at Wulverghem. After resting and cleaning their quarters, the soldiers began to explore and became acquainted with the Indian soldiers who were billeted close by, being invited to share their food with them. It is very unlikely that any of the Territorials had seen or tasted any meal as exotic before, and their impressions were recorded in their letters home.

In a joint letter written to their father, who lived at Albion Street in Brierley Hill, **9077 Lance-Corporal Charles Marsh** and his brother, **9064 Private James Marsh**, who served with "A" Company of the 1/5th South Staffords, described meeting Indian troops on their arrival at Ouderdom:

"We are at a different place now, and for two days our 'neighbours' were Indians. Very interesting they proved. They were very friendly, and invited us to their bivouacs and we sat down with them round their fires, they made tea for us in their own peculiar way, and gave us food which it is beyond me to describe, as the shape and taste were all peculiar."[53]

The 1/6th North Staffords had also marched to Ouderdom at the same time as the 1/5th South Staffords, and an unidentified soldier of the battalion wrote to Rev. H. W. Gilbert, Vicar of Branstone, recounting the meal that he had shared:

"I have just had some tea with the Indians – the Sihks (sic)... The tea consists of boiled peas – not the same as we have in England, but quite as nice."[54]

The same soldier also transcribed in his letter a version of "It's a Long Way to Tipperary" that he heard sung in Punjabi:

"Burra, due hai Tipperary,

Bahoot Lumbah knouch wo

Burra, due hai Tipperary,

Sake pas Powchenay ko,

Ram, Ram, Piccadilly!

Salaam, Leicester Square!

Burra, Burra dur hai Tipperary

Lakin del hoe-aye lah gah."

[53] County Express, 24 July 1915.
[54] Burton Daily Mail, 1 July 1915.

D/2601 Corporal Archibald John Vanson and *5536* **Sergeant Robert Henry Vanson**, were brothers who served together in the 1ˢᵗ (Royal) Dragoons, were both killed on 30 October 1914. The sons of Henry and Frances Vanson, their father had previously been a soldier but on leaving the Army was employed as a prison warder at Canterbury Gaol.

Born at Bangalore in 1888, Archibald Vanson was working as a porter when he attested for the Royals at Dover on 18 July 1905. He served with his brother in India and South Africa.

Robert Vanson was born at Agra and was aged 18 years and one month when he attested at Canterbury on 21 November 1901. Working as a labourer at the time of his enlistment, Robert joined the Depot of the 1ˢᵗ (Royal) Dragoons at Shorncliffe the following day. Vanson was awarded his first Good Conduct Badge on 21 November 1903 and was posted to India on 27 January 1904. While stationed at Lucknow he was appointed as a Lance-Corporal on 17 January 1906 and was awarded his second Good Conduct Badge on 21 November. He also passed a railway guards' certificate while stationed in India, possibly with a view on taking up employment there on his transfer to the Reserve. Vanson was promoted to Corporal on 5 November 1908 and, while quartered at Muttra, advanced to Sergeant on 4 November 1909.

On 13 March 1911, he re-engaged to complete 21 years with the Colours and in November the Royals left India for South Africa, where the regiment was stationed at Robert's Heights in Pretoria. By this time Sergeant Vanson was also an instructor at the regiment's Riding School. During July 1912, the Royals were deployed to Pretoria on strike duty. The strike soon descended into rioting and Sergeant Vanson was noted for his steady conduct under difficult circumstances in which the Royals had 22 Officers and Other Ranks injured and four horses killed and a further 14 wounded. The regiment moved to Potchefstroom in February 1913 and Sergeant Vanson married Flora Ada Goldsmith there on 26 February 1914.

The Vanson brothers returned from South Africa to Southampton on 19 September 1914 and Robert's wife, Ada, moved into lodgings at 55 Havelock Street in Canterbury. They landed at Ostend with the Royals on 8 October.

Corporal Archibald Vanson died of wounds received while in trenches north of Hollebeke Chateau, while his brother, Robert, was later recalled by one of his comrades, Jack Cusack, as having been killed while serving with the Headquarters of 6th Cavalry Brigade, carrying the pennant for the Brigade's commander, Brigadier-General Ernest Makins, who was the former commanding officer of the Royals.[55]

Archibald and Robert Vanson are commemorated on Panel 5 of the memorial. The register records that their parents lived at 22 Hope Street in Maidstone, and that Robert's widow, Flora, had remarried and lived at 54 Havelock Street after the war.

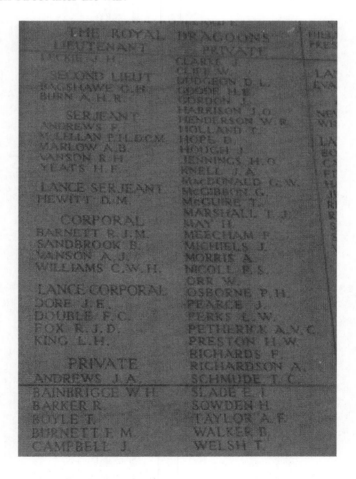

---

[55] Cusack, J. & Herbert, I. *Scarlet Fever: A Lifetime with Horses* (London, Cassell, 1972), p.36

358298 Private John Eddy Hartley
1/10ᵗʰ (Scottish) Battalion, The King's (Liverpool Regiment) (Territorial Force)

Private John Hartley was killed on 31 July 1917 during the attack mounted by 1/10ᵗʰ King's on Capricorn Trench, to the north-east of Wieltje. He had volunteered on 27 June 1916, leaving his job as a cashier at Harling and Todd's foundry in Burnley. At first it was reported that he was missing following the fighting, and news was reported in The Burnley News on 5 September 1917:

ONE OF SIX BROTHERS.

Fate of Well-Known Burnley Soldier in Doubt.

"Uncertainty surrounds the fate of Private John Eddy Hartley, 114, Cog-lane, Burnley.

On Thursday, a communication reached Mrs Hartley for a captain at the Front, stating that her husband was reported missing as from 31ˢᵗ July. The writer heard that Pte. Hartley had been instantly killed by shrapnel. No definite ground were given for this belief, and the anxiety of the wife was somewhat relieved when official intimation reached her yesterday morning to the effect that her husband was reported "missing."

Private J. E. Hartley, aged 32, was formerly engaged in the clerical department of Messrs. Harling and Todd's foundry, and joined up about 16 months ago. He was sent to France last November, and was afterwards confined to hospital with trench fever. It was when he was recovering that he discovered that he possessed a good baritone voice. His musical ability soon became known and he was invited to join the "Jollies' Concert Party," which he eventually did. So great was his success that he was allowed to continue as an entertainer of his comrades for a considerable time.

Five brothers are serving in the Army."

Private Hartley's parents, who lived at 21 Mizpah Street, received a letter from Captain J. A. Roddick, who confirmed that their son had been killed on 31 July, which was reproduced in The Burnley Express on 5 September:

"I am very sorry to tell you that Pte. (358298) J. E. Hartley, who went over with us in the great attack on the enemy on July 31, and was subsequently reported missing, is now confirmed as having been killed instantaneously by a piece of shell. He is buried 400 yards north-east of ---------- (Wieltje). It is very sad for his officers, N.C.O.'s and men, but the loss we, his comrades, feel can be as nothing to your own bereavement, and I wish you to accept on our behalf this expression of sincerest sympathy. He was a gallant and brave soldier, and met his end doing his duty nobly for his King and country. I have been on active service nearly two years and I can assure you that it is the continued loss of such fine fellows which makes us all the more determined to thoroughly thrash these savages, and thereby reap a rich revenge."

To mark the first anniversary of his death, his widow, Florrie, placed a notice in The Burnley Express on 27 July 1918:

HARTLEY – In loving memory of Pte. John E. Hartley, Liverpool Scottish, who was killed in action on July 31st, 1917.

If those who caused this cruel war
Were the only ones to fight
This world would be the brighter,
And less aching hearts to-night.

- From Wife and Child, 114, Cog-lane.

Private Hartley is commemorated on Panel 6 of the Ypres (Menin Gate) Memorial. The register for the memorial records that his widow, Florrie, remarried and lived at 118 Cog Lane in Burnley after the war.

8773 Private Frank Ashton, who served with "D" Company of the 2nd Battalion, The Suffolk Regiment, was listed as missing on 26 August 1914 following the Battle of Le Cateau. A regular soldier, Frank had been stationed at the Curragh when war was declared and had disembarked at Le Havre on 17 August. His fate uncertain for many months, it was reported by The Bury Free Press on 31 July 1915 that he had died while in captivity in Germany:

"Mr and Mrs A. Ashton, 17, St Edmund's Place, Bury St Edmund's, have received official notification that their fifth son, after being in the list of missing since the battle of Le Cateau on 26 August 1914, has died in Germany on April 9th. The deceased soldier, who was 18 years of age, left Ireland for France at the commencement of the war in D Co., 2nd Suffolk Regiment."

Although reported to have died as a prisoner in Germany, Private Ashton is commemorated on Panel 21 of the Ypres (Menin Gate) Memorial together with his brother, **13039 Lance-Corporal William Ashton**, who had been killed with serving with the 1st Battalion, The Suffolk Regiment on 8 May 1915, when the battalion was holding trenches on the Frezenberg Ridge and repulsed two German assaults, but lost heavily. William had only been with the 1st Suffolks for a matter of days, having been part of a draft sent to the front from the 3rd (Special Reserve) Battalion at Felixstowe.

The death of William was reported in the same article in The Bury Free Press:

"Lance-Corpl. W. Ashton, third son of Mr and Mrs Ashton, is also officially reported killed in action on May 8th, being attached to the 1st Suffolk Regiment. He was buried near Ypres. He joined Kitchener's Army in August last, leaving Felixstowe on April 22nd, 1915. The deceased was formerly in the employ of the G.E.R., and was much respected by all his fellow work-men. He was 27 years of age. Much sympathy is felt for Mr and Mrs Ashton and family in their very sad bereavement, and they wish through our columns to thank all for the expressions of sympathy they have received. Mr and Mrs Ashton have two other sons, Horace and George, serving with the colours."

Frank and William were the sons of Alfred and Alice Ashton.

A Model "Ranker"

"Second-Lieutenant Frederick C. Hatton, who has been killed in action while serving with the 2nd Battalion Alexandra, Princess of Wales's Own Yorkshire Regiment, was a model "ranker" officer, and only got his commission a month ago. He was a native of Parkhurst, Isle of Wight, and married a daughter of the last Q.M.S. Thewlis (Royal Dublin Fusiliers), and niece of Alderman Thewlis, an ex-Lord Mayor of Manchester. Mr Hatton was 38 years of age, and enlisted at Portsmouth as a boy of 14. He was a lance-corporal after four years' service, and became a full sergeant in 1900, orderly room sergeant, 1903, Q.M.S., 1906, and sergeant major (warrant officer) last year. Mr Hatton was Hon. Secretary of the Green Howards' Association. His father was formerly sub-editor of the first English newspaper printed in Japan, and the deceased and his two brothers (one of whom a medical man frequently contributes to the "Lancet") were very clever writers."[56]

---

[56] Portsmouth Evening News, 19 November 1914.

Second-Lieutenant Frederick Charles Hatton was 3620 Regimental Sergeant-Major F. C. Hatton at the outbreak of the war, stationed on Guernsey with the 2nd Battalion, Alexandra, Princess of Wales's Own (Yorkshire Regiment).

Born on 9 April 1878 at the Barracks in Parkhurst, his father was a Lance-Sergeant serving as canteen steward to the 2nd Battalion, 19th (1st Yorkshire North Riding – Princess of Wales's Own) Foot at the time of his birth, and Frederick joined The Princess of Wales's Own (Yorkshire Regiment) on Boy Service in 1892. He held the rank of Corporal when he saw active service in South Africa during the Boer War and was wounded during the Battle of Driefontein on 10 March 1900. Invalided back to England, Hatton was issued with the Queen's South Africa Medal on 28 August 1901, with clasps for Relief of Kimberley, Paardeberg and Driefontein.

Frederick married Elsie Thewlis in 1902 and during his service with the Yorkshires held a number of appointments: Gymnastics Instructor, Drill Instructor at the Regimental Depot at Richmond, Pay Sergeant, Orderly Room Sergeant, Canteen Accountant, and Regimental Quartermaster-Sergeant. Hatton was awarded the Long Service and Good Conduct Medal in Army Order 254 of October 1910, and was appointed Regimental Sergeant-Major to the 2nd Battalion in 1913.

The 2nd Yorkshires sailed for Southampton on 28 August 1914, and on 4 September moved to Lyndhurst in the New Forest, where the battalion joined 21st Brigade of 7th Division. R.S.M. Hatton disembarked at Zeebrugge on 6 October and three days later, while the 2nd Yorkshires were at Bruges, was commissioned in the field as a Second-Lieutenant.

Second-Lieutenant Hatton was acting as Adjutant of the 2nd Yorkshires when he was shot and killed by a German sniper on 30 October beside the Commanding Officer, Lieutenant-Colonel Charles Arthur Cecil King (who was also killed by a sniper) while directing the battalion in a counter-attack near Zandvoorde against the advancing Germans. Frederick Hatton has no known grave and is commemorated on Panel 33 of the Ypres (Menin Gate) Memorial.

His widow, Elsie, and their son, Frederick Arthur, are recorded as living at 4 West Terrace at Richmond after the war. Second-Lieutenant Hatton's 1914 Star was issued to Elsie on 20 February 1920, and the clasp for the medal was sent to her on 20 January 1921.

2513 Lance-Corporal Lawrence Burr Merson, who served with "D" Company of the 1/4ᵗʰ Battalion, The Gordon Highlanders (Territorial Force), was killed on 25 September 1915, aged 21, during the diversionary attack mounted by 3ʳᵈ Division at Hooge.

His parents, Stuart Anderson and Jessie Merson, who lived at 17 Mount Street in Aberdeen, later received a letter from the sister of a German soldier who had found their son dead in a trench in their third line, elements of "D" Company having been cut off there following the enemy counter-attack. The letter had been sent from Frankfurt-am-Main to an Uncle of the German soldier who lived in Switzerland, who then sent it on 2 October to Lance-Corporal Merson's family. The letter was printed in The Aberdeen Evening Express on 8 October:

"It is a very sad matter I am writing you. My brother sent home a letter from the front and begged me to write you.

He stands in the West, and it was in his first letter since the hard fights there. My eldest brother was killed last year at Ypres, so that I know how glad we were to hear any details of his death. I think you have already heard that Lawrence B. Merson, whom I believe to be your son, did not come back from the last fight. We were enemies, but pain and mourning are uniting us. So thought my brother, too, for he wrote everything about your son he could find out. I just will translate it to you –

"We led the way to our position, and found there a dead Highlander, who had a deep wound above the right eye, probably by a thrust of the bayonet. We found the following objects:- Book of payment, mark of distinction, a small sketch, and an instrument against the gases. The dead Englishman (sic) had his gun with the bayonet at it (and there were spots of blood on it) on his right side. He was a Highlander with a kilt, and bare knees."

My brother sent these photos. I am sure my brother and his comrades did all honour to their enemy who died in their tracks."

The German soldier's uncle also added a note to the letter:

"My brother is a clergyman for French Protestants in Frankfort, and his son is in the German Army, although we are of old Swiss origin, and he sent the intimation to his sister in Frankfort. Your son did his duty for his country, and he will find his reward. God help you in these dark days."

Included with the letters were Lance-Corporal Merson's pay book, identity disc and other letters and photographs that the German soldier had found on his body. Lawrence Merson, who had worked as a postman at Blairs Post Office, has no known grave and is commemorated on Panel 38 of the Ypres (Menin Gate) Memorial. The Commonwealth War Graves Commission record that he was aged 20 when he was killed.

7425 Private James Stallard
8303 Private John William Stallard
2ⁿᵈ Battalion, The Oxfordshire and Buckinghamshire Light Infantry

John and James Stallard were the sons of James and Florence Stallard. Both James and John were born in the Hockley district of Birmingham, where their father was employed as a railway lamp maker. The Stallards later moved to North Buckinghamshire, where their father worked at the Wolverton Railway Works. The family set up home at 67 St Mary Street in New Bradwell. As well as their two sons, James and Florence had another boy, Sidney, and six daughters.

James Stallard joined The Oxfordshire Light Infantry at Oxford in 1905, and his brother John enlisted five years later. The brothers served together with the 1ˢᵗ Battalion in India before James was transferred to the Reserve and returned home to England.

Following the declaration of war James was mobilised from the Reserve, leaving his job as a carpenter in Northampton and his wife and baby daughter. John was in England preparing for a boxing competition and the brothers were posted to the 2ⁿᵈ Battalion at Aldershot before embarking for France, landing at Boulogne on 14 August 1914.

Letters sent home by James were published in The Wolverton Express on 16 October 1914:

STANTONBURY MEN'S LETTERS FROM THE FRONT.

"Interesting letters have been received from the fighting line by Mr and Mrs James Stallard of St Mary's Street, Stantonbury, from their sons, Privates James and Jack Stallard, both of whom are serving with the Oxfordshire and Bucks Light Infantry.

Jim is a reservist who, when war broke out, was employed in Northampton where his wife and child live. There is another brother who is in the Army and he, Sidney, rejoins his regiment, the King's Royal Rifles, in a few days. Jack Stallard is a boxer of repute in the Army and had gone into strict training for a big match at the National Sporting Club when war broke out. Because of his prowess with the gloves he was known amongst his comrades in India as "The Mad Mullah".

These two brothers, Jim and Jack Stallard, are fighting shoulder to shoulder in the trenches. When they first entered the firing line, twenty-five comrades separated them. One by one the twenty-five have dropped out, either killed or wounded, until the brothers brushed shoulders and together they have been for many days.

The first letter is dated 24th September, the following being an extract:

"I beg for the finish of this war, and it is war. hell cannot be worse. It is just like waiting for death, but still, we are lucky enough to escape so far, and can safely say it is a game of luck, and trust luck will be with us to the end. Whoever is spared will have thoughts and "memories" of a war the like of which has never been before in history. One has only to think of the countries involved, the up-to-date guns we all have in action, and the range and power of the weapons in use, and try and form opinions of the result. We are not against a lot of farmers but against a nation of fighting material.
One of the most touching events I have seen in this war was in Belgium, in our advance and retirement on and from Mons. There we saw the most unfortunate people leaving what had once been their homes, with a bit of food all tied up in anything they could carry. Aged, young and babies, all destitute. We met them in the woods, in the fields, and in fact everywhere we went we found the poor terrified folk. It was heartrending. At one large house, as we advanced on Mons, the family were just leaving, and with eyes much swollen by crying, one young girl, about 22 or 23, unable to hold herself in check, ran forward at the sight of our troops and before we were aware of her intentions, had kissed several of us on both cheeks. That sort of thing tends to touch even the hardest of hearts. The people of Belgium behaved to us splendidly. Never to my dying day shall I forget their kindness."

In a letter dated 4th October it is stated:

"The Special Reserve have joined us, and young Nash and Syrett from Bradwell came past me the other day and spoke. I also received a message from Frank Levitt of the Rifle Brigade but have not seen him. I was also recognised when we passed the Northamptons, but donít know who it was (it was night). I see some of the Wolverton chaps here, several in our Company. Mr Webber, in the Time Office, has a son here in our platoon, so we have a good chat together. I also came across Hobson of the Berks, he was a fireman on an engine in the yard at Wolverton Works, and two fellows from Stony are in our Company.

A few words regarding our advance and the state the Germans left the places they came through when we were following them up. They looted everything and everywhere; hardly a house escaped their evil work. They threw things about that were not a bit of use to them, smashed open the doors, and broke everything they could lay their hands on. Tables were carried out of the houses, cloths spread, and plates, etc. were used in the open. Lamps, beds, everything from the houses were scattered in the roads and the street. Never have I seen or even dreamed of such sights. Farms were in an awful state; they absolutely emptied them and destroyed every mortal thing. On place we came through I particularly noticed. All children's and women's clothes were thrown about from the houses; mirrors, lamps, beds, furniture all broken and scattered in the streets, fancy chairs, in fact the entire contents of good houses, so you can perhaps picture the sights.

But as we got further, instead of household things lying about, it was the Germans themselves lying in all directions. At first it appears rather a ghastly sight, but one has to get used to more than this, things I am not allowed to speak of. We can hear them (shells) screaming as they come but, worse luck, don't know where they are going to settle (settle, what a word!). It is all bobbing up and down (we hear some of the boys shout "Look out!").

Still, it is surprising how the boys keep up their spirits. It is beautiful to see and hear them; there is plenty of life in them. We are all the same;set faces one minute, joking and laughing the next. Still, it is a good game of luck, nothing else. Jack and I are still side by side. We are both all gay. The winter will be awful, I bet, it is terrible at nights now."

Another letter sent by James to his wife in Northampton was published by The Northampton Mercury on 30 October:

"Mrs Stallard, the wife of Private James Stallard, one of two Bradwell brothers who are in the firing line, has received a second letter from her husband, in the course of which he speaks of the unnerving effect of the German artillery fire.

"The terrific noise, the shake and smoke, and the waiting for them to drop as one hears them coming, is a thing I cannot explain. It is awful waiting to hear and feel the explosion so as to be able to breathe once again freely and wait for the scream of the next one. If only you could see the awful destruction caused by their shells on buildings out here – I think in numerous cases necessary – it would, I am sure, cut you to the heart.

What with the different things I have seen since the Germans started to retreat and also here – is too much. I used to picture different things that could possibly happen among the natives of India and Burmah during the time I was there, but never did I dream that anything like we see here could be done by a European race. It was an awfully sad sight for us to see as we came through the villages and towns.

"A Game of Luck"

The writer continues: "The fight is really a game of luck, which I shall be glad to be out of. There is now doubt our boys are in wonderful good spirits. Perhaps we may be sitting down in the trenches holding a mother's meeting when, all of a sudden, one of our big guns may fire from right behind us, and noticing which way it is fired first, it is sport to see us all bob down. Then when we have found out our mistakes a good laugh ends the meeting. It is sport of a good sort, played slowly, but only let me scrape through safely and I shall always think of all the boys and their splendid spirits. When we have had the chance to buy a loaf of bread out here we have to pay as much as 1s. 2d. for it. Still I expect we must not grumble."

The brothers died together during the successful counter-attack at Nonne Bosschen, during which the 2nd Ox and Bucks defeated the 1. Garde-Regiment zu Fuß for the loss of five killed and 25 wounded. News of their deaths appeared in The Wolverton Express on Christmas Day 1914:

BRADWELL
-
TWO BROTHERS KILLED

"The following has not yet appeared on our official lists: Pte. J.F. Stallard, Oxon. and Bucks L.I., killed. Mrs Stallard, who resides at 48 Grafton Street, Northampton, has received an official intimation that her husband, Private J. F. Stallard, was killed in action on 11th November. The last she heard from her husband was a letter written by him on 10th November, the day before his death. There is one child, six months old. Private Stallard was a native of Bradwell. He worked at Messrs Smith, Major and Stevens, St James', Northampton, and was called up with the reserve in August. He had been through all the fighting on the Continent since the landing of the British Expeditionary Force. He was brother to Private Jack Stallard of the same regiment, a well-known boxer, who was in training for an important competition at the date of mobilisation and who is also unofficially reported killed."

James and John Stallard are commemorated side-by-side, as they had died, on Panel 39 of the Ypres (Menin Gate) Memorial, and also on the war memorial at New Bradwell Cemetery

The War Memorial at New Bradwell

2548 Private Ernest Freeman, of the 1/1ˢᵗ Battalion, The Cambridgeshire Regiment (Territorial Force), was killed during the early hours of 5 May 1915, when "A" Company was working in Sanctuary Wood digging a communication trench. Aged 24, Private Freeman had attested for The Cambridgeshire Regiment shortly after the outbreak of the war, leaving his job in the kitchens at Christ's College.

His father, 257 Sergeant Frank Freeman, who in civilian life was a compositor at the Cambridge University Press, had originally attested for the 3ʳᵈ Volunteer Battalion, The Suffolk Regiment on 18 January 1889 and had re-engaged for the Territorial Force on the formation of The Cambridgeshire Regiment on 1 April 1908. Frank Freeman did not serve alongside his son, on account of his age, but remained at home with the 62ⁿᵈ Provisional Battalion.

2352 Private Herbert George Hunt, who served alongside Ernest in "A" Company, wrote to Private Freeman's parents at 84 Hemingford Road in Cambridge and described the circumstances in which he had been killed, and how he had been buried by his comrades:

"I have taken it on myself to write this letter to you, which is meant for one of sympathy and condolence from one and all of his comrades, drawn together by the close association and hardships, and suffering, and occasionally happy moments, which, in spite of all the hardships and horrors, still creeps into our lives out here in this sorely stricken country of Belgium.

You have, no doubt, learnt the sad tidings from his officer and the War Office. We, his comrades, felt his death very much. The shell struck down with one fell blow so many of our number, for up to that time we were very fortunate compared to others, and had only one killed.

One of our corporals got permission the next night to take a small party and fetch poor Ernie's body in from the place where he fell, about one mile away. The corporal asked for volunteers for this expedition, and, of course, I responded at once, and was followed by others. We crept out with much doubt and misgiving, and succeeded in recovering his body. We dared not show a light, and it was a pitch dark night, but as we gently placed him on the stretcher, some German rockets and flare-lights shot up from the trenches near by and lit us all up for a few seconds.

His face was as calm in death as it was in life, and the body lay as if in a deep sleep. A corporal read a short passage of scripture, and we committed Ernie's body to the earth. We stood with bared heads, and then with heavy hearts we turned sorrowfully away."[57]

Private Freeman's grave was lost during subsequent fighting in the area and he is commemorated on Panel 50 of the Ypres (Menin Gate) Memorial and also on the war memorial at Cambridge Guildhall.

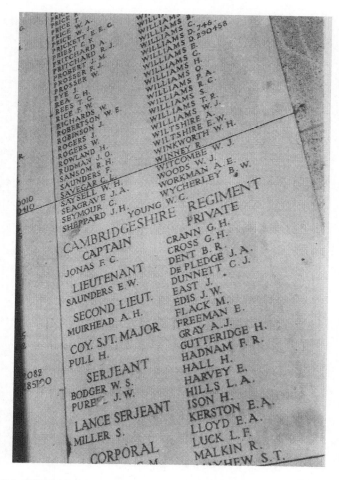

Panel 50 of the Ypres (Menin Gate) Memorial, including the name of Private Ernest Freeman. The photograph was taken in 1940 by a German serviceman following the invasion and occupation of Belgium.

[57] Cambridge Indepdendent Press, 28 May 1915.

108 Sergeant Leonard Arthur Johnson M.M.
27th Infantry Battalion, Australian Imperial Force

Born at Adelaide on 17 September 1891, Len was working as a stockman and was the son of William Arthur and Miriam Caroline Johnson, who lived at "Hazelmere" on 15th Street in Renmark in South Australia. He was aged 23 years and five months when he passed through the Recruiting Office at Renmark on 5 February 1915,[58] and attested for the Australian Imperial Force at Keswick Barracks three days later. Posted to "C" Squadron of the Light Horse Base Details, Private Johnson was transferred to "A" Company of the 24th Infantry Battalion on 1 April 1915. He was transferred to the 27th Battalion, which formed part of 7th Brigade of 2nd Division, and was posted as a Driver to the Transport Section. Johnson embarked at Adelaide on board the Vestalia on 29 June 1915 for Egypt. He remained with the battalion Transport Section at Heliopolis when the 27th Battalion was sent to Gallipoli in September, and rejoined them at Tel-el-Kebir on 10 January 1916. He was appointed a Lance-Corporal while encamped at Ismailia on 22 January 1916 and was posted to "B" Company. Lance-Corporal Johnson sailed from Alexandria on 15 March and landed in France six days later.

---

[58] Murray Pioneer, 29 July 1915 & 4 May 1916.

The 27th Battalion entered the front line for the first time on 7 April in the La Chapelle d'Armentieres sector and the following month Johnson wrote to his local newspaper, giving an account of his experiences since leaving Egypt. His letter was printed by The Murray Pioneer on 14 July:

FROM THE TRENCHES IN FRANCE.

"Cpl. L. A. Johnson (B. Coy., 27th Batt.) writes, under date May 13, from France, "in the trenches."

I thought perhaps a few lines from the Front might interest some of your readers. Well, we left Egypt on the 15th of March, and sailed for France on a lovely boat, with good accommodation for troops. We had an excellent trip, although we were chased by a submarine. After nine days on the water we landed at Marseilles, in the south of France. Then we all entrained and travelled right through France, which took 3½ days. The journey was most interesting and very enjoyable, and the welcome we got in France was more than words could explain. When we reached our destination we were all billetted in empty houses, for some two weeks.

I might mention that we were the first Brigade of Australian Infantry to land in France and go into action. The life in the trenches for the first few weeks was very miserable, nothing but snow, mud and water. We were often knee deep in mud and slush, but we overcame all these difficulties and now the weather is most favourable, much like the spring in our own little land.

The warfare in France is waged much different to that at the Dardanelles, although it's very rough at times. Well I've been chosen for a Batt. Patrol, also being the N.C.O. in charge of B. Coy. Patrol. I have along with me a lad by the name of J. Gilford, a brother of F. Gilford, late of Renmark, also another lad by the name of J. McLean, from Wallaroo, South Australia. Both these lads are very brave. They have proved themselves already. I might mention we have had some narrow escapes, like a lot more, but one gets accustomed to all this. We have a lot of Renmark lads in this Battalion, also Sergt. J. Dillon, of Mildura. We are all quite well, but looking forward for our homeward trip. My duty calls me now so I must ring off, trusting you and all friends are quite well."

In June, the 27th Battalion moved with the rest of 2nd Australian Division a few miles north into Belgium and took over the Wulverghem sector, facing Messines. Johnson took part in a trench raid mounted by the battalion on the German positions at Ontario Farm. The battalion War Diary recorded the sequence of events:

"During night our raiding party entered enemy trench at Ontario Farm under artillery barrage & did some damage, killed 17 enemy and taking 4 prisoners. Retaliation by Bosche Artillery severe."[59]

The 27th lost two Officers wounded and four Other Ranks killed and another 26 wounded during the action. Among them was Lance-Corporal Johnson, who had received a severe gunshot wound to his back.

Admitted to 73rd Field Ambulance, he was evacuated to No. 1 Canadian Casualty Clearing Station before being transferred to the Anglo-American Hospital at Wimereux on 1 July. Johnson sailed from Boulogne to England on board the H.M.H.S. Western Australia on 3 July and was admitted to 2nd Southern General Hospital at Bristol the following day. He remained there until he was discharged on 4 August, and was ordered to report to the Officer Commanding the A.I.F. Training Camp at Bhurtpore Barracks in Tidworth.

Granted leave, Johnson arrived at No. 1 Command Depot at Perham Down on 23 August. While convalescing, he was admitted to hospital on 9 October suffering from venereal disease. Johnson was transferred to 1st Australian Dermatological Hospital at Bulford on 16 November for further treatment for his condition. He was discharged on Boxing Day and posted to Perham Down. On 5 January 1917, Lance-Corporal Johnson was charged as having been absent without leave between midnight of 4 January until 1.30 p.m. that afternoon. He was reprimanded by Lieutenant H. E. Shaw for the offence, and forfeited one days' pay as punishment.

Lance-Corporal Johnson was placed on a draft for France and embarked on the Princess Clementina at Folkestone on 24 January 1917. He arrived at 2nd Australian Division Base Depot at Etaples the following day and rejoined the 27th Battalion on 5 February. Johnson reported sick on 25 February and was admitted to 3rd Field Ambulance. Diagnosed as suffering from mumps, he was transferred to 2nd Field Ambulance and after treatment he returned to the 27th Battalion on 12 March. Johnson was promoted to Corporal the same day, and was again promoted, to Sergeant ten days later, in charge of the

---

[59] AWM4 23/44 War Diary, 27th Infantry Battalion.

Battalion's Scouts, following the death of 703 Sergeant Herbert James Teesdale.[60]

Sergeant Johnson was awarded the Military Medal for his actions during the fighting around Bullecourt. The citation for the award reads:

"During the period 19th April to 6th May 1917, before the HINDENBURG LINE East of BULLECOURT, this N.C.O. acted as Scout Sergeant. He was employed on this trying duty for at least seventeen nights. he penetrated the wire in front of the HINDENBURG LINE on several occasions, and made most valuable and accurate reports on its condition. He displayed unusual initiative and courage on many occasions, and had several encounters with enemy patrols all of which were engaged and driven in. On the night of 26/27th April, he led the party of Engineers and Infantry who destroyed portion of enemy's wire with Bangalore Torpedoes."[61]

The award was confirmed in 1st Anzac Corps Routine Order No. 57 of 2 July 1917, and announced in The London Gazette on 6 July. News of his award was printed by The Murray Pioneer on 10 August:

"Congratulations are due, and will be heartily given, to the relatives of Sgt. Len Johnson, of Renmark, who has been awarded the Military Medal for gallantry in action in France."

Another reference to Johnson being awarded the Military Medal was made in an article published by The Murray Pioneer on 24 August:

"Sergeant L. A. Johnson, who as mentioned a week or two ago, has been awarded the military medal for conspicuous service on the battle field, has been serving with the colours for quite a long time, and is now a veteran campaigner. He was wounded in France twelve months ago last July as a result of which he spent six months in hospital in England. He has seen a lot of fighting since he returned to France, and on one occasion he mentions that he was in charge of six German prisoners whilst writing his letter. In a letter which his parents recently received from him he mentions that they (the Allies) had achieved a big won on the night before writing. He also incidentally mentions that he had won a decoration for bravery, and that he had been mentioned in army despatches, and also that they had experienced much hard fighting but he was thankful that he had come through all right.

---

[60] 703 Sergeant Herbert James Teesdale (alias Herbert James McInerney) was killed on 21 March 1917 and is buried at Vaulx Hill Cemetery: Plot I, Row K, Grave 21.
[61] Commonwealth of Australia Gazette No. 189, 8 November 1917.

He sent home a piece of ribbon used for suspending the Military Medal. He mentioned that the battalion to which he was attached was then very strong and that all the men were looking fit. He had seen Ralph Jury and Harry Brand and they wished to be remembered to all Renmark friends."

Sergeant Len Johnson M.M. was killed on 20 September 1917 during the assault mounted by 7th Brigade from Westhoek Ridge into Polygon Wood.

His death was reported in The Adelaide Advertiser on 27 October:

THE LATE SERGEANT JOHNSON M.M.

"Mr and Mrs W. A. Johnson, of Renmark, have been notified that their eldest son L. A. Johnson (Len) was killed in action September 20. He left in June, 1915. He was wounded in 1916, but returned shortly to duty. He won the Military Medal in August last. He was widely known, and greatly esteemed by many friends. He was 26 years old."

Len's family also placed a notice in the same edition of the newspaper:

JOHNSON. – On the 20th September, in France (sic), Sergeant L. A. Johnson, eldest beloved son of W. and M. Johnson, of 15th-street, Renmark, aged 26 years and three days. Dearly loved, sadly missed. – Inserted by his parents, sisters, and brothers.

Sergeant Johnson's family continued to mark the anniversary of his death by placing a notice in The Adelaide Chronicle well into the 1920s.

Among the documents preserved with his service record held by the National Archives of Australia is a letter written by his mother, Miriam, which indicates that the family were unaware that Len's remains had not been identified and buried in a marked grave:

Hazelmere
15th St.
Renmark

March 6th 1922

Dear Sir

I have filled the enclosed form, I hope all particulars are satisfactory. Would you please oblige me by giving me a little more personal information concerning the probable cost of the inscription on the grave of my son, as I want to be prepared to meet the cost when required. Thanking you in anticipation & hoping for a reply at your earliest opportunity.

I remain,

Yours sincerely,

M. Johnson.[62]

Sergeant Len Johnson M.M. is commemorated on Panel 23 of the Ypres (Menin Gate) Memorial.

---

[62] NAA B2455/1827231

Ypres Town Cemetery and Extension

A short walk from the Ypres (Menin Gate) Memorial is Ypres Town Cemetery and its Extension. The stories of those buried in both locations offer insights not only into the lives of the men who fought in the Ypres Salient during the Great War, but also the fighting that took place in May 1940 and the small British community that lived and worked in Ypres as the city was rebuilt in the years following the Armistice.

The Town Cemetery was used by the British to bury their dead shortly after 7th Division and 3rd Cavalry Division arrived in October 1914, with 21st Field Ambulance taking the bodies of men who had died of wounds for interment there as well as units in the front line bringing back their dead, mostly officers, to be committed for burial in spaces between the civilian graves. There are 145 burials in the main Town Cemetery, most of which date from 1914 and the early part of 1915, scattered in small plots.

The most well-known grave in the cemetery is that of **Lieutenant Prince Maurice Victor Donald of Battenberg K.C.V.O.**, who served with the 1st Battalion, The King's Royal Rifle Corps and was killed on 27 October 1914 near Zonnebeke. He was the youngest grandchild of Queen Victoria and was the third son of Prince Henry of Battenberg and Princess Beatrice. His funeral took place days later and one of those present was **P/182 Lance-Corporal William Henry Dyer** of the Military Mounted Police:

"I was one of the four mounted police who attended the funeral of the young Prince Maurice, besides the escort of the King's Royal Rifles. The General and his Staff were there. I have a button from his serge, and I also took a piece of a yew tree by the side of the grave. He was buried on October 30 at about 3.30 p.m., and not far away the German big guns were firing on our trenches, and our guns were doing their best to put them out of action. The guns were making such a noise that you could not hear the chaplain's voice. It was a soldier's funeral amidst the noise of battle."[63]

---

[63] Liverpool Daily Echo, 16 November 1914. Lance-Corporal Dyer came from the Isle of Wight and had enlisted as a Special Reservist on 29 September 1914, being drafted to the front on 10 October. He was discharged on 13 November 1916 as a consequence of sickness and was subsequently issued with a Silver War Badge.

The grave of Prince Maurice of Battenberg, set on its own close to the Extension, can be found in Plot I.B.

The Ypres Town Cemetery Extension was also established in October 1914 and contains the graves of 604 soldiers who died during the Great War. This number includes 367 graves that were concentrated in the cemetery from smaller cemeteries and isolated burials from around the former Ypres salient, including the remains of **Lieutenant Charles Sackville Pelham, Lord Worsley**, the Officer Commanding the Machine-Gun Section of the Royal Horse Guards (The Blues), who was killed near Zandvoorde on 30 October 1914. There are 141 unidentified soldiers from the Great War buried in the Extension, as well as sixteen Special Memorials commemorating men believed to be buried with them. Following the fighting around Ypres in May 1940 a further 43 soldiers were buried in the Extension, thirteen of whom are unidentified.

In addition to the military graves, both Ypres Town Cemetery and the Extension contain graves of several employees of the Imperial (later Commonwealth) War Graves Commission who lived and worked in and around Ypres following the Great War, as well as their families and other members of the British community.

The graves of two employees of the Commonwealth War Graves Commission who are buried at Ypres Town Cemetery – 8 August 2018

In 1922 **William John Wheatley** made a visit to Ypres Town Cemetery and the Extension, and later described his impressions for an article published in The Kent and Sussex Courier:

"We went to the Communal or Town Cemetery, with its extenstion, and in the latter are buried several hundred of our own men, with a few French on one side. I had a look at the register of names, and one grave contained the remains of Sapper Culshaw, of the Kent (Fortress) Engineers, who I believe was a Southborough man.[64] This Cemetery is also beautifully kept, and a profusion of flowers brighten it up. M--- told me that thousands of headstones would be soon erected, and took me to one part where there was a large stack of them ready to be placed in position. A little farther on I found two or three rows already concreted. How neat they looked, and all of a uniformity.

On looking at the stone I noticed the inscription. A cross, the name of the soldier, a verse or text (chosen by the relatives), and beneath the words "A Soldier of the Great War." Two stones were pointed out at me where the bodies beneath had not been identified. The inscription on these stones was "An Unknown Soldier," "Known only to God (sic)."[65]

At one end was the grave of Prince Maurice of Battenberg, a grave corresponding with the others, and no distinction made between high, low, rich and poor.

But in one or two cases I saw what to a visitor seemed to spoil the harmonious effect. A few friends at home had had erected an extra private stone in front of the provided one, and that seemed to disarrange the uniformity of the rows.

On passing through a gateway I entered the Ypres Town Cemetery, and in one part there are a few graves of British soldiers. But what a contrast to the other part of the Cemetery! This being the Cemetery for the town, many had been buried there for some years, and some handsome monuments and

---

[64] **170529 Sapper William Culshaw**, who is mentioned in the extract, was serving with 497th (3rd Kent) Field Company in 29th Division when he died on 28 September 1918. Culshaw was not from Southborough, as Wheatley stated, but came from Southport and had formerly served in The Durham Light Infantry before being transferred to the Royal Engineers. He was the son of William and Sarah Culshaw, who lived at 115 Shakespeare Street in Southport and had been the husband of Amelia St George Hopwood (formerly Culshaw), who had remarried and resided at 14 Delhi Street in Wigan after the war. Sapper Culshaw is buried in Ypres Town Cemetery Extension: Plot III, Row A, Grave 16.
[65] The correct inscription is "Known Unto God."

stones had been erected. But now they were in many cases heaps of rubbish, battered about by shell-fire. British guns had been placed in this Cemetery. The grass was not mown, and the place seemed neglected.

A strange thing happened here, and we read of similar cases during the war. In the centre of the Cemetery is a large wooden Crucifix. Although the tombs and stones around are battered to pieces, yet this Crucifix stands high above everything else, with the image only damaged by bullet marks."[66]

Born on 15 April 1863, William Wheatley was headmaster of St John's Church of England School in Tunbridge Wells for forty years until his retirement in 1928. During the Great War he served as a Special Constable and also took a great interest in his former pupils who served in the forces, several of whom died. As a result of his wish to remember the old boys of his school he made several visits to France and Belgium and gave latern slide lectures on his trips to the former battlefields to local groups in and around Tunbridge Wells.[67] William died on 14 March 1948.

[66] Kent and Sussex Courier, 15 September 1922 & 22 September 1922.
[67] Ibid, 13 February 1925 & 23 March 1928.

1688 Corporal William Arthur Claybyn, of The Royal Horse Guards (The Blues), came from Axminster and was the eldest son of Mr E. and Mrs S. Claybyn, who lived at 3 Trinity Terrace. Born at Fowey in Cornwall, he had previously served with the Royal Horse Guards for twelve years, his regimental number being 753.

As a Lance-Corporal he had served in South Africa with the Household Cavalry Composite Regiment, for which he later received the Queen's South Africa Medal with clasps for Johannesburg, Diamond Hill, Cape Colony and Orange Free State, and was a member of the Escort to King Edward VII at his Coronation on 9 August 1902. On his discharge on the completion of his period of engagement, by which time he held the rank of Corporal, William became an Inspector for the Royal Society for the Prevention of Cruelty to Animals in Newmarket.

On 31 August 1914 Claybyn volunteered to return to his old regiment, even though he had no liability for additional service, and attested at Regent's Park Barracks on 3 September. Initially serving as a Trooper, he was appointed a Lance-Corporal on 10 September and promoted to the rank of Corporal five days later. Corporal Claybyn disembarked at Zeebrugge with the Blues on 7 October.

On 18 October, while on an advance guard moving towards Oostnieuwkerke, Corporal Claybyn was mortally wounded when his patrol clashed with a party of German cyclists, receiving a gunshot wound to his right arm and a compound fracture. He was taken back to Ypres and admitted to 21st Field Ambulance R.A.M.C., but died the same day. A very brief mention of his death appeared in The Exeter and Plymouth Gazette on 6 November 1914, but an obituary published in The Cambridge Independent Press on 20 November 1914 stated that; "His upright, soldierly figure is well remembered in Newmarket, although he was there only a few months." Corporal Claybyn, who was aged 36 when he died, is buried at Ypres Town Cemetery: Row D1, Grave 6. He is also commemorated on the war memorial in Axminster.

7715 Private George Henry Prowse
2ⁿᵈ Battalion, The Oxfordshire and Buckinghamshire Light Infantry

Born at Dartmouth (some records state Brixham) in Devon in 1883, George was the son of Robert James Prowse and Hannah Prowse. Recorded as working as a labourer, residing with his family at 15 Bridge Street in the St Ebbe's district of Oxford in the 1901 Census, George was employed as a railway porter when he attested for The Oxfordshire Light Infantry at the Regimental Depot on 3 October 1904.

He returned to Oxford on being transferred to the Reserve, and was still residing at 15 Bridge Street when he married Nellie Rose Bampton Blay at St Ebbe's Parish Church on 9 October 1909. George and Nellie are recorded in the 1911 Census as residing at 35 Donnington Road in Cowley with Nellie's widowed mother, Emma, and their nine-month old son George. George senior was at this time still employed as a railway porter by the Great Western Railway.

Mobilised following the declaration of war, George was posted to the 2nd Battalion at Aldershot and disembarked at Boulogne on 14 August 1914. He was severely wounded during the fighting near Langemarck and died at Ypres on 23 October. Private Prowse is buried at Ypres Town Cemetery: Row D1, Grave 20. The register for the cemetery records that his widow Nellie lived at 73 Magdalen Road in Oxford after the war and the following inscription was carved at the base of his headstone:

Gone From Our Home
But Not From Our Hearts
At Rest

George Prowse is also commemorated on the brass memorial plaque inside St Ebbe's Church, on the wooden tryptich memorial to the men of the parish of St John's in Cowley who died during the Great War, which is located inside St Mary and St John Church, and his name is also recorded in the City of Oxford Roll of Honour.

5701 Lance-Sergeant John Henry Grey
1ˢᵗ (Royal) Dragoons

Born at Meare in Somerset on New Years' Day 1889, John was the son of Walter Henry and Rosa Helena Grey and was baptised at St Mary's Church on 3 February of that year. He attended the Boys' National School in Evercreech before winning a Junior County Scholarship and moving to Sexey's School (School of Science) at Bruton.

John was living with his family at Ivy Cottage in Evercreech when he attested for the Dragoons of the Line at Taunton on 2 October 1903, aged 14 years and nine months, on Boy Service. Sent to join the Cavalry Depot at Canterbury on the supernumerary strength of the 1ˢᵗ (Royal) Dragoons, he attained his 3ʳᵈ Class Certificate in Education on 26 November 1903 and passed his 2ⁿᵈ Class Certificate on 27 June 1904. Boy Grey was posted to the 2ⁿᵈ Dragoons (Royal Scots Greys) on 1 July 1904, passing his 1ˢᵗ Class Certificate in Education on 27 May 1905, before being drafted to the Royals in India on 7 September 1905, joining the regiment at Lucknow. On reaching the age of eighteen on 1 January 1907, Grey converted to Adult Service and became a Private, being awarded his first Good Conduct Badge on 2 October. On 7 October 1909, a few days after he had received his second badge for Good Conduct, Private Grey was appointed an unpaid Lance-Corporal and the following month the Royals changed station and moved to Muttra. He was appointed a paid Lance-Corporal on 8 March 1910, but later reverted to Private. While in India Grey had been bitten by a wild dog, but had survived the experience, and also contributed regularly to the regimental journal, "The Eagle," which had been first published in 1907.

On 8 November 1911 the 1ˢᵗ (Royal) Dragoons left Muttra for Bombay, where they embarked for service in South Africa. The regiment relieved the 3ʳᵈ (King's Own) Hussars at Robert's Heights in Pretoria and on 11 November 1912 Grey was re-appointed as a paid Lance-Corporal. The Royals left Pretoria in February 1913 and moved to new quarters at Potchefstroom, deploying to Johannesburg in July on riot duty during the Rand Miners' Strike. On 11 November 1913 John married Amy Potter, a British immigrant, at Potchefstroom and he was promoted to Corporal on 14 April 1914. Corporal Grey was still stationed at Potchefstroom when war was declared, but the Royals were recalled to England shortly afterwards, disembarking at Southampton on 19 September 1914. After training at Ludgershall, the Royals sailed for the continent, landing at Ostend on 8 October as part of 6ᵗʰ Cavalry Brigade of 3ʳᵈ Cavalry Division. Amy also returned to England, expecting their first child.

Appointed a Lance-Sergeant, John Grey was serving with "B" Squadron of the 1ᵗ (Royal) Dragoons when he was mortally wounded while fighting dismounted in trenches positioned between Hollebeke and Zandvoorde. He died after being admitted to 21ᵗ Field Ambulance at Ypres on 25 October 1914 and his death was recorded in the Births, Marriages and Deaths column of The Shepton Mallet Journal on 6 November:

"Sunday, October 25th, 1914, at the Hospital of the 21st Field Ambulance Corps (sic), with the Expeditionary Force, of wounds received in battle, Sergeant John Henry Grey, 1st (Royal) Dragoons, aged 25 years, the beloved husband of Amy Grey, and eldest and beloved son of Mr and Mrs W. H. Grey, of Evercreech. Buried on the same day in the cemetery at Ypres. For eleven years a faithful "Soldier of the King.""

Lance-Sergeant Grey is buried at Ypres Town Cemetery: Plot A1, Grave 17. The following inscription was carved on the base of his headstone:

A Devoted Son, Husband
Great Will Be
The Joy Of Meeting

Lance-Sergeant Grey's widow Amy gave birth to their son, Leslie Charles Grey, on 6 January 1915 at Cirencester, and the register for the cemetery records that she lived at "Melrose" in Evercreech after the war. Their son Leslie was later employed as a santitary labourer with the Royal Air Force and was residing at 8 Choseley Road in Knowl Hill in Berkshire at the time of his death in 1968.

7295 Sergeant Harry Underhill
2ⁿᵈ Battalion, The South Staffordshire Regiment

Born in 1885, Harry Underhill attended Brockmoor Council School and had attested for the South Staffords at Lichfield in 1905.

He disembarked at Le Havre on 13 August 1914. Sergeant Underhill was severely wounded during fighting on the Broodseinde-Becelaere Road, and died of his wounds at Ypres on 28 October. His brother, **7239 Private Alfred Underhill**,[68] wrote home:

"I am writing this in the trenches, only 150 yards from the Germans, and it seems a hot corner we are in – shells flying all day long, and the rattle of the guns enough to make one deaf. I expect you know about Harry, but I am not sure whether he is dead or wounded. I could not go and see, though I was close to him. But don't worry too much. If he is dead, he died fighting."[69]

When official news of his death was received at Brockmoor, a memorial service was held at St John's on 6 December at which members of the 5th South Staffords, Boy Scouts and the St John Ambulance attended. However, some confusion was caused to members of Sergeant Underhill's family when the name of **7469 Sergeant Claude Underhill** was published in a casualty list, as reported in The Birmingham Daily Gazette on 27 February 1915:

MISSING OR KILLED?

"In December last the War Office officially notified the family of Sergeant John Henry Underhill, of Brockmoor, Brierley Hill, that he had been killed in action. Sergeant Underhill's brother, Private Alfred Underhill, has since written to say that he saw Sergeant Underhill wounded, and afterwards had searched for his grave, but had not been successful in finding it.

On Thursday morning a Sergeant Underhill, of the South Staffords, was officially reported as missing. The family of the Brockmoor sergeant are hoping that the missing soldier is he who was officially reported "killed in action.""

Harry Underhill is buried at Ypres Town Cemetery: Plot A2, Grave 14.

---

[68] Alfred Underhill was a reservist, attesting on 4 January 1905, and had been drafted to the 2nd Battalion with the First Reinforcement on 27 August 1914. He was later wounded and transferred to the 9th Training Reserve Battalion, his service number being TR5/32375 and was discharged as being no longer physically fit for war service on 5 March 1917. Alfred was later issued with a Silver War Badge and died in 1968.

[69] Birmingham Daily Gazette, 16 November 1914.

Sergeant Underhill's Medal Index Card mistakenly states that he died of wounds on 20 October 1914, and that E. Rawley, who lived at New Building, New Tower at Brockmoor, applied for his 1914 Star on 9 July 1919.

7469 Sergeant Claude Vincent Underhill, who had been reported as missing, served with the 1st Battalion and was born in Birmingham on 27 June 1887. The son of Edward and Caroline Underhill, he was baptised at St Augustine's in Edgbaston on 20 July. Claude attested for the South Staffords at Birmingham in 1905 and in 1911 was serving as a Lance-Sergeant attached to the 3rd (Special Reserve) Battalion at Whittington Barracks. Underhill later qualified as an Army Schoolmaster. At the outbreak of the war, Sergeant Underhill was serving with the 1st Battalion at Pietermaritzburg and went to Belgium on 4 October, disembarking at Zeebrugge three days later. He was initially reported as missing, but had been killed on 27 October near Kruiseecke and is commemorated on the Ypres (Menin Gate) Memorial. Claude's sister applied for his 1914 Star on behalf of his mother on 15 January 1919, and it was issued to her at 119 Frederick Road in Aston Manor.

4364 Sergeant Frederick David Curl, of the 10ᵗʰ (The Prince of Wales's Own) Royal Hussars, was born at St Albans in 1878 and had enlisted at Swindon on 15 January 1900. He was working as a game-keeper at the time of his attestation. Curl had served in South Africa during the later stages of the Boer War and had been wounded in action at the Vaal River on 7 May 1901. For his service in South Africa he later received the Queen's South Africa Medal with five clasps and, while in India, was awarded the 1911 Delhi Durbar Medal. Sergeant Curl was stationed at Potchefstroom in South Africa at the outbreak of the war and landed in Belgium on 8 October. He was killed on 30 October 1914 while serving in trenches east of Klein Zillebeke and is buried at Ypres Town Cemetery Extension: Plot II, Row B, Grave 1. He was married and the register for the cemetery records that his widow, Mary, lived at 25 Trewint Street in Earlsfield. Frederick Curl is also commemorated on the war memorial at Flamstead.

On 11 February 1915, shortly after being relieved from the front line at Zillebeke, the billets of the 1ˢᵗ Life Guards on the Rue des Chiens at Ypres were shelled by German artillery. A house where a troop of "D" Squadron was billeted received a direct hit and half of the building was demolished. Six soldiers were killed and nine wounded inside the house, all of whom were Reservists from regiments of Dragoon Guards and Dragoons who had been posted to the 1ˢᵗ Life Guards early in the war.

One of the soldiers inside the house was **5792 Private George Gilman**, a Reservist of the 6ᵗʰ (Inniskilling) Dragoons, described the shelling in a letter sent to Mr E. Clement Davies, the son of the managing director of the Crown Copper Works:

"I only returned from the trenches last Saturday after ten days in them. I am very lucky to be here alive. We were billeted in a house and the house was shelled, killing three of my mates and wounding nine altogether. My Princess Mary box was battered by a shell, and there were three bullet holes in it. My serge was riddled with bits of shell, and my rifle also was badly damaged. Eight civilians also were among those killed, so I am very lucky."[70]

24241 Sapper Arthur Thirlwell, who served with 3ʳᵈ Field Squadron, Royal Engineers, also witnessed the shelling of the billets at Rue des Chiens and recounted the scene in a letter to his sisters, who lived at 6 Ropery Walk at Seaham Harbour:

---

[70] Liverpool Daily Echo, 26 February 1915. Born at Garston, George Gilman had attested for the Dragoons of the Line at Warrington on 25 September 1906. At the time of his enlistment he was aged eighteen years and eight months and was employed as a labourer. He also served in the 3ʳᵈ Militia Battalion of The King's (Liverpool Regiment). Gilman was posted to the 6ᵗʰ Dragoons at Ballincollig on 27 September, but was sent to military prison on 16 November. He was released on 29 November, shortly before the regiment sailed to Egypt. He went on to serve in India and was appointed an Acting Lance-Corporal on 29 September 1911 before being transferred to the Reserve on 11 December 1913. On being mobilised at the outbreak of the war, Gilman reported to No. 4 (Western) Cavalry Depot at Newport and was posted to the 1ˢᵗ Life Guards at Knightsbridge Barracks on 8 August. He landed in Belgium in October 1914 and remained at the front until he was posted to the 1ˢᵗ Life Guards Reserve Regiment on 3 May 1917. Gilman was transferred to the Guards Machine Gun Regiment on 10 May 1918, his regimental number being 3231, and was drafted back to France on 16 May to join No. 1 (1ˢᵗ Life Guards) Battalion. George Gilman was transferred to the Class Z Army Reserve on being demobilised on 1 March 1919, giving his home address as 20 Allen Place at Boughton in Cheshire, and died in 1945.

"We had a bit of trouble the other night, for a few shells began to burst beside our billets, killing a lot of women and children and six soldiers and wounding several others, but let me ease your mind for the time being by telling you that I am all right and we are having a rest."[71]

The six soldiers who died on 11 February 1915 are buried together in Plot II, Row C at Ypres Town Cemetery Extension:

5644 Corporal Herbert Thomas Cordery   Grave 3
6th (Inniskilling) Dragoons

5972 Private James Henry Smith   Grave 4
1st (King's) Dragoon Guards

5128 Private Maurice Sullivan   Grave 5
2nd Dragoon Guards (Queen's Bays)

5400 Private Patrick Corcoran   Grave 6
6th Dragoon Guards (Carabiniers)

6445 Private James Hall   Grave 7
2nd Dragoon Guards (Queen's Bays)

G/2501 Private Robert John Williams   Grave 8
6th (Inniskilling) Dragoons

The graves of the six soldiers killed in their billet on the Rue des Chiens
8 August 2018

[71] Sunderland Daily Echo, 24 February 1915. Arthur Thirlwell had joined the Royal Engineers on 13 January 1913 and landed in France on 24 October 1914. He was discharged from the Section B Army Reserve due to sickness on 1 May 1919 and was issued with a Silver War Badge.

Richard "Dick" Collick

Born at Illogan near Redruth in Cornwall on 9 March 1891, Dick Collick was employed as a carpenter and joiner when he enlisted for the Royal Naval Air Service on 28 October 1916, being issued with the service number F22840. Sent to H.M.S. President II for training, he was posted as an Air Mechanic 1ˢᵗ Class to Dover Aerodrome on 6 March 1917, and then to Mullion Aerodrome, on the Lizard in Cornwall, on 24 July. Collick was sent to the R.N.A.S. Naval Seaplane Training School, H.M.S. Daedelus at Lee-on-Solent, on 21 October before returning to Cornwall.

A.M.1 Collick was serving at Mullion Aerodrome on 1 April 1918 when the Royal Naval Air Service became part of the new Royal Air Force and was transferred to the new arm, being issued with the service number 222840. On 4 April he was posted to Wormwood Scrubs to attend a course at the former R.N.A.S. Stores Depot, before returning to Cornwall on 19 April. Reclassified as a Leading Aircraftsman on 1 January 1919, Collick was posted to Plymouth on 24 February but returned to Mullion on 1 August, where he was remustered as a L.A.C. (Carpenter and Rigger). He was sent to the Dispersal Centre at Fovant on 28 November before being demobilised and transferred to the R.A.F. Reserve on 21 December. Dick Collick was finally discharged on 30 April 1920.

After leaving the Royal Air Force, Dick found employment as a carpenter with the Imperial War Graves Commission and went to work in Ypres. He married Jeanne Desmadryl, a seamstress, in May 1926 and they were still residing at 15 Brugesweg when they celebrated their Golden Wedding Anniversary in 1976.

It was Dick who taught the buglers of the Ypres Brandweer (Fire Brigade) to sound the Last Post and Revielle in the style that he had known while serving with the R.N.A.S. and R.A.F.

Dick Collick died on 21 March 1986, aged 95, and is buried at Ypres Town Cemetery Extension together with his Belgian wife Jeanne and their daughter Cynthia, who died on 27 October 1933, aged four.

The grave of Dick Collick, his wife Jeanne and their daughter Cynthia.

Hooge Crater Museum

The Hooge Crater Museum is a private collection established in 1994 and is housed in a former chapel and school building built during the 1920s. Very much an old-style museum, the collections of Niek Benoot and Philippe Oosterlinck tell the story of the fighting in the Ypres Salient during the Great War and include amongst its displays a variety of artefacts, arms, ordnance, equipment and dressed figures arranged by nationality. Attached to the museum is a cafe and shop.

Across the N8 Menenweg, the old Menin Road, is Hooge Crater Cemetery. First established by the Burial Officer of the 7th Division in early October 1917 and the original 76 graves form Rows A to D in Plot I. Following the Armistice the cemetery was greatly expanded as the remains of soldiers buried in a number of smaller cemeteries around the Salient, as well as those found on the battlefield, were concentrated there. There are in total 5,915 soldiers buried in the cemetery, of whom 3,570 are unidentified, and these include British, Canadians, Australians, New Zealanders and two Privates of the 3rd Battalion, The British West Indies Regiment who died in October 1917:

3029 Private Arthur Norman Reid, who came from Jacksontown in Jamaica. The son of James and Arabella Reid, Arthur was aged 20 when he died on 3 October 1917 and was originally buried at Map Reference I.18.a.9.8. His remains were exhumed and reinterred in Plot II, Row DD, Grave 8.

3260 Private Nathaniel Stoddart, who came from Montego Bay in Jamaica and was the son of Samuel and Angelina Stoddart. Private Stoddart was killed on 26 October 1917, aged 27, and was originally buried at Pillbox Cemetery, which had been established at a recently-captured German position near Zonnebeke following the fighting there. His body was later exhumed and reburied in Plot XIV, Row D, Grave 12.

Also buried in the cemetery is **3774 Private Patrick Joseph Budgen V.C.**, of the 31st Battalion, Australian Imperial Force, who was killed on 28 September 1917 and is buried in Plot VII, Row C, Grave 5.

Another soldier whose remains were moved to Hooge Crater Cemetery after the war was **5909 Lance-Corporal John Syme**, who served with "B" Squadron of the 11th (Prince Albert's Own) Hussars and was killed on 24 May 1915. News of his death was reported in The Daily Record on 11 June:

Hooge Crater Cemetery
September 1992

"Mrs Syme, 133 Monkswood, Newtongrange, received official intimation yesterday that her son, Private John Syme, of the 11th Hussars, had been killed in action in France. He was previously employed at the Lothian Coal Company's mines at Newbattle, and as a reservist was called up at the beginning of the war. He was 34 years of age and unmarried."

Lance-Corporal Syme was buried close to where he was killed, at Map Reference: I.24.b.7.9. In 1919, his grave was located and his remains were identified by the inscription on the cross that still survived over his burial place. Symes was exhumed and reburied at Plot XV, Row H, Grave 1.

The name of the cemetery derives from the series of mine craters that scarred the area around the remains of the former Chateau at Hooge. The scene of fierce fighting throughout the course of the war, it was close to this location that the Germans first employed the flammenwerfer, or flamethrower, against troops of 14th (Light) Division on 30 July 1915. After changing hands many times Hooge was finally retaken on 28 September 1918 by the 9th (Scottish) Division and 29th Division.

Hooge Chateau – 31 October 1914

On 31 October 1914 the situation for the British and French troops defending the approaches to Ypres was dire. On the frontage held by I Corps of the British Expeditionary Force the Germans had managed to penetrate the line around Gheluvelt. The recently-promoted Lieutenant-General Samuel Lomax, the General Officer Commanding 1ˢᵗ Division and Major-General Sir Charles Monro, in command of 2ⁿᵈ Division, were in conference with senior staff officers of both formations in an annexe of Hooge Chateau, planning a counter-attack with the meagre resources available to them.

At around 1.15 p.m. a German aeroplane was seen flying over the Chateau. Shortly afterwards a heavy artillery shell exploded in the garden, and as the assembled officers moved towards the windows and open doors to see where it had landed a second shell pierced the roof of the building and exploded, killing and wounding several officers and men, including General Lomax. Major-General Monro was knocked unconscious by the blast but was able to recover sufficiently to retain command.

Acting as a despatch rider, **L/3884 Lance-Corporal Thomas Copsey** of the 16ᵗʰ (The Queen's) Lancers was inside Hooge Chateau when it was shelled and described the scene in a letter to his mother in Tunbridge Wells:

"I am still keeping A1. Really it is the mercy of Providence that I am able to sit and write this letter, because since I wrote I have seen a sight that I hope never to see again. It was like this. The headquarters were billeted at a large chateau, which was used as a reporting centre for everybody. We had been there all morning, but things got so hot that at 12 o'clock we had orders to move. We were on the point of going when two awful "coal-boxes" dropped right among us. After pulling myself together I looked round, and what met my eyes I cannot describe. Poor Wally Marchant, my chum. It really broke my heart. I had not left him two minutes when it happened. Poor old Wally was buried in the chateau. He was a favourite with everyone. I am still among the "coal-boxes" and "Jack Johnsons," but hope to be among the Germans before long."

As the result of one shell the Headquarters Staff of two Divisions were rendered destroyed and the formations were leaderless. General Sir Douglas Haig, the commander of I Corps, hastily appointed Major-General Edward Bulfin to take over 1ˢᵗ Division but as he was unable to assume control immediately temporary command Brigadier-General Herman Landon, the commander of 3rd Brigade, stepped in temporarily to lead the formation.

By pushing all available troops forward, and the mounting of a successful counter-attack later that afternoon by the 2nd Battalion, The Worcestershire Regiment at Gheluvelt, the front was stabilised and the Germans were held.

Lance-Corporal Copsey's friend was **20630 Gunner Walter Marchant**, who served with 35th Heavy Battery, Royal Garrison Artillery. He came from Tunbridge Wells and had worked as an upholsterer when he attested at New Cross on 29 August 1904. Gunner Marchant is buried at Ypres Town Cemetery Extension: Plot III, Row AA, Grave 1.

Buried alongside Gunner Marchant are five members of the Headquarters Staff of 1st and 2nd Divisions who were also killed during the shelling of Hooge Chateau:

Lieutenant-Colonel Arthur Jex Blake Percival D.S.O.   Grave 2
The Northumberland Fusiliers
Attached to 2nd Division Headquarters Staff

Major George Paley   Grave 3
The Rifle Brigade
Attached as G.S.O. 2,[72] 1st Division Headquarters Staff

Colonel Frederic Walter Kerr   Grave 4
Late 1st Battalion, The Gordon Highlanders
Attached as G.S.O. 1,[73] 1st Division Headquarters Staff

Major Francis Maxwell Chenevix Trench   Grave 5
Royal Field Artillery
Attached as Brigade Major to the Commander, Royal Artillery
2nd Division Headquarters Staff

Captain Rupert Ommanney   Grave 6
Royal Engineers
Attached as G.S.O. 3,[74] 2nd Division Headquarters Staff

---

[72] General Staff Officer, Grade 2.
[73] General Staff Officer, Grade 1 (Staff Colonel).
[74] General Staff Officer, Grade 3 (Staff Captain)

Two more officers died of their injuries shortly afterwards:

Captain Graham Percival Shedden, who served with 35th Heavy Battery R.G.A., died of his wounds the following day at Ypres and is buried in the Town Cemetery in Row E2, Grave 14. His grave is marked both by a Commonwealth War Graves Commission headstone, which is placed in front of a private one erected shortly after the war.

Captain Robert Giffard, Royal Field Artillery, who was the Aide-de-Camp to Lieutenant-General Lomax, also died of the wounds he received at Hooge on 1 November and is also buried in Ypres Town Cemetery: Row E1, Grave 12.

Lieutenant-General Samuel Holt Lomax did not recover from the wounds that he received at Hooge on 31 October 1914 and died some months later on 10 April 1915 in London. He was cremated at Golders Green Crematorium and his ashes were interred at Aldershot Military Cemetery, the home of 1st Division in peacetime.

Hooge - 30 July 1915

"The 30th July I shall never forget. They started on us at three o'clock in the morning with flames of burning liquid. It was most horrible. We lost nearly all our officers and men. How I got out of that lot God knows – I don't, but still, here I am. I have not been right since... We are getting nothing but big guns and bullets for our meals, and the same through the night. They promoted me to Sergeant-Major after."[75]

7603 Company Serjeant-Major Albert Baldock
8th (Service) Battalion, The Rifle Brigade

Albert Baldock was born at Stockingford, near Nuneaton, in 1876 and had attested for The Rifle Brigade on 23 February 1900 at Warwick. He was posted to the 4th Battalion from the Rifle Depot at Winchester on 1 September 1900 and was appointed an Acting Corporal two days later, before being transferred to the 3rd Battalion on 22 December. Baldock reverted to the rank of Rifleman at his own request on 10 January 1901, but was again appointed an Acting Corporal on 3 December. He was awarded his first Good Conduct Badge on 23 February 1902. Baldock received a second badge on 23 February 1905 before being promoted to Corporal two days later. After completing eight years' service, Baldock was transferred to the Class A Army Reserve on 23 February 1908. As he neared the completion of his period of engagement, Albert re-enlisted for the Section D Army Reserve on 9 November 1911.

He was employed as a park attendant by the Coventry Corporation when he was mobilised following the declaration of war and reported to the Rifle Depot at Winchester on 6 August 1914. Baldock was posted, as a Corporal, to the 8th (Service) Battalion on 8 October and was promoted to Serjeant the same day. He had arrived in France on 21 May 1915 as a Serjeant and was promoted to Warrant Officer Class II on 31 July, following the flamethrower attack at Hooge.

Company Serjeant-Major Baldock was awarded the Military Cross for actions performed during the fighting on the Somme in 1916, and the citation for the award was published in The London Gazette on 14 November:

---

[75] Coventry Evening Telegraph, 6 September 1915 & Coventry Herald, 10 September 1915. C.S.M. Baldock was writing to his mother, Mrs Mary Ann Baldock, who lived at "Ashdene," 114 Sir Thomas White's Road in Coventry.

"For conspicuous gallantry in action. He assumed command of and led his company with great courage and determination, gaining his objective and consolidating the position. He set a splendid example."

Baldock was also twice Mentioned in Despatches. He was posted to the Rifle Depot at Winchester on 25 February 1917 and married Emma Parker at St Thomas's Church on 25 May. Baldock was discharged as unfit, suffering from myalgia, on 12 November 1917 and was issued with a Silver War Badge. He had six younger brothers, five of whom served in the Army and one in the Royal Navy.

Albert Baldock M.C. was killed, aged 64, on 28 October 1940 at 97 Broomfield Road in the Earlsdon district of Coventry during an air raid.

"Our brigade happened to the trenches at the time the Germans started. We had just lay down to get a rest and had to dash to help those who were in the other trenches, the German curs had massed thousands of troops to try and break through. They sent over flames of burning oil. Talk about being in Hell! If it can be like what we have been through we have had a taste. We held on, thank God, although our lads were dropping down, and we did not give way until we were burnt out, as they set fire the tops of our trenches.

Then we had to get in our next line. Later in the day we were told that we had got to try and get back the trenches. We dashed out over our parapet, meaning to sacrifice our lives if we had to drive the murderous lot back. What a hell to be in! We had to dash up a slope for about 500 yards, and they had got machine guns going at us as fast as ever they could. The bullets came from everywhere. -------- dropped almost first with a bullet in his muscle. I said 'Get back,' and he managed to, although I don't know how, and then – dropped with one through his head. Then I think I must have gone mad, and it makes me feel sorry to write it, we could not do what we wanted, that is, take the trenches back, as there was only a little band of us left. One or two got in, but we could not hold it so we had to retire, and then we went at it again. However a man came back I don't know. When we got back the captain looked at us. He came to me and the few who were still alive, and said, 'How are you, lads? Such a fine company as I had – the best lads I ever had under me.'

Then we held on to what we had, as we knew we had to do as the reinforcements had not come yet. We carried on until night came, and then it was 'off again.' But we had our own back. There were sixteen of us and a gun to keep the devils back, and as they sent their fire over us I thought it was all up this time, when up came the other battalions to help us, and we gave the curs a gruelling this time. Our artillery smashed them up in heaps, and when it had stopped, what was left of our boys were sent back, and here we are having a well-earned rest. It makes me ill to look around and see the boys sitting and thinking about their pals that have gone. The fight is still going on, but there are plenty of our troops up now, and they are giving it the dogs, I can tell you. Our men have driven them right back again and tanned them terribly."[76]

A/990 Rifleman James Butler
7th (Service) Battalion, The King's Royal Rifle Corps

"We had a very hot time. When the bombardment started we fixed our bayonets and had to go through a wood that was being heavily shelled to a trench on the other side. In doing so we lost a lot of men, and then the Germans started squirting burning tar and other liquids into our trench. So we had to fall back. We got into another trench, where there were reinforcements, and we didn't half give it the Germans after that. Things went a bit slack after the hard fight except for the bombardment, which continued all the day. In the afternoon we charged them, and took some trenches, but I don't know how many, as I was injured before it was finished."[77]

B/265 Rifleman Arthur Gresty
8th (Service) Battalion, The Rifle Brigade

---

[76] Birmingham Gazette, 4 August 1915. Rifleman Butler was writing to his wife, Sarah, who lived at 32 Moland Street in the Gun Quarter of Birmingham. Born in 1889, he had been employed as a cycle polisher, he had attested for The King's Royal Rifle Corps at Birmingham on 18 August 1914. Butler was discharged, as a consequence of wounds, on 19 July 1917 and was later issued with a Silver War Badge.

[77] Manchester Evening News, 12 August 1915. Rifleman Gresty had disembarked with the 8th Battalion at Boulogne on 21 May 1915. He described his experiences in a letter to his relatives, who lived at Beech Terrace in Chorlton-cum-Hardy. Gresty was later discharged and issued with a Silver War Badge.

Lieut. H. N. L. RENTON,
9th King's Royal Rifles.

Lieutenant Harry Noel Leslie Renton
9th (Service) Battalion, The King's Royal Rifle Corps

Harry Noel Leslie Renton, who served as a platoon commander with "C" Company of the 9th (Service) Battalion, The King's Royal Rifle Corps, was aged 20 when he was killed near Hooge on 30 July 1915. The son of James Henry and Louise Renton, who lived at Aspley Guise in Bedfordshire, Lieutenant Renton is commemorated on the Ypres (Menin Gate) Memorial. An obituary for him was published in The Bedfordshire Times and Independent on 6 August 1915:

"News reached the village on Wednesday of the death of Mr Harry Noel Leslie Renton, Lieut., 9th King's Royal Rifles, killed in action on July 31st (sic). He was the second son of Mr and Mrs J. H. Renton, and was well-known in the village, and had several times helped the Cricket Club when on holidays.

He was born in Ceylon, and educated at The Knoll, Woburn Sands, and Harrow School, was a monitor at Harrow, head of his house, and in the Upper VI. He was house cricket and football captain, a member of the school cricket eleven, and kept wicket in the Eton and Harrow match at Lords in 1914. He was to have entered Oxford University in October, 1914, but on the outbreak of the war he joined the Army, and was gazetted second-lieutenant in the 9th King's Royal Rifle Corps on Sept. 23rd, 1914, and lieutenant on Feb. 13th, 1915. He left for the front on May 21st."

However, in November 2015 the author came across evidence that Lieutenant Renton is buried as an "Unknown Lieutenant" of The King's Royal Rifle Corps at Oosttaverne Wood Cemetery. The specific information regarding his burial was contained in a letter that was printed in The Essex County Chronicle on 12 November 1915:

BRAINTREE SOLDIER

KILLED IN COMMUNICATION TRENCH.

"Letters giving information of the death of Corpl. E. Wiffen, of the King's Royal Rifles, and a resident of Braintree, have been received by his relatives. Sergt. Percy W. Thomson, of the same regiment, who has since also been killed, wrote as follows:-

"In the absence of his officer, I regret to have to inform you that Corpl. E. Wiffen was killed in action on August 1st. He got his head over the parapet, and I cannot say exactly whether he was hit by a sniper's bullet or a piece of shrapnel; in any case his death was instantaneous. I know nothing I can say will alleviate the awful blow this will be to you, but I have soldiered with him ever since he first gave his services to his country. We all thought worlds of Wiffen, and I miss him terribly. He was buried by myself and a corporal before we left the trenches, together with an officer and three more. Your brother's death was not an individual one – the battalion was given a very important work to carry out, and we lost heavily; it was coming through this that the casualty happened. The N.C.O.'s of A Company and men of his platoon have lost a soldier and a man, who, to use their own words, was a 'jolly good fellow.' The only thing of importance he had on him was his watch, but everything is being handed in and will be sent off as soon as possible."

Another letter from the same writer stated:

"Corpl. Wiffen, who at the time of his death was my second in command, was buried on the left of the Menin Road near Ypres, and **was laid by me by the side of one of our officers, Lieut. Renton, whose photograph appeared in a recent illustrated paper, and who was killed in the same action.** I am a city fellow, and in the event of my ever reaching England I shall most certainly call upon you and tell you the things you must all be burning to know. The fighting is too furious, and it was too dangerous to make any semblance of a grave, or I would certainly have done so. Anyhow, as a second before he was joking. He was British, and you at home must be the same."

A little later Sergt. Thomson sent another letter, this time to the deceased's brother, Mr L. W. Wiffen, of South Street, Braintree, which read:

"Corpl. Wiffen was killed in a communication trench leading up the Zouave Wood against the Chateau at Hooge, about which you have read such a lot. He was buried at the Ypres end of the communication trench on the right-hand side of the Menin Road. **He was buried with one of our officers; this grave is not marked.** Wiffen did not speak after he was hit; the last words he spoke were, "Well, we're jolly old warriors, still sticking it." This was mentioned as I passed his traverse. I believe he then said, "Well, this is my last cigarette to-night." He was seen to stoop down to pick something off the ground, and when the nearest man reached him he was dead. I examined him, and he was hit in the heard; whether it was a bullet or shrapnel I cannot say; he was quite dead. I searched him and handed everything he had into the orderly room. He was killed about six o'clock in the evening.

His grave was not marked, and it was a very risky job getting him buried at all. I might here tell you the incidents which led up to his death. We were resting in some dug-outs behind the firing line when the news reached us that the English had lost some trenches. This news was followed up a few minutes later with the news that our battalion had been specially honoured and that we were given the opportunity of re-taking the lines. Wiffen, who, as I have previously said, was my second, and myself had a lump of ginger cake. I told him what I wanted done, and with six more N.C.O.'s and myself we started up under a perfect hail of shell fire, and our noble little platoon.

All the other N.C.O.'s, with the exception of Wiffen and myself, were knocked out before we reached our destination. We retook the trenches, covered ourselves with glory, and the evening before we were relieved poor old Wiffen was killed. The Germans, who were furious, tried their best to smash us up; it was fearful, but we hung on. Now came the time to look after Wiffen; I intended burying him in a grave at the back of the trenches with an officer, but no sooner had we shown ourselves than snipers and machine-guns forced us to get back into the trenches as it was asking to be killed. We had no other opportunity that night, as they started an attack at dusk and kept on until daybreak. Of course, we were done up, but we had another try, and just management to get him buried a few minutes before our relief arrived. So we had no time to mark his grave, although should we ever go there again I shall mark it with a wooden cross, as I am sure he would have done anything for me. I was absolutely done up, and was glad to get away from the place. Really, we did our level best. I can assure you I miss him terribly, as his nature was very similar to my own, and we had many things in common. Our laughs over his parcel of flea powder, some of which he sent me with his compliments, I shall never forget."

R/3000 Corporal Edgar Wiffen served with the 9th (Service) Battalion, The King's Royal Rifle Corps and was the son of William and Martha Wiffen, who lived at 7 Notley Road in Braintree. He was aged 21 when he was killed.

When the author searched for Corporal Wiffen's burial or commemoration, the Concentration of War Graves return included with his record confirmed that his body was found in 1926, together with those of R/478 Rifleman George Edward Deakin, who came from Handsworth; A/2227 Rifleman James Ingley from Tamworth; and an unknown Lieutenant of The King's Royal Rifle Corps.

Having recently come across Serjeant Thomson's letter, the author was intrigued to find out if the Lieutenant was Renton. Renton's details were then checked on the CWGC website and found that he had no known grave and was commemorated on the Ypres (Menin Gate) Memorial. At the time the remains were found, Corporal Wiffen's name had been included with those soldiers to be commemorated on the Ypres (Menin Gate) Memorial. Corporal Wiffen was reburied at Oosttaverne Wood Cemetery: Plot V, Row K, Grave 11. As the four bodies were found at the same map reference, and Serjeant Thomson implicitly identified Lieutenant Renton as having been buried next to Corporal Wiffen, the case for identification is compelling.

The entry for Lieutenant Renton contained in Volume 1 of de Ruvigny's Roll of Honour intriguingly states that he **"was killed in action near Hooge, 30 July 1915, during the capture of a German trench; unm, Buried there."** This reference also seems to support Serjeant Thomson's account.

The writer of the letters, **R/335 Serjeant Percy Walter Thomson**, was killed on 25 September 1915, aged 21. He was the son of Charles Daniel and Caroline Thomson, who lived at 1 Sussex Road in Southsea. Serjeant Thomson has no known grave and is commemorated on the Ypres (Menin Gate) Memorial.

As well as Renton, there were five Lieutenants of The King's Royal Rifle Corps who died between 30 July and 1 August 1915:

- Lieutenant Roger Wentworth Watson – "C" Company, 8th (Service) Battalion. Buried at Sanctuary Wood Cemetery: Plot II, Row D, Grave 4.

- Lieutenant F. Seymour – 7th (Service) Battalion – Commemorated on the Ypres (Menin Gate) Memorial.

- Lieutenant Sidney Henry Snelgrove – 14th (Reserve) Battalion, attached 7th (Service) Battalion – Commemorated on the Ypres (Menin Gate) Memorial.

- Lieutenant Arthur Bertram Findlay – 15th (Reserve) Battalion, attached 7th (Service) Battalion – Commemorated on the Ypres (Menin Gate) Memorial.

Renton is the only Lieutenant of the 9th (Service) Battalion recorded as having been killed during this period of the fighting near Hooge, and with the evidence provided by Serjeant Thomson's letter, the reference to his burial provided by the entry in de Ruvigny's Roll of Honour, and that the body was found with three soldiers of the 9th Battalion in which he served, it appears likely that the "Unknown Lieutenant" buried at Oosttaverne Wood Cemetery was in fact Lieutenant Renton.

The evidence for the identification of Lieutenant Renton's remains is (three years after the evidence was submitted) still being considered by the War Graves Adjudicator and the Commonwealth War Graves Commission.

Hooge – 9 August 1915

"You would read in the papers about the British success at Hooge. Well I am proud to tell you that it was our battalion that charged the Germans out of their position. We came out of the firing line after over a fortnight of hot work, expecting about a week's rest, but two days later the Divisional Commander paid us a visit, and addressing us said he was sorry to tell us that the British had lost their position at Hooge, and that it was of such strategic importance that unless retaken the whole of the British line south of Hooge would have to retire, and that Sir John French had selected our division for the job. You can guess our excitement when we were told we had been selected to lead the attack.

And what an attack it was! After half-an-hours' artillery fire we charged like one man, and although there were three different regiments of Germans they shouted for mercy, but our fellows replied with shouts of 'gas' and 'Lusitania,' and in less than ten minutes there was hardly a German that hadn't been bayoneted or clubbed. We could have taken more ground, but it wasn't policy. They tried to form up their reserves well behind the lines in order to make a counter-attack, but we had shown such determination in our charge that all the stuffing was knocked out of them, and they would not budge.

When they saw it was hopeless trying to get their infantry to tackle us they tried to shell us out of it. They used all kinds of shells, also aerial torpedoes, and although they kept it up for 20 hours, we still hung on. When darkness set in we were relieved by another regiment, only 297 returning unscathed out of about 1,000 but the greater part of the wounded will be all right again in a few weeks.

What a sight when we came down the line! Men of all kinds of regiment who had been watching the fight nearly wrung our hands off – some actually kissed us – and as we were marching away next day the road was lined with artillery, cavalry, A.S.C., Medical Corps and infantry, who cheered us time after time. All our casualties were caused by artillery, and those who were watching the fight told us afterwards they thought we would be compelled to retire under such a bombardment, but you see we surprised the enemy and our own men too by hanging on... In the first hour of the bombardment I was practically buried, and my rifle smashed to pieces. Of course I was badly shaken, but soon recovered and managed to scrape through all right. What was left of my rifle I put in my pocket, and am keeping it for a souvenir. I have also a German belt and bayonet. Nearly all of us got German helmets, but they are awkward things for infantry to carry about, so we sold them to other corps."[78]

8733 Lance-Corporal Walter Spencer
2nd Battalion, The Durham Light Infantry

"I had just given orders to my men to stick together, when I got a stinging blow on my right arm, knocking my rifle up in the air. I knew then that I was hit by a piece of shell, and was bleeding from the main artery. A comrade got my bandage out, and I instructed him where to tie it to stop the bleeding, and he did his best, but he seemed to lose his nerve on seeing the blood rushing out, and as I knew he had not stopped it, and I was getting faint. I made it to the dressing station. After going fifty yards I had, however, to lie down; then I pulled myself together and dashed on for about 100 yards and fell into a trench. I lay there thinking I was done. Then I shouted for a stretcher-bearer, and luckily one came along and stopped the bleeding, and then another arrived with a stretcher and they put me on. They lifted me up, when a sniper sent a bullet through the head of one, and a second bullet grazed the head of the other bearer. I was left in the open, so I rolled off the stretcher into the trench, where I lay for about three hours. I was wounded at 3.30 a.m., and arrived at the dressing station properly done up at 2 p.m."[79]

8724 Corporal John William Straughan
2nd Battalion, The Durham Light Infantry

Corporal Straughan came from Sunderland and had enlisted on 15 January 1904. He had landed at St Nazaire with the 2nd D.L.I. on 10 September 1914. Wounded on 9 August, Straughan wrote his account of the fighting at Hooge while being treated for his wound at a hospital in Cambridge. He was discharged as unfit for further war service on 31 October 1916 and issued with a Silver War Badge.

---

[78] Burnley News, 22 September 1915. Lance-Corporal Spencer was writing to his parents, Mr and Mrs Thomas Spencer, who lived at 34 Albion Street in Earby. Spencer had disembarked at St Nazaire on 10 September 1914. He was later promoted to Serjeant and was commissioned as a Second-Lieutenant in The Durham Light Infantry on 14 May 1917.
[79] Newcastle Daily Journal, 3 September 1915.

"We have just come out of the trenches, which we captured from the Germans and I can tell you I am not sorry as it was hell upon earth. The Huns used 17-inch sells, aerial torpedoes, liquid fire and gas, but they all failed. We captured a big line of trenches. It was at a dear cost to our regiment; but, with the help of God, I came out all right. If it was a dear cost to us, it was ten times dearer for the Germans. They were lying in heaps, and in one trench alone I saw them three and four deep. There were Saxons, Bavarians, and Prussians all mixed up. I distinctly saw them bayoneting our wounded, and after doing that they would fling their hands up and shout 'Mercy.' They got mercy! It was God help them. They either got the bayonet or the bomb. Our lads were shouting, 'Remember the Lusitania,' and they struck everything that came in their way. Saxon prisoners told us that they did not want to fight against us. They said it was not their wish, and that they had been reinforced in order to make an attack. After the battle Sir John French addressed us, and said we had been mentioned in dispatches. We had had the honour of being the chosen regiment to lead the attack, and that we had undertaken and accomplished a most difficult task."[80]

3/9716 Private Thomas Munroe
2nd Battalion, The Durham Light Infantry

A native of Jarrow, Private Munroe was a Special Reservist and had been drafted to the front from the 3rd (Special Reserve) Battalion on 29 June 1915. He was killed on 19 April 1916 and is commemorated on the Ypres (Menin Gate) Memorial.

"I am simply "in the pink" after having been engaged in a hard fight at Hooge. We drove the Germans back with bombs and the bayonet. You should have heard them yelling when we laid hold of them for the purpose of taking them prisoner. We took about 200, and they were very fortunate to escape death. It was not in the advance that we suffered, but after we succeeded in taking the position, as we were responsible for holding it under heavy shell-fire. They were sending over the largest shells at their disposal, such as "coal-boxes," air torpedoes, and heavy shrapnel. It was something terrible. The whole earth trembling and rocking like a cradle, so you will have a slight idea of the size of the shells. We won the trenches in spite of all, and held them for two days without a drink of water or a bite to eat, as we felt obliged to give all our water to the wounded."[81]

---

[80] Dundee, Perth, Forfar and Fife's People's Journal, 28 August 1915.
[81] Dundee Evening Telegraph, 7 September 1915.

3/21893 Private Albert Henry Anderson
2nd Battalion, The Durham Light Infantry

Private Anderson, who came from Gateshead, was writing to his father, Joseph Aloysius Anderson. He also wrote to his brother, who lived in Felling, regarding his experiences on 9 August:

"At present we are having a rest after the fight we had at Hooge. We are right proud of the fact that General (sic) French, accompanied by several other Generals, addressed us about the battle, and they remarked that it was a capital fight and was praiseworthily carried out from start to finish. They expressed their satisfaction and spoke highly of the Durhams."[82]

Private Anderson's conduct during the action at Hooge was brought to the notice of the General Officer Commanding 6th Division, and he received a card from him:

"Your Commanding Officer and Brigade Commander have informed me that you distinguished yourself on the 10th August, 1915, near Hooge. I have read their report with much pleasure.

Walter Congreve V.C.
Major-General."

Albert, who was appointed Lance-Corporal shortly after the fighting, had been drafted from the 3rd (Special Reserve) Battalion on 23 June 1915. He was killed, aged 18, on 19 April 1916 and is buried at Essex Farm Cemetery: Plot II, Row K, Grave 12. The register for the cemetery records that his father and mother, Grace, lived at Wallsend after the war.

---

[82] ibid.

From Hooge

THE RED, RED ROAD TO HOOGE

"On parade – get your spade;
Fall in the "Shovel and Pick Brigade;"
There's a "Carry Fatigue" for half a league,
And a trench to dig with a spade.
Through the dust and ruins of Ypres town,
The "Seventeen Inch" still battering down;
Spewing death with its fiery breath;
On the red, red road to Hooge.

Who is the one whose time has come.
Who won't return when the work is done.
Who'll leave his bones on the blood-stained stones
Of the red, red road to Hooge?
Onward the Staffords – never a stop;
To the sand-bagged trench, and over the top;
Over the top, if a "packet" you stop.
On the red, red road to Hooge.

The burst and the road of a hand grenade,
Welcome us on to the death parade;
The Pit of Gloom –the Valley of Doom.
The Crater – down at Hooge.
Full of many a soldier from the Rhine
Must sleep to-night in a bed of lime,
'Tis a pitiless grave for a brave or a knave,
Is the Crater – down at Hooge.

Hark to the stand to fusillade.
Sling your rifle, bring your spade,
And fade away, 'ere break of day,
Or a hole you'll fill at Hooge.
Call the roll – and another name
Is sent to swell the Roll of Fame;
So we carve a cross to mark the loss
Of a chum who fell at Hooge.

Not a deed for the paper man to write,
No glorious charge in the dawning light;
The "Daily Mail" won't tell the tale
Of the night work out at Hooge.
But our General knows, and his praise we've won,
He's pleased with the work the Staffords have done,
In the shot and shell at the gates of hell,
On the red, red road to Hooge."[83]

---

[83] The poem is stated to have been written by 8962 Private William Woolley, who served with the 1ˢᵗ Battalion, The North Staffordshire Regiment, which was published in The Burton Daily Mail on 12 October 1915. The poem also appeared in The Derby Telegraph on 7 October 1915, written by a "Derby soldier" and again in The Burton Daily Mail on 6 December 1915. Many other versions of the same poem also exist.

The Tyne Cot Memorial and Cemetery

Tyne Cot, 10 November 1994

The origin of the name "Tyne Cot" is shrouded in myth. Evidence from British Army trench maps shows that the ruined buildings on the Broodseinde Ridge were marked as "Tyne Cottages" long before the accepted story that the position was christened "Tyne Cot" by troops of the 50th (Northumbrian) Division during 1917, as they were said to resemble miner's cottages from their home area. By that time the buildings had been pulverised by artillery fire and replaced by the Germans with four concrete pillboxes, consisting of a command blockhouse and three machine-gun positions. The pillboxes made for a formidable obstacle for any attacking force, having interlocking fields of fire that were able to dominate the slope below them. The position was captured by troops of the 3rd Australian Division on 4 October 1917 during the Battle of Broodseinde.

The Bronze Wreath on the Cross of Sacrifice, 7 August 2018

Three of the blockhouses are preserved within the boundaries of the cemetery, the command pillbox being used as the foundation for the Cross of Sacrifice, at the suggestion of King George V. Part of the original blockhouse is exposed and contains a bronze wreath recording its capture by the Australians, although the original inscription attributed the taking of the position to the 2nd Division A.I.F. This was corrected to the 3rd Australian Division during the 1990s. Following its capture, Australian and British units used the command blockhouse as a Regimental Aid Post, and the original cemetery can be found to the east of the Cross of Sacrifice, retaining the irregular layout of a battlefield cemetery. The 343 graves include British Canadian and German soldiers, and also includes twenty Special Memorials commemorating soldiers whose graves were destroyed by shell fire.

Graves at Tyne Cot Cemetery, 7 August 2018

Tyne Cot Cemetery is the largest Commonwealth War Graves Cemetery in the world and contains in total of 11,968 graves. The cemetery was greatly expanded by concentrating burials from around the Ypres Salient and further afield, and it was not until 1922 that the work of reinterring the remains was completed. Of the nearly 12,000 graves only 3,605 are identified. There are also over eighty Special Memorials to soldiers believed to have been reburied at Tyne Cot when their remains were moved there, as well as headstones recording multiple burials in the same grave.

Australians, Canadians, New Zealanders, South Africans and Channel Islanders all rest together with British soldiers, airmen and sailors and Royal Marines who served with 63rd (Royal Naval) Division. Also among those soldiers who have identified graves in Tyne Cot Cemetery are two Australians and a Canadian soldier, all posthumously awarded the Victoria Cross. The most recent burials in the cemetery took place on 6 November 2018, when the remains of two Australians and a soldier of The Lancashire Fusiliers were interred there. Their bodies had been found in December 2015 while roadworks were being carried out near Passchendaele.

One of the surviving German blockhouses at Tyne Cot Cemetery,
7 August 2018

A view of part of Tyne Cot Cemetery, with the Memorial at the rear, taken by a former soldier from Spalding who revisited the battlefields in July 1929.

Charles Preston, a journalist, returned to Tyne Cot in August 1928. He had been there ten years previously as 241276 Private C. W. Preston, serving with 1ˢᵗ Battalion, The Queen's Royal West Surrey Regiment:

"Almost ten years ago the writer stood in the trenches at Passchendaele in fighting kit with a gas mask at the alert, shells screaming overhead, the country around him shell-holed and water-laden, discoloured by gas. Last week he stood at the same spot, or as near as it was possible to reach, and there were fields of golden corn, level country and an almost unbroken stretch of rich prosperous country. The harvest of death has ceased – the harvest of man was in progress. Passchaendaele in those seeming far-off days beggared description by reason of its utter ruin and desolation, its stark nakedness, to-day it excels in the glory of its fertility, the industry of its farmers and a tribute to the perseverance of a nation that has arisen from the ashes of Armageddon.

A little further on I stood in Tyne Cot Cemetery, one of the largest of the graveyards of the British Army. The foundation of the Cross of Remembrance is a German Pill Box – Tyne Cot was its name, and during our turn in the line it was our Battalion Headquarters – the 1ˢᵗ The Queen's – and it held us safely during fierce barrages and gas attacks. Who can ever forget the beauty of the British cemeteries. Roses, the flower of England, bloom before each headstone, the grass is as well kept as a lawn, loving care is bestowed by the gardeners. No parent, wife, or sister need fear that their loved one's grave is neglected, and the write pays grateful tribute to those who tend with exquisite care the resting place of his comrades."[84]

Tyne Cot Cemetery and Memorial, 23 March 2018

[84] Surrey Mirror, 17 August 1928.

28721 Corporal Arthur Long
7th Division Signals Company, Royal Engineers Signals Service

The earliest dated burial at Tyne Cot Cemetery is that of **28721 Corporal Arthur Long**, who came from Birmingham and served with 7th Division Signals Company, Royal Engineers Signal Service. He was accidentally killed on 18 October 1914 while serving as a despatch rider.

Arthur was born on 3 May 1890, the son of Arthur John Long, a builder, and Clara Long, and was baptised at St Thomas in the Moors Church in Balsall Heath on 2 July of that year. He had lived with his parents at 1 Oakwood Road in Sparkhill and worked as a carpenter and joiner before joining the Royal Engineers at Chatham in September 1914, having made several previous attempts to enlist. While training on Salisbury Plain he exchanged places with another despatch rider so that he could go the front earlier, and Corporal Long disembarked at Zeebrugge with 7th Division on 7 October. On receiving the news of his son's death at the front, Arthur's father stated to a newspaper reporter in Birmingham that he believed that his son had been killed as he was deaf and had failed to hear the challenge of a sentry.[85]

Originally buried at Kruiseecke German Military Cemetery, Corporal Long's remains were exhumed in March 1921 and reburied in Plot LXIII, Row J, Grave 16.

8119 Drummer George Wheeler, of the 1st Battalion, The South Staffordshire Regiment, was a regular soldier from Birmingham and was working as a labourer when he attested for the regiment on 27 September 1907. At the outbreak of the war he was station with at Pietermaritzburg. Following the declaration of war Wheeler returned with the 1st South Staffords to England, landing at Southampton on 19 September 1914, and after training at Lyndhurst in the New Forest sailed for the front, disembarking at Zeebrugge on 7 October.

Drummer Wheeler was killed on 22 October 1914 while his battalion was in positions of the Zonnebeke Ridge, and is recorded as one of the first fatalities suffered by the 1st South Staffords. News of his death at the front, together with a tribute paid to him by one of his officers, was published in The Staffordshire Advertiser on 16 January 1915:

---

[85] Birmingham Daily Post, 3 November 1914.

8119 Drummer George Wheeler
1st Battalion, The South Staffordshire Regiment

A DRUMMER OF THE 1ˢ BATT. SOUTH STAFFS. REGIMENT

BRAVERY & COOL MARKSMANSHIP

"Please accept my sympathies, which are the most heartfelt, for the loss of a really brave and true man, a fine soldier, who died doing his duty as a man should. I am proud to have known him."

In these simple yet consoling words, eloquent of the comradeship among all ranks of the British Expeditionary Force, Lieut. C. Wilmot Evans, of the 1ˢ South Staffordshires, concludes a letter addressed from the trenches to L-Corp. Harry Wheeler, describing how his brother, Drmr. George Wheeler, of 4 Peel Terrace, Wynn Street, Birmingham, was killed by a sniper's bullet during a hot encounter at Zonnebeke on or about Oct. 20.

"I am pleased to say he was a credit to the flag", writes the officer, "Mothers should be proud to give their sons for their country if they be as the whole regiment knew Drmr. Wheeler to be. We were all very fond of him and offer to you our condolences. I never knew such a splendid fellow as he was. I was awfully fond of him, as he was always cheerful and willing to help anyone during those trying hours we had then. He was brave, and did awfully well. He was shot through the temple by a sniper while we were holding trenches just in front of a forest. I was standing by him at the time, and he himself was firing at the Germans as they came out of the wood. Of course, we did our best for him, but he died almost immediately. We could not take his body out of the trench until dark, as the Germans were attacking the whole of the time. Then we moved it after dark and covered it up. The next day we were driven out of the trenches, as we were the only regiment left in the line and were practically surrounded. So I sorry to say the body fell in German hands. He is deeply mourned by officers and men of the battalion, as he was very deservedly a general favourite. He was in our platoon and I have never had a nicer man under me. Please tell his family how well he died and what excellent work he did before his death. The regiment was so badly cut up that all records of casualties were lost. I am the only officer left of 30 which came out with the battalion."

Drummer Wheeler was buried by the Germans close to where he was killed, and after the war his remains were located at Map Reference D.29.c.65.45 and identified by a surviving identity disc. He was then reinterred at Tyne Cot Cemetery: Plot XXXI, Row F, Grave 20.

On 4 October 1917, the 1ˢᵗ Battalion, The South Staffordshire Regiment took part in 7ᵗʰ Divisions' push towards Reutel, as part of the Battle of Broodseinde.

The 1ˢᵗ South Staffords attacked at 6.00 a.m. and advanced to their first objective, the Red Line, which ran along the road from Reutel to Broodseinde, and soon found many German positions concealed by brushwood, which the Staffords quickly cleared at the point of their bayonets.

The battalion then commenced their advance to the Blue Line, their second objective, and moved forward to capture Jolting Trench, but came under enfilade fire from their right flank due to 21ˢᵗ Division not having kept pace with 7ᵗʰ Division's advance.

By nightfall the South Staffords had secured their flank, with two companies positioned along Jolting Houses Road facing south, one company in Jetty Trench and another in reserve at the Buttes in the remains of Polygon Wood. The 1ˢᵗ Battalion lost 3 Officers and 36 Other Ranks killed and 223 wounded during the days' fighting.

Born at Aberdeen, **32638 Private John McFarlane** was the son of James and Jeannie McFarlane, who lived at 9, Overdale Avenue in the Langside area of Glasgow. Private McFarlane had originally attested for the Army Ordnance Corps at Glasgow, his corps service number being 012518, but was transferred to the South Staffords and drafted to the 1ˢᵗ Battalion. He was reported as missing following the fighting on 4 October.

On 4 October 1920, three years to the day since he had been reported as missing, Private McFarlane's remains were found by a working party from 126ᵗʰ Company of the Labour Corps at Map Reference J.14b.7.4. and were identified by his surviving identity discs. His body was exhumed and brought to Tyne Cot Cemetery for reburial. Private John McFarlane now rests in Plot XXXIII, Row B, Grave 15.

32638 Private John McFarlane
1ˢᵗ Battalion, The South Staffordshire Regiment

Men of The South Staffordshire Regiment commemorated on the Tyne Cot Memorial. The names of 407 soldiers of the regiment are carved on Panels 90 to 92, 162 and 162A.

On the eastern side of Tyne Cot Cemetery is the Tyne Cot Memorial, which commemorates 34,997 British and New Zealand servicemen who died while serving in the Ypres Salient between 15 July 1917 and 29 December 1918 and have no known grave.

Designed by Sir Herbert Baker, with sculptures executed by Joseph Armitage and Ferdinand Victor Blundstone, the names of the servicemen are carved on Portland stone panels that are mounted on walls faced with flint. The memorial forms a semi-circle on the boundary wall, with two pavilions at each end.

There are also two rotundas and in the centre of the memorial stands the New Zealand Memorial Apse, which commemorates 1,166 members of the New Zealand Expeditionary Force who fell between 30 September and 30 October 1917 and whose remains were not identified. Among the men commemorated on the Tyne Cot Memorial are 450 sailors of the Royal Naval Volunteer Reserve and Royal Marines who died while fighting with 63rd (Royal Naval) Division during October and November 1917, as well as three soldiers who were awarded the Victoria Cross.

The Tyne Cot Memorial and the Cross of Sacrifice were inaugurated on 20 June 1927 by Captain Gilbert Joseph Cullen Dyett C.M.G., the National President of the Returned Sailors' Soldiers' and Airmens' Imperial League of Australia. In a speech delivered at the ceremony, Captain Dyett said:

"We are assembled here today to pay the tribute of our homage and gratitude to the tens of thousands of heroes who fell valiantly fighting in the Ypres Salient. This cross will preserve their memory for ever."[86]

Tyne Cot has been the setting of many ceremonies since then commemorating notable anniversaries of the 1917 battles, the most recent being held on 31 July 2017.

Names of members of the Scots Guards, among the 68 soldiers of the regiment commemorated on Panel 10 of the memorial.

---

[86] Aberdeen Press and Journal, 20 June 1917.

32756 Private George Eric Galtress was killed on 25 October 1917 during an assault on German positions near what remained of Polderhoek Chateau. At the time of his death Galtress was serving with the 15ᵗʰ (Service) Battalion, The Royal Warwickshire Regiment (2ⁿᵈ Birmingham), but was a former cavalryman of the 4ᵗʰ (Royal Irish) Dragoon Guards.

George Galtress was born at Stantonbury on 31 August 1894, the son of Robert and Margaret Galtress, who lived at 80 Spencer Street. He had been an apprentice blacksmith at the Wolverton Carriage Works before enlisting in the 4ᵗʰ (Royal Irish) Dragoon Guards at Bletchley in 1911. Issued with the regimental number D/7218, Private Galtress was stationed at Tidworth at the outbreak of the war and landed in France on 16 August 1914.

In the book "Tickled to Death to Go: Memories of a Cavalryman in World War I", a former comrade, Ben Clouting, stated that Galtress suffered from shell-shock in May 1915 but no mention of this was made in the following extract from a report that appeared in The Wolverton Express on 11 August 1916:

"... Mr. Galtress's second son, George, is serving with the 4th Royal Irish Dragoons. He landed in France on August 15, 1914, and although slightly wounded at Mons, has so far passed through the rest of the fighting on the Western Front without receiving a scratch..."

Private Galtress was transferred to the infantry in August 1917 and was part of a draft of former cavalrymen that was posted to the 15ᵗʰ Royal Warwicks. He has no known grave and is commemorated on Panel 26A of the Tyne Cot Memorial. George's name can also be found on the war memorial at New Bradwell Cemetery and the memorial tablet inside St James's Church.

15307 Sergeant Albert Edward Essery M.M., of the 8ᵗʰ (Service) Battalion, The Leicestershire Regiment, was killed on 1 October 1917 while fighting in Polygon Wood near Zonnebeke.

Albert was born on 23 January 1881, the third son of John and Mary Ann Essery, who lived at Mill Green at Turvey in Bedford. He attested at Melton Mowbray on 15 September 1914 and was rapidly promoted. Albert was appointed as a Lance-Corporal on 15 October 1914, promoted to Corporal on 7 November and advanced to Sergeant on 7 December. He was appointed a Company Sergeant-Major on 13 March 1915, but reverted to the rank of Sergeant at his own request on 17 May. Essery landed in France on 29 July 1915 and was awarded the Military Medal in 1916, the announcement being published in The London Gazette on 27 October.

News of the death of Sergeant Essery was reported in The Grantham Journal on 27 October 1917, the first anniversary of the announcement that he had been awarded the Military Medal:

"It has been reported for a week or two past that Sergt. A. E. Essery, of the Leicestershire Regiment, formerly of Melton Mowbray, had been killed in action, and confirmation of this has now been received from several who knew him, as well as a letter from an Army Chaplain to his parents who reside at Bedford. Sergt. Essery, it appears, was killed on the 1st October. It was after an early morning attack, through which he had come safely, but on emerging from a shell hole he had not proceeded more than three or four yards when he was shot in the stomach by a sniper, death ensuing within a minute or so. Three others fell in just about the same spot at the same time. Sergt. Essery was buried on the battlefield. Lance-Corpl. Butteriss, of the same regiment, son of Mr Chas. Butteriss, Thorpe-end, Melton Mowbray, who is at home at the present time on special leave, though he did not actually see Sergt. Essery killed, was with him shortly before the sad occurrence, and saw him again directly after he died. The late Sergt. Essery before joining the Leicesters shortly after the outbreak of war, was butler to Capt. Bertie Sherife, of Goadby Hall, prior to which he was for some years with Mr A. V. Pryor, Egerton Lodge, Melton Mowbray. He had been out at the front for about two years, and was at Melton on leave in June. Every sympathy will be felt for his relatives and friends at his death."

Sergeant Essery is commemorated on Panel 50 of the Memorial.

3/8862 Acting Company Sergeant-Major William Arthur Beech M.M.
1ˢᵗ Battalion, The South Staffordshire Regiment

William Beech came from Smethwick and lived on Brasshouse Lane. He had originally joined the 3ʳᵈ (Special Reserve) Battalion of The South Staffordshire Regiment at Birmingham in 1908 and at the outbreak of the war was mobilised. In peacetime, Beech was employed at Best and Lloyds Ltd. in Handsworth. A Corporal when he was drafted to France on 17 December 1914 to join the 1ˢᵗ Battalion, Beech was wounded during the Battle of Loos in September 1915 and was awarded the Military Medal for his gallantry during the fighting on the Somme the following year while serving as a Sergeant with the 1ˢᵗ South Staffords, his award being announced in The London Gazette on 1 September 1916. He was subsequently appointed as a Colour-Sergeant and an Acting Company Sergeant-Major.

William Beech was killed on 26 October 1917 when the 1ˢᵗ South Staffords attacked Joist Trench, Berry Cottage and Hamp Farm, which lay south of Gheluvelt. He has no known grave and is commemorated on Panel 90 of the Tyne Cot Memorial. One of his brothers served with The Royal Berkshire Regiment during the Great War.

200357 Corporal Charles Anker was killed on 27 April 1918 while serving with "C" Company of the 4ᵗʰ (Extra Reserve) Battalion, The South Staffordshire Regiment. He had been transferred to the 4ᵗʰ Battalion on the disbandment of the 2/5ᵗʰ South Staffords on 30 January 1918 and had seen action during the Easter Rising in Dublin. News of his death was reported by The Walsall Observer on 1 June:

"Corporal Charles Anker is officially reported to have been killed in action in France (sic) with the South Staffords on April 27. Formerly employed by Messrs. J. Cliff & Co., Portland Street, he enlisted in 1914, and served a long time in Ireland before going to France, where he saw eighteen months' active service. He was a single man, 21 years of age, and his home was at 51, James Street."

Corporal Anker was the son of Charles and Ellen Anker, and had lived with his widower father in the Ryecroft district of Walsall prior to his enlistment. He is commemorated on Panel 90 of the Tyne Cot Memorial.

CPL. CHARLES ANKER,
51, James Street.
(Killed in action.)

PRIVATE ABRAHAM LITTLEWOOD
(2nd South Staffords),
Spout Lane.
(Recommended for D.C.M.)

29222 Private Abraham Littlewood served with the 8th (Service) Battalion, The South Staffordshire Regiment and was killed on 12 October 1917, aged 40. He had already served at the front with the 2nd Battalion but, on being discharged on the termination of his period of engagement, rejoined his old regiment and was drafted back to France. From the Caldmore district of Walsall, Private Littlewood had disembarked at Le Havre on 13 August and served with "A" Company of the 2nd South Staffords. The act of gallantry for which he had been recognised had taken place at Moussy on 15 September, and was recorded by Captain Morris Boscawen Savage in his diary:

"Private Littlewood, of the Company, showed great pluck in going for the stretchers on two occasions along the road to Moussy under a hail of shells and bringing them back with him and removing the wounded."[87]

Recommended to receive the Distinguished Conduct Medal, Littlewood instead was given the lesser award of being mentioned in despatches. His actions were reported by The Walsall Advertiser on 24 October 1914:

"The honour of being mentioned in despatches by General French has fallen to the lot of a Walsall soldier in the person of Private A. Littlewood, of the 2nd Battalion, South Staffs. Regiment, whose home is at 11, Spout-lane. Out of the whole Battalion only six were mentioned, these being the Commanding Officer (Lieut.-Colonel Davidson), Capt. Savage, and four men.

The act which won for Private Littlewood this proud distinction was one of conspicuous gallantry – assisting wounded men out of the trenches under a very heavy shell fire.

Place Alive With Shells.

A letter was recently received by his wife, stating that his Commanding Officer had told him he should recommend him for the Distinguished Conduct Medal "And," he added, "I hope and trust I shall live to wear it." He mentions that at the time he was assisting the wounded the place was alive with shells, and in another part of the letter he states, "We are under fire all the time, but are used to it now."

---

[87] Lichfield Mercury, 15 January 1915. Private Littlewood's original regimental number was 6676.

Private Littlewood enlisted in the Staffords in 1902, and shortly afterwards was drafted to his regiment then in India, afterwards proceeding to South Africa. His term in the reserve had only two months to go when war broke out, and he proceeded to France with the first Expeditionary Force, taking part in all the big battles from Mons to the Aisne.

Walsall has indeed cause to be proud of the manner in which its sons are conducting themselves in the firing line, but particularly so of Private Littlewood's heroic action, and the hope he expressed that he should live to wear his medal will, we feel sure, be re-echoed by all our readers. Well done, Littlewood!"

The announcement that Private Littlewood had been Mentioned in Despatches was published in The London Gazette on 9 December 1914.

Private Littlewood returned home to Walsall on leave in February 1915 and was interviewed by a journalist from The Walsall Observer about his experiences. An article was subsequently published in the 20 February edition of the newspaper:

"PRUSSIAN COWARDS."

Caldmore Soldier's Opinion of Kaiser's Favourites.

"With a face tanned through continual life in the open air, and looking none the worse because of six months amid the hardships of the war, Private Abraham Littlewood, 2nd South Staffords (whose photograph we published last week), has returned from the Front on short leave, and, when seen at his home in Spout Lane, showed the "Observer" representative numerous war souvenirs. During the fierce bombardment of the village of Moussey, in the early stages of the battle of the Aisne, Private Littlewood rendered humane service by bringing in wounded under a hail of fire, and, as a recognition of his bravery, was recommended for the D.C.M. It was during those hot times that he had a succession of narrow escapes, and was not far away when that unexpected "Jack Johnson" wrought such havoc among "Tommies" assembled round the pump in the village square. On Christmas Eve he and a comrade narrowly escaped death. They were out reconnoitering the German trenches, when they fell over a trip wire. This must have given some alarm, for they had hardly fallen flat than a volley rang out from the enemy's positions.

"They peppered away in the darkness," he says, "and the bullets were whizzing all round, but we lay extended and face downwards. After some minutes, which seemed like hours, they stopped firing, evidently judging that they had put an end to our careers. But we were very much alive. I whispered, 'Are you ready?' to my comrade, and we decided to chance our luck. The officer was surprised when at last we managed to get back to the trench. When he heard the Germans fire, he never expected to see us alive again."

"Talk about the Prussian Guards being brave," said Private Littlewood, with a sarcastic smile, "why, they're the biggest cowards who ever walked the earth." A body of the Kaiser's much-vaunted regiment sought refuge in a wood, and, when fired upon, never so much as returned a shot. He confessed that when leaving the firing line after receiving his furlough papers he dreaded walking along a certain canal bank, which was very much exposed.

"But it was the only way," he said, "and it had to be done. Well, I was trudging along, thinking of home, when, honour bright, a bullet whizzed straight across my face – pang! Oh, the shock took two stone off my weight. But," he added, meanwhile gripping his rifle, "I'll pay 'em out when I get back. Although being one of the Staffords, I perhaps oughtn't to say it, but you can take it from me they've done some grand work out there, and mean to do a bit more before this job's finished. Without any boasting, the 2nd South are the finest regiment in the British Army."

We have several pieces of shrapnel at our offices as rather grim keepsakes from Private Littlewood."

Private Littlewood is commemorated on Panel 91A of the Memorial. His widow lived at 11 Spout Lane in the Caldmore district of Walsall.

Second-Lieutenant Christopher Hollins Lucas served with the 8th (Service) Battalion, The North Staffordshire Regiment, and was killed on 10 April 1918 when his battalion were involved in trying to stem the German advance along the Messines Ridge on the second day of the "Georgette" Offensive.

Christopher was the son of Christopher, who was a Birmingham City Councillor, and Florence Lillian Lucas, who lived at 28 Cambridge Road in King's Heath in Birmingham. After serving in ranks he was commissioned in The North Staffordshire Regiment on 28 March 1917 and landed in France on 26 May.

On 1 April 1918 Second-Lieutenant Lucas wrote to his parents:

"As you have doubtlessly noticed, our division (the 19th) has received special commendation for its work in the great battle still raging, and though I, of course, am not permitted to tell you anything about it just now, I can say that we were in the thick of it from the very first day, and once again we have come through with remarkable good luck, and, incidentally, I trust, given old Fritz something to remember us by. It has been, of course, the most wonderful, exciting, and awful experience that has yet befallen me, and the same applied to practically everybody, for it is by far the most stupendous battle ever waged in the world's history of war. Still, here we are, still unbeaten, hale, hearty, and cheerful, and all the boys going strong. We ourselves had six days of it, solid, on the go in action the whole time, day and night, though I must admit that, despite all, we fed remarkably well in the circumstances."[88]

His death at the front was reported by The Birmingham Daily Post on 23 April 1918:

"Sec. Lieut. C. H. LUCAS, North Staffordshire Regiment, son of Councillor C. Lucas, 28, Cambridge Road, King's Heath, was killed in action on April 11 whilst leading his men. He was twenty-one years of age, and was educated at Camp Hill Grammar School and Birmingham University, where he joined the University O.T.C., but resigned in December 1916, and became a Sergeant-Instructor to a battalion of the Worcestershire Regiment. In March 1917, he received a commission, and went out to France in May, 1917, and took part with his battalion in all their engagements from that time, including the great battle that commenced on March 21, in reference

---

[88] Birmingham Daily Post, 15 April 1918.

to which he wrote a letter describing the troops as "unbeaten, hale, hearty and cheerful," which appeared in the 'Daily Post' on April 15."

Second-Lieutenant Lucas has no known grave and is commemorated on Panel 124 of the Memorial. His medals were sent to his mother on 13 October 1921, and were sold, together with his memorial plaque, at auction in 1995.

1254 Private Richard Spensley served with XIV Corps Cyclist Battalion but was attached to 22nd Squadron, Royal Flying Corps at the time he was reported as missing on 18 October 1917.

Born at Long Newton in County Durham in 1893, Richard was the son of Thomas and Sarah Spensley. Employed as a colliery labourer above ground, he lived with his parents at 47 Tower Street West in the Hendon district of Sunderland before attesting for The Durham Light Infantry in 1911. Private Spensley was stationed at Whittington Barracks near Lichfield with the 2nd Battalion when war was declared, and embarked for St Nazaire with the 6th Division Cyclist Company on 9 September 1914. While fighting in France in November 1914, Private Spensley wrote to his mother:

"You are right when you say the Germans are getting it hot, it is a case of come out and go under with them. The boys have only got to wait and when they do come out they are in a bunch and a tenth class shot could not miss them. I heard a good yarn the other day: A German officer and a soldier were captured and as they were being brought past our guns the officer asked was that all the men there were to the guns. They told him it was all and he turned to the private and said: 'What would the Kaiser think if he knew that?' The private said, 'To the devil with the Kaiser; I want to get back to London!' They said he had been living in London. I see poor old Sunderland won (!) again 1-7; there is always someone chewing the rag about football, it keeps us lively now and again."[89]

Spensley transferred to the Army Cyclist Corps on its formation in 1915, and remained with the 6th Division Cyclist Company until it left the Division in June 1916. It was not until April 1918 that his death was presumed, and he is commemorated on Panel 154 of the Memorial.

---

[89] Sunderland Daily Echo, 3 December 1914.

Passchendaele and Crest Farm

The Canadian Memorial at Passendale
23 March 2018

The Canadian Memorial in Passchendaele (now Passendale) marks the site of Crest Farm, a German position captured by the 72nd (Seaforth Highlanders of Canada) Battalion, Canadian Expeditionary Force on 30 October 1917 after fierce fighting. The 72nd killed 50 Germans, took another 25 prisoner and four machine-guns. The Battalion's History described the conditions in which they had fought:

"It was one vast quagmire of shell-holes and of the debris of war. Roads were practically non-existent and had had to be replaced with "duck mats" – sparred pathways of wood laid on the yielding surface. Let it be remembered too that there had been no time to build defensive gun emplacements. Moreover, the Germans had every spot registered and kept it under continual shell-fire. The Canadians had been asked to do an almost impossible task. That they accomplished it shows their superiority to the picked troops brought against them."[90]

The location for the memorial, west of the centre of Passchendaele, was one of three granted in Belgium to Canada by the Imperial War Graves Commission in 1920, and takes the form of a granite block designed by Percy Nobbs, the Architectural Advisor to the Canadian Battlefields Memorials Commission.[91] The memorial is inscribed in both English and French, the English inscription being:

THE CANADIAN CORPS IN OCT - NOV 1917 ADVANCED
ACROSS THIS VALLEY
THEN A TREACHEROUS MORASS
CAPTURED AND HELD THE PASSCHENDAELE RIDGE

"Passchendaele" a name synonymous with the commonly-held perceptions of the Great War: mud, slaughter, and futility, is also often used to refer to the entire Third Battle of Ypres, fought from 31 July to 10 November 1917. In fact there were two battles of Passchendaele that were part of the final weeks of the offensive, the First Battle taking place on 12 October and the Second Battle between 26 October and 10 November.

The ruins of the village of Passchendaele were finally captured by the 4th Canadian Division on 10 November 1917, but on entering the village the Canadians encountered the bodies of troops of the 66th (East Lancashire) Division, who had entered the village on 9 October but had withdrawn. A memorial window in memory of those members of the 66th Division who died during the Great War was later subscribed to by the Old Comrades' Association and unveiled inside the reconstructed church in 1928.

The British held the Passchendaele Ridge until April 1918, when the German offensives on the Lys compelled the Second Army to withdraw to positions much closer to Ypres. The village was finally captured by the Belgian Army on 28 September 1918.

---

[90] B. McEvoy & Captain A. H. Finlay M.C. History of the 72nd Battalion, Seaforth Highlanders of Canada, (Vancouver, Cowan & Brookhouse, 1920), p.80.
[91] The memorials are sometimes informally referred to as "Nobbs' Cubes."

Hill 60

A spoil heap that was created by the excavation of the nearby cutting for the railway between Roulers and Ypres during the 19th Century, the hill gained its name because it stands sixty metres above sea level. It had been known before the war as "Lover's Knoll," but by the time the German 39. Infanterie-Division captured the hill took the hill from the French on 10 December 1914 its reputation became far from romantic. The strategic importance of Hill 60 was evident to the Germans, as it provided excellent observation over the low-lying ground towards Ypres. On the south side of the same railway cutting was another spoil heap, which was christened "The Caterpillar" by the British.

The British 28th Division, composed of units recently arrived from garrison duties in India, took over responsibility for the sector from the French in February 1915, and they were in turn relieved by 5th Division in April. On 17 April, assisted by the firing of five charges placed under the German trenches by British tunnellers, units of 5th Division stormed the hill and captured the crest and the mine craters. Savage fighting took place for the next three weeks for possession of Hill 60, the Germans launching a gas attack against the British on 1 May, followed by two more on 5 May which resulted in them recapturing the position. A British counter-attack was made on 7 May, but this failed and Hill 60 remained in the possession of the Germans for just over two years, but in addition to the routines of trench warfare an active underground battle continued between British, and later Canadian and Australian tunnellers against their German counterparts as they mined and counter-mined under the trenches, exploding charges under the opposing positions and camouflets to collapse each other's galleries and shafts.

In August 1915, 175th Tunnelling Company, Royal Engineers began deep mining operations against the Germans on Hill 60, the entrance of the shaft being dug into the railway cutting some 220 yards behind the British front line trench. The 3rd Canadian Tunnelling Company took over responsibility for the sector in April 1916 and commenced work on pushing a second set of galleries towards The Caterpillar. Two charges totalling 53,300lbs of explosives were placed into position by the Canadian, and they were relieved by 1st Australian Tunnelling Company in November 1916, who continued with the work of maintaining the tunnel system

At 3.10 a.m. on 7 June 1917 the two mines were fired, and infantrymen of the 23rd Division rushed and captured the two craters, securing both Hill 60 and the Caterpillar.

The concrete bunker that is preserved on Hill 60 was constructed during January and February 1918 by 4th Field Company, Australian Engineers, commanded by Major J.H. Jolly, and used as its base an existing German bunker that had been taken on 7 June 1917. Following the German advances following the Lys Offensive which opened on 9 April 1918, Hill 60 was given up on the night of 15-16 April, with the British troops withdrawing to a new defensive line some 400 yards to the west. The position was finally recaptured on 28 September 1918.

In March 1920 Lieutenant-Colonel Edward Percy Cawston, who had served with the 1/9th Londons on Hill 60 in 1915, purchased Hill 60, and a few months later sold a half-share to John Calder, who was the Managing Director of Samuel Allsop and Sons Brewery in Burton-on-Trent. After reports in the press appeared that Calder was planning to develop the site for tourist purposes, criticism was directed at both men and they were compelled to state that their intention was to preserve Hill 60 for future generations.

Cawston later sold his interest in Hill 60, following the erection of the memorial to his old regiment, and seven years after the site was purchased Allsop offered it to the nation. The matter was reported on by The Scotsman on 28 July 1927:

"Lt.-Colonel E. P. Cawston, of Bromley, who was associated with Mr J. J. Calder in the original acquisition of Hill 60, yesterday made the following statement:-

"I purchased the summit of Hill 60 in March 1920, at a cost of about 15,000 Belgian francs, and sold a half-share a few months afterwards to Mr J. J. Calder. The area held by us jointly comprises about 15,000 square metres. On the highest point of the hill there was a very substantial concrete pill-box, which was purchased with an area of about 100 square metres by the Queen Victoria Rifles, who subsequently erected upon it a granite memorial. This London regiment is particularly interested in the hill because – as a unit of the 13th Brigade, 5th Division – in the spring of 1915 they were engaged in the very heavy fighting on the hill, and one of their young subalterns, now the Rev. G. Woolley, received the first Territorial V.C. for gallantry on the now historic hill.

ORIGINAL INTENTION.

"What I originally had in mind in purchasing Hill 60 was that by purchasing other prominent points, such as at Messines, Hooge, Poelcappelle, and so on, a series of Martello towers could be created to indicate the general line held by British troops defending the salient.

"Some time ago Mr Calder and I came to the conclusion that, in view of the historic importance of the hill, there was no better course than to present the hill to the nation, and with this object in view, and on that understanding, I surrendered to Mr Calder my interest in such portion of the hill as we jointly owned. I have not yet disposed of the 'approaches' to the hill from the Ypres or 'British' side."

OFFER UNDER CONSIDERATION.

Mr John J. Calder's offer to present Hill 60 to the nation is still under consideration by the War Office, the Press Association understands. It was explained yesterday that, assuming the War Office decided at once to accept the offer, it could not, as a Government Department, hold the land. Other Departments of the Government have first to be consulted, and the offer is being discussed by the officials concerned. There will be no unnecessary delay in coming to a decision, but the matter is one which cannot be settled immediately."

The urgent need for the site to be preserved was hastened due to locals collecting salvage from the Hill to sell for scrap. This included chipping the lead lettering from the memorial to 1st Australian Tunnelling Company. The activities of the scavengers were reported on by The Sheffield Daily Telegraph on 22 June 1925:

"At Hill 60 there were two lots of men at work. Some were searching for brass and other metal, out of the sale of which they make a living. This search for valuable metal is a little too thorough at times. There is a simple monument to some Australian tunnellers, who were killed in mining operations. The lettering on the stone was filled in with lead. Some of this lead has been picked out! One party of men still continues the sad search for the bodies of our soldiers. Thirty were found a week or two ago. They included those of two men still in full equipment, with steel helmets, crouching together as they sought shelter at the bottom of a trench. A heavy explosion had buried them. The bodies were remarkably preserved, and it should be quite possible to identify some of them at any rate."

Hill 60 was eventually handed over to the care of the Imperial War Graves Commission in 1930.

Although the Hill itself was not subject to development as a tourist attraction, enterprising individuals saw the potential of the site as the numbers of visitors to the battlefields increased during the 1920s. Prior to 1939 two rival "trench museums" existed on the edge of Hill 60, but the relationship between the owners of the attractions was far from cordial.

Matters came to a head, as recorded by The Newcastle Sun (New South Wales) in an article published on 22 February 1939:

2nd BATTLE OF HILL 60

Disputes Between Belgians

"The second Battle of Hill 60 is over.

It has resulted in a victory for Mrs Ted Moon, Belgian-born wife of a British ex-soldier, over her Belgian neighbour. During the war a shell struck the house in which the present Mrs Moon, then the belle of Zillebeke, was living. She was draffed to safety by Rifleman Ted Moon, from the Old Kent-road. After the war they married, and Mr Moon became a War Graves gardener, settling down at Zillebeke.

Mrs Moon foresaw the large influx of tourists and erected a war-style canteen at the foot of Hill 60. The café prospered. Then a Belgian neighbor opened a system of war-time tunnels and trenches. Tourists were attracted to these, and Mrs Moon's business began to wane. But she discovered tunnels and trenches at the back of her canteen, opened them up, and prospered again.

Unfounded Charge

Then the second Battle of Hill 60 began in earnest. It culminated in an allegation by the Belgian, on a large notice board, and in three languages, that Mrs Moon's trenches and tunnels had not been dug during the war. Mrs Moon took the matter to the court at Ypres, and now they have found the allegation untrue, and awarded Mrs Moon damages of 500 francs, and costs. Mr Moon said: "When it became known that my wife was going to take the matter to court, we received letters from all parts of the British Isles wishing us good luck. A notice of apology is being inserted in the Belgian papers by our neighbour."

"Trenches and Dugouts on 'Hill 60,' near Ypres, Belgium, Monday 22nd July 1929." A photograph taken by George Reuben Bertram Owen, who lived at 7 Nelson Avenue in Monton Green, Eccles, who visited the area on a battlefield tour.

German veterans visiting the trenches near Hill 60 in 1937.

Hill 60 was briefly fought over again in May 1940 as the Germans advanced towards Ypres and following the Second World War only one trench museum and café, christened the "Hill 60 (Queen Victoria's) Museum," remained to cater for visitors to the site. That museum closed in January 2006 and the collection of artefacts was transferred into the care of the Memorial Museum Passchendaele 1917 at Zonnebeke.

During 2015 Hill 60 was extensively landscaped, with boarded walkways and information panels being installed to provide information to visitors. At the same time access to the mine crater at the Caterpillar, which had previously been on private property, was opened.

The memorial to 14th (Light) Division, which is positioned close to the entrance of Hill 60, was not an original feature and was moved to this location in 1978 from Railway Wood where it had been in danger of being damaged by subsidence.

The memorial to 14th (Light) Division in July 1998.

A photograph of Hill 60, taken in July 1929 by an ex-serviceman from Spalding who had served in the area with 46ᵗʰ (North Midland) Division in 1915.

A former soldier, Percy George Arnold died at Chelmsford Hospital on 2 January 1931. Employed as an insurance agent at the outbreak of the war, Percy George Arnold joined the 1ˢᵗ Birmingham Battalion of The Royal Warwickshire Regiment on 8 September 1914. He was issued with the regimental number 14/351, and disembarked at Boulogne with the 14ᵗʰ Royal Warwicks on 21 November 1915. Private Arnold was wounded in 1917 while serving in the Ypres Salient and was discharged as physically unfit for war service on 11 October 1918, aged 39. He was later issued with a Silver War Badge.

Percy married May Maria Arnold, who was a midwife, at Warwick in 1921 and at the time of his death lived with his wife at 311 Yardley Road in the Little Bromwich district of Birmingham. He had requested that his ashes be scattered on Hill 60 and the story behind his request was widely reported in the press, including The Birmingham Daily Gazette of 12 January 1931:

"The cremated remains of Mr Percy G. Arnold, who, up to the time of his death, was chief steward at the Birmingham City Hospitals, are, in accordance with one of his dearest wishes, to be scattered over Hill 60.

Mr Arnold, who was 51 years of age, died on 3 January (sic) in a Chelmsford nursing home from hemorrhage caused by war wounds.

WITH THE CITY BATTALIONS.

During the war in which he served in one of the Birmingham City Battalions he was in some of the fiercest fighting which centred round the historic Hill 60, and it was there that in 1915 (sic) he was shot through the lungs – a wound which resulted in him spending over two years in hospital.

Many of his friends fell in the region of Hill 60, and it always figured much in his memories of the war.

WEDDING DAY WISH.

On his wedding day in 1921 he asked his wife to see that his ashes were taken and scattered there when he died.

Mrs Arnold at present is lying ill at her home in Yardley-road, Little Bromwich, and her husband's ashes are in a casket reposed in St Gregory's Church, Small Heath.
There the casket is to remain until Mrs Arnold is sufficiently recovered to carry out his request – which she intends to do."

It is not known if Maria Arnold was able to travel to Belgium to scatter her husband's ashes at Hill 60, but she died at 113 Aubrey Road in Small Heath on 23 January 1934.

"The night of the taking of Hill 60 an officer that was along with us recommended me for a D.C.M. for holding the trench myself after they had all left me. I was left on this part of the trench myself because the Germans were creeping up on us. I kept firing on them, and stopped their rush until the rest got away.

It was a terrible place to be in - nothing but dead men all around you. I was sitting on the top of a dead man firing all the time. It was terrible watching your chums being shot through the head and you could do nothing for them.

I was back at the rest camp, and was there for two days when I got the order to get ready and march back to Hill 60, as the regiment that was holding the hill retired from it, and we were told we had to take back the hill again. That was a 'jaw breaker' for us, as we were done up with what we came through before. The Cheshires were holding the position, and had to run out of it because of the gas. They were left with only 50 men out of 1000. On Wednesday, 5ᵗʰ (May), we were told to attack the hill at ten o'clock at night. There were only two companies of us – D Company and C Company. We charged across the open and chased the Germans out of it. The other two companies were to support us at the back after we got there. That was all the men who came with us. The other two companies had lost their way coming up to the trench. We were in a fix, and were shot down like rabbits as we were going into the German trenches on either side, and they were shooting at us from our backs. We were about two hours in the trench and there was only one officer with five men left where I was. We kept firing away until we had no more ammunition. We did not know what to do. We got into a veritable death-trap.

Then we got the order to retire, and this movement was worse than the attack. I said to myself, 'Well, old boy, you got across all right; you will have to go back again.' I said my prayers that night. I am out of it safe and sound. The only thing I am vexed at was the taking the trench from them and then losing it again through having to retire. I wanted one of the sergeants to get all the men he could together to hold the trench, but it was no use; we had to go. I only hope I shall not have to go through the same again.

All my chums at my side were shot, and we could do nothing for them but let them lie. Thousands of men are lying on Hill 60. It isn't fighting; it's pure murder. Three hard fights in three weeks is bad, and only twenty-four hours' rest out of that shows what kind of stuff the regiment is made of.

We got more congratulations to-day from the Generals of brigades for our work. There was some lucky star guiding us, because it was simply raining bullets, with machine gun fire on each side of us, and the Germans were also firing in front of us. You can think what it would be like.

There were some funny thoughts running through my head. I could not tell you the sensation that comes over you when you are told to charge. We lost 132 men and 10 officers out of two companies. I don't know yet how many of us got back. We were never told how the trenches lay or where we were to run to or anything about it. We charged in the dark. I consider myself lucky being able to write this. I have two or three souvenirs I am going to send home."[92]

16884 Private John Sinclair
2nd Battalion, The King's Own Scottish Borderers

John Sinclair was employed as a mine contractor at the Station Pit in Denny when he attested on a Short Service Engagement at Berwick-on-Tweed on 3 December 1914 and was drafted from the 3rd (Special Reserve) Battalion, The King's Own Scottish Borderers to the front on 17 February 1915. The recommendation for the award of the Distinguished Conduct Medal for his actions on Hill 60 was unsuccessful. Private Sinclair later received a gunshot wound to the left forearm and on his recovery was posted to the Depot at Berwick on 9 March 1916, before returning to the 3rd Battalion on 12 May 1916. Sinclair returned to France as part of a draft on 28 September 1916 and was sent to No. 21 Infantry Base Depot, before being posted to the 1st Battalion on 30 October. He was transferred to the Class Z Army Reserve on 23 February 1919 on his demobilisation. A son served with the Highland Cyclist Battalion.

---

[92] Falkirk Herald, 22 May 1915.

Born at Bromley on 20 January 1886, **S/4936 Private Bertram Baldwin** attested for the 3rd (Special Reserve) Battalion, The Queen's Own (Royal West Kent Regiment), on 9 August 1908. At the time of his enlistment he was employed as a valet. Bertram was five feet, three inches tall, and had brown eyes and dark brown hair, and stated that he was a Baptist. He was appointed a Lance-Corporal, but reverted to Private at his own request in 1910. Four years into his six years' period of engagement, Baldwin re-enlisted for further service on 29 May 1912. He was employed as a waiter when he married Florence Hart at Lyminge on 14 June 1912, and their daughter, Lilian May, was born the following year.

Baldwin was mobilised on 8 August 1914 and joined the 3rd Battalion at their war station in Chatham. He had been drafted to France on 20 September 1914 and joined the 1st Battalion. On 11 April 1915, Baldwin was sentenced to 14 days' Field Punishment No. 2, but the necessities of war intervened and he did not complete it.

On 17 April, Private Baldwin took part in the assault on Hill 60 and was severely wounded. On reaching the 1st Eastern General Hospital in Cambridge, Private Baldwin wrote the account of his experiences at Hill 60 to his wife, Florence, at their home at 39 Rossendale Road in Folkestone:

"It does seem a treat to be able to write and to say what we like, to send off a letter any time, and to be in England. No doubt you have read of the terrible slaughter at Hill 60 near Ypres. This is one of the places where I have been engaged since February. Papringe (sic – Poperinghe), St Eloi, Yser Canal, and other places – I was there last November.

When I arrived in France in September last I went to Neuve Chapelle and La Bassee. Our regiment suffered terribly. I was there five days – terrible time. I left there for ------------, ----------, and Messines; saw some terrible times here after we were strengthened by reinforcements. At these places right through the winter. I have since been in the vicinity of Ypres.

On Saturday, April 17th, our regiment met the King's Own Scottish Borderers, made a charge, and captured the German trenches and prisoners as soon as Hill 60 was blown up by the Engineers. It was hell – the worst I have witnessed. Our regiment has always been in the thick of all the fighting.

Our regiment this time has been cut up terribly, besides others. My company's officer had his head blown off. There were dead and dying all around me, and we were at close quarters with the Germans, the Prussian Guard. I was wounded in four places; thank God my life was spared. I was at first wounded through the hand. A bullet pierced my hand, going right through, and I was hit by shrapnel. A lump about 2½ inches by 2½ inches pierced my leg, went through the calf, and stuck in the top of the bone on the top of my leg, going right through. The others were slight wounds. I lay in agony for 36 hours, among strange sights and awful suffering, all the time without food. Eventually I was taken with others on stretchers by the Bedfords out of it.

I travelled on to Boulogne, remaining at the General Hospital from the 19th till the 26th. The doctors and nurses were very kind to me. My wounds were attended to here. The doctor told me it meant my life or my leg. Blood poisoning set in, so I was compelled to have my leg taken off. I have since improved wonderfully well. I am now feeling a treat. I am very comfortable here. The nurses are kind, and the food is good and lovely weather. I am glad to be in England after being in France and Belgium for over seven weary months of terrible hardships and awful fighting. I have done my bit. Thank God, I am hoping soon to be home again when I am well to see my little family. I shall get a pension for losing my leg."[98]

As a result of having his leg amputated, Bertram was discharged on 30 September 1915 and issued with a Silver War Badge. Baldwin received the clasp and roses for his 1914 Star on 22 March 1920.

Bertram and Florence lived in Lewisham after the war and later at 40 Brandon Street in Walworth. Bertram died on 4 March 1980 and Florence, who was born on 10 August 1892, died the following year.

---

[98] Folkestone, Hythe, Sandgate and Cheriton Herald, 22 May 1915.

"7/5/15

Pte. G. H. Bland 7450
"D" Company,
1ˢᵗ Beds. Regt.
British Expeditionary Force.

Dear Mother,

Just a few lines hoping you are all well, as it leaves me in rather a queer state. After the gas, which the brutes sent over to us on the 3ʳᵈ and the 5ᵗʰ, the first we have had since the taking of the famous Hill 60, which we are still holding, but we had to retire owing to the gas but the good old Bedfords stopped them. We had rather a hard time since Hill 60, only been out of the trenches three days, but were released by the Irish Rifles on the 7ᵗʰ, when we came back for a short rest.

Our casualties are as great as Hill 60, but the gas used in shells there, had not half the effect as this which they pumped out of the bottom of their trench. I myself am wearing a silver ring on my little finger, which the gas has cankered. But we gave them an (sic) horrible job to get that which the Devons had to leave. Not a man could stand, owing to the the terrible stuff which streamed from their trench to ours, but the breeze changed and drove it back into their trench, then our machine guns got into them, so they were forced to retire from their own trench, then we laughed, you can bet. We have named them 'old gas bags.'

On Hill 60 they prayed for mercy. Well, I am sorry to say my old mate Harry Cox⁹⁴ was killed by one of our own shells that dropped short on the 5ᵗʰ, during the recent battle, and if possible let Mrs Cox know. I felt quite down-hearted over it.

I must now draw to a close, but they tell me the 1ˢᵗ Rifles have regained the lost trenches on the other side of Hill 60 (not losing the Hill). Goodbye mother and all, brothers and sisters.

---

⁹⁴ 7898 Private Harry Cox was aged 30 and is commemorated on the Ypres (Menin Gate) Memorial. His widow remarried after the war and is recorded in the register for the memorial as living at Queen Street at Stotfold.

I omitted to say that Capt. Gladstein[95] got wounded later in the day of Harry's death. Goodbye mother, I will write more next time. I received letter and parcel. I hope you got my P.C.

Harry."[96]

3/7450 Private George Henry Bland
1ˢᵗ Battalion, The Bedfordshire Regiment

Private Bland wrote his letter shortly after arriving at rest billets in Ouderdom after coming out of action at 2 o'clock that morning. Before the war, George had worked as a farm labourer and also for Openshaw's Builders in Letchworth. His mother, Eliza Bland, was landlady of the Railway Tavern at Arlesey while his father, George, was serving with the 5ᵗʰ Battalion, The Bedfordshire Regiment at Newmarket. Harry Bland, who was originally from the 3ʳᵈ (Special Reserve) Battalion, was drafted to France on 4 January 1915.

During fighting on the Somme in July 1916, Bland distinguished himself in action by entering an enemy trench with his Lewis Gun and engaging the Germans under difficult circumstances, and also secured two German helmets as trophies. In recognition of his bravery he was later awarded the Military Medal, the decoration being announced in the London Gazette on 1 January 1917. He received a gunshot wound to the knee in the action and was treated at a hospital in France for ten weeks before returning to the 1ˢᵗ Bedfords.

Bland was again wounded on 23 April 1917, suffering shrapnel injuries to his left side, left shoulder and right thigh, during the attack mounted on La Coulotte and was later admitted to Fort Pitt Military Hospital in Chatham. He returned to the front in August with a piece of shrapnel still in his left shoulder.

---

[95] Captain Sheldon Arthur Gledstanes, who had commanded his men in the defence of a section of trench on the right of the Bedford's positions that had been isolated by the German counter-attacks on 5 May. For two days, despite their position being shelled and attacked with hand-grenades and gas, Captain Gledstanes and his men held on, dealing with any Germans who entered their trench in desperate hand-to-hand fighting, using bombs and bayonets frequently. Captain Gledstanes was wounded but continued to direct the defence of the position and encourage his men. On 7 May, the remaining Bedfords were relieved, and Gledstanes was evacuated to hospital. His wounds proved to be mortal and he died on 9 May at Bailleul.
[96] Biggleswade Chronicle, 14 May 1915.

Hooge Crater Cemetery
July 1998

Lance-Corporal Bland M.M. was killed on 4 October 1917 during the fighting for Polderhoek Chateau. In 1920, his remains were removed from their original burial place and reinterred at Hooge Crater Cemetery: Plot XVIII, Row A, Grave 7. He is also commemorated on the war memorial at Arlesey.

The Queen Victoria's Rifles Memorial

Unveiled on 9 September 1923, the memorial on Hill 60 commemorates the part played by the 1/9th (County of London) Battalion, The London Regiment (Queen Victoria's Rifles) (Territorial Force) in the fighting for Hill 60 in April 1915. The ceremony was reported by The Sheffield Daily Telegraph two days later:

FIRST TERRITORIAL V.C.

War Memorial Unveiled on Famous Hill 60.

"The highest point of Hill 60, says a Reuter message from Ypres, was the spot chosen for the site of the memorial to the officers and other ranks of the Queen Victoria's Rifles, which was unveiled on Sunday by General Sir Charles Fergusson, Bart. K.C.B. It was here that the regiment fought their first engagement after trench work, an engagement in which they lost 12 officers and 180 men killed and wounded.

The clergyman who officiated on Sunday, Captain the Rev. G. H. Woolley, V.C., M.C., was the first Territorial to win the coveted bronze cross. He was then a lieutenant in the Queen's Victoria Rifles, and at the time of the withdrawal from the Hill was the only officer left. On the spot where he won the V.C. years ago as a lieutenant he returned as a clergyman to conduct the memorial service to his fallen comrades.

In his unveiling address, General Sir Charles Fergusson referred to the great sacrifices on Hill 60 and the glorious traditions of the regiment."

The Reverend Geoffrey Harold Woolley V.C., M.C., who conducted the memorial service at the unveiling ceremony, had been ordained in 1920. In 1914, Woolley was serving as a Second-Lieutenant with the 1/9th Londons and disembarked with "B" Company at Le Havre on 5 November 1914. He was awarded the Victoria Cross the following year, the first member of the Territorial Force to receive the award, and the citation was published in The London Gazette on 22 May 1915:

"For most conspicuous bravery on "Hill 60" during the night of 20th-21st April, 1915. Although the only Officer on the hill at the time, and with very few men, he successfully resisted all attacks on his trench, and continued throwing bombs and encouraging his men till relieved. His trench during all this time was being heavily shelled and bombed and was subjected to heavy machine gun fire by the enemy."

The Memorial is erected by Queen Victorias Rifles
To the Glory of God and in everlasting memory
of their comrades who fell in the battle of
HILL 60
on april 20-21-1915, also of all other Q.V.R.S
Who gave their Lives for their country in
The Great War.
1914 - 1918

G. Pottier OSTENDE

Woolley applied for his 1914 Star on 11 September 1919, and for the clasp and roses on 13 July 1920, which were issued to him on 2 September.

Woolley served with the Royal Army Chaplain's Department during the Second World War and was appointed an Officer of the Most Excellent Order of the British Empire (O.B.E.) for his service. He became President of the Harrow and Wembley Branch of the Old Contemptibles' Association shortly after taking up the parish of St Mary's at Harrow on the Hill in 1944. He moved to West Grinstead in 1952, and retired six years later.

The Reverend Geoffrey Harold Woolley V.C., O.B.E., M.C., died on 10 December 1968, aged 76.

The original memorial was destroyed in May 1940 as the Germans advanced towards Ypres, although the exact circumstances under which this happened are unclear and open to conjecture. A new memorial was later built on the site and incorporated some of the stonework that remained of the old one. The inscription was also modified to include reference to those members of the Queen Victoria's Rifles who had died during the Second World War.

A pilgrim photographed beside the Q.V.R. Memorial on Hill 60, c.1930

"I was very lucky to escape without a scratch from two battles in which the casualties have been very heavy. The experience was wonderful, and the scenic effect of shrapnel and grenades bursting on the hill on the night of April 20th was magnificent, just like a brilliant display of fireworks. But there was another side of the spectacle, which, although a terrible sight, affects one very little in the heat of the fight. It is not until all is over that one fully realises what has happened... I am enclosing three pressed flowers (a violet and two cowslips). The former I plucked outside my 'dug-out' in the wood just before the Germans commenced the bombardment which preceded their furious attack to regain the hill. The latter on the ground where the so-called Second Battle of Calais was fought."[97]

2766 Rifleman Alan Volt
1/9th (County of London) Battalion, The London Regiment (Queen Victoria's Rifles) (Territorial Force)

Rifleman Volt served under the alias, his real name being Alan Mowbray Wilson. Born in 1893 in Nottinghamshire, he had arrived in France as part of a draft for the Q.V.R. on 10 February 1915. Commissioned as a Second-Lieutenant in the 3rd (Special Reserve) Battalion, The East Surrey Regiment on 4 September 1916, he was killed on 19 November with the 8th (Service) Battalion during the fighting for Desire Trench on the Ancre Heights. Alan Wilson is commemorated on the Thiepval Memorial.

---

[97] Middlesex Chronicle - 15 May 1915.

"You will observe from the above date that it is ten days since your letter was written. I can, however, offer a very good excuse for the apparent delay. As a matter of fact, during this period my Battalion has done some excellent work by taking part in attacks and repelling advances on the part of the enemy. We have worked day and night with scanty rations and an extremely small amount of rest. On one occasion, while one Company was charging in a battle which will make history, my platoon was in support on the English side of a large, natural mound of earth. The Huns were quite unable to shell our firing line, owing to the risk to their own men, so, they shelled the supports. My dear sir, the bombardment was terrible. One man humorously called it "Hell with the lid off." We could neither get relief or relieve others (had we been needed). It is said the bombardment was the worst since Mons, and I can quite believe it. After spending five days under these circumstances we were relieved at 5 one morning (one mass of nerves), and marched off to another part of the line to push the Germans back where they had broken through. As luck favoured us, we were not wanted for the first line, in spite of the fact that we had extended ready for the advance; but other Battalions of our Brigade did the necessary work. We were not exempt from duty, however, but were placed on the bank of a canal, absolutely "done" to spend the night in the open, with no ground sheet, pack or other necessities. At the expiration of our canal bank experience we were again marched off in broad daylight to take up a very advanced position. Here we were spotted by the enemy's artillery observers, for directly the head of our column was visible we were met by a rain of shell and shrapnel. It was worse than murder to see my old pals and comrades mown down by the terrible fusiliade. Those of us who were left eventually took up our position, where we were compelled to dig ourselves in, still under heavy fire. I could not possibly give you a graphic account on paper of our experiences. I must thank Providence that I am alive and untouched, but absolutely run down. It is quite possible you will see the name of my Battalion mentioned with honours as having taken part in some very important affairs out here... (censored), and I am sure we can safely console ourselves that we have done our bit. Why don't they send some of the slackers – of which you speak in your letter – out here to do their little bit? We should be glad of a long rest to recuperate."[98]

2710 Rifleman Harry Neithercott
1/9th (County of London) Battalion, The London Regiment (Queen Victoria's Rifles) (Territorial Force)

---

[98] Kent and Sussex Courier, 14 May 1915. Harry Neithercott emigrated to the United States following the war and died in Pinellas County, Florida, in 1963.

Second-Lieutenant Walter Nelson, of the 1/6th Battalion, The South Staffordshire Regiment (Territorial Force), taken in No. 41 Trench, facing Hill 60, in August 1915. (Courtesy of the late Jake Whitehouse)

Commissioned as a Second-Lieutenant on 11 March 1915, Walter Nelson did not join the 1/6th South Staffords in Belgium until August, as recalled by the authors of the history of the battalion:

"(his) hatred of everything German was relentless. Lord Kitchener's general request had been sole cause of his being taken out of the Legion Etrangere, and nothing had delayed his coming out to the front again except the slow grinding of the War Office mills."[99]

Posted to "B" Company, Nelson was killed leading his platoon on 13 October 1915 during the attack on the Hohenzollern Redoubt, reportedly while trying to cut a gap through barbed wire entanglements to allow his men to move forward. His death was reported by The Leamington Spa Courier on 22 October:

"We have to record, with extreme regret, the fact that Second Lieutenant Walter Nelson was killed in action in France on the 13th inst. He obtained a commission last March in the 6th Battalion South Staffordshire Regiment, but had previously spent 16 weeks in the trenches with the French Foreign Legion, having joined a Company of English Volunteers in Paris. Forty-five years of age, he was the third son of the late Mr George H. Nelson, of Warwick, and was a director of the firm of Nelson, Dale and Co., Ltd.

For the past seven or eight years he had been one of the Emsote representatives on the Warwick Town Council, and for a time acted as Chairman of the Corporation Farm Committee. He was one of the most active workers in connection with the Warwick Pagent of 1906, being one of the stage managers as well as impersonating King William III in the final Episode. A strong supporter of Tariff Reform, he was hon. Secretary of the Warwick Branch of the Warwick and Leamington Tariff Reform League, of which his uncle, Sir E. Montague Nelson, is president. He was a graduate of Cambridge University, and member of the Shakespeare Lodge of Freemasons."

Walter Nelson has no known grave and is commemorated on the Loos Memorial, as well as on the war memorials at Warwick and Trysull.

---

[99] A Committee of Officers, *War History of the 6th Battalion, The South Staffordshire Regiment (T.F.)* (London: Heinemann, 1924), p. 80.

"Some of those trenches in which we have been working have been used by the French and Germans months before, and it is not a very pleasant job digging in the dark, sometimes up to your knees in mud. The stench is terrible at times, for you will hear the chaps shout that they have found the corpse of a German or a Frenchman.

The men have been killed and not properly buried, the body being placed in the loose soil that has fallen down the side of the trench, or which has been blown in by a shell. The sights are enough to make one's blood boil, for there are lots of ruined houses not far behind our firing line, and you can see some poor souls in the debris. Under some bags which form part of the parapet in the firing line a man's boots protrude, and here and there bodies of horses as well have been found. These have to be removed to make it better for us."[100]

9604/20118/242560 Private William Giles
1/5th Battalion, The South Staffordshire Regiment (Territorial Force)

Born in 1885, William Giles was a native of Old Hill living at 79 Clifton Street, and was employed as a fitting striker at a tube works when he attested for the "Rowley Regis Company" of the Reserve Battalion of the 5th South Staffords on 12 October 1914. He was a member of the "Gallant Eighty," the name given to the recruits who enlisted at Old Hill on the same day. He was transferred to the 1/5th Battalion and landed in France on 3 March 1915.

Private Giles was sent for training as a bomber at the 137th Brigade Bombing Class between 18 and 24 September, and went on to take part in the fighting for the Hohenzollern Redoubt on 13 October as a member of one of the two bombing parties drawn from the 1/5th Battalion. He was appointed as a paid Lance-Corporal following the action, on 14 October.

On 20 February 1916, shortly after arriving back in France from Egypt, Giles was reported as sick. Admitted to No. 19 Casualty Clearing Station on 1 March, he was transferred to No. 16 General Hospital the following day and diagnosed as suffering from influenza and trench feet. Giles was sent home on board the H.M.H.S. Dieppe on 14 March and admitted to a hospital in Bermondsey the following day, being discharged at the end of his treatment on 1 April. Posted to the 3/5th Battalion, Lance-Corporal Giles was later placed on a draft for France, embarking at Folkestone on 3 December 1916 and arriving at Boulogne the same day. He was sent to No. 9 Infantry Base Depot and transferred to the 1/6th South Staffords, joining the battalion on 22 December. Giles was transferred to the Class "W" (T.F.) Reserve on 7 March 1917 as his civilian skills were required for war work, and was finally disembodied on demobilisation on 14 December 1918.

William Giles died in 1966.

---

[100] County Express, 25 September 1915.

On 9 October 1915, The London Gazette published the announcement of the award of the Distinguished Conduct Medal to two soldiers of the 1/6th Battalion, The North Staffordshire Regiment: **350 Sergeant Frank Wallbank** and **1206 Lance-Corporal Joseph Cronise**, who served with 137th Brigade Mining Section. Their act of gallantry took place in mine workings underneath Trench 37 near Hill 60. 137th Brigade Mining Section, which supported 175th Tunnelling Company, Royal Engineers on defensive mining tasks under Hill 60.

The citation for Lance-Corporal Cronise's award read:

"For conspicuous gallantry and devotion to duty on the 10th September 1915 near Ypres. The enemy blew a mine, burying two men. Another Non-Commissioned Officer who was in the mine sent all the uninjured men to the shaft, and then attempted to reach the buried men, with no protection save his smoke helmet, which was useless against the gas caused by the explosion. Driven back by gas, he repeated the attempt, accompanied by Lance-Corporal Cronise. Later in the day it was decided to camoflet the enemy, and although the gas overcame most of the men working in shifts, Lance-Corporal Cronise continued working until he had to be carried to the shaft. Both Non-Commissioned Officers showed the greatest bravery and devotion."

Sergeant Wallbank's citation:

"For conspicuous gallantry and devotion to duty on the 10th September 1915 near Ypres. The enemy blew a mine, burying two men. Sgt. Wallbank, who was in the mine, sent all the uninjured men to the shaft, and then attempted to reach the buried men, with no protection save his smoke helmet, which was useless against the gas caused by the explosion. Driven back by gas, he repeated the attempt, accompanied by another Non-Commissioned Officer. Both were badly affected by the gas, but managed to reach the shaft. Later in the day it was decided to camoflet the enemy, and although the gas overcame most of the men working in shifts, his companion continued working until he had to be carried to the shaft, while Sgt. Wallbank remained until the work was finished, but collapsed on reaching the surface. Both Non-Commissioned Officers showed the greatest bravery and devotion."

Born on 1 June 1886 at Rugeley, Frank Wallbank was the son of the Francis and Mary Wallbank. Frank worked as a colliery loader, and before his marriage resided with his parents at 12 Lion Street. He was also a member of his local Congregational Church and the Ancient Order of Foresters (Court 2003) in the town.

Frank had joined "D" Company of the 2nd Volunteer Battalion of The North Staffordshire Regiment at Rugeley in 1902, and in 1907 was awarded a prize of 2/6d for passing his certificate in signalling and semaphore while at annual camp. Transferring to the 6th North Staffords on the formation of the Territorial Force in April 1908, Wallbank was appointed a Lance-Corporal and in December 1909 was awarded a silver guard for proficiency in musketry.

Frank Wallbank was serving as a Corporal when he embarked for France on 3 March 1915 with "A" Company of the 1/6th North Staffords. He was appointed a paid Lance-Sergeant on 10 May and promoted to Sergeant on 8 June, being posted to "B" Company five days later.

The news that he had been awarded the Distinguished Conduct Medal was reported in The Staffordshire Advertiser on 30 October 1915:

"D.C.M. for Rugeley Sergeant. – Sergt. Frank Wallbank, of the 1st-6th North Staffordshire Regiment, has the distinction of being the first Rugeley man to win the Distinguished Conduct Medal for conspicuous gallantry and devotion to duty in the field. Sergt. Wallbank attempted near Ypres on Sept. 10 to rescue some men who had been buried as a result of the explosion of a mine, having no protection other than a smoke helmet, which was of little use against the gas caused by the explosion. Sergt. Wallbank, who is the son of Mr and Mrs Wallbank, Lion-street, has served in the Volunteers and Territorials for about 13 years. At the outbreak of the war he offered himself for foreign service and went to France early this year attached to the 137th Brigade Mining Section, North Staffordshire Regiment, Territorial Force."

Sergeant Wallbank was killed during the attack on the Hohenzollern Redoubt on 13 October 1915 and is commemorated on the Loos Memorial.

His widow, Lizzie Wallbank, lived at 22, Market Street in Rugeley. His baby daughter was baptised on 15 November 1915 and on the same day his widow was awarded a grant from the Cannock Chase and Pelsall Miners' Relief Fund.

Frank Wallbank is commemorated on the war memorials at Rugeley and that of the Ancient Order of Foresters, located in Cannock.

Joseph Walter Cronise was a former student of Alvecote College and had been employed at Alvecote Colliery before the war. He served with "C" Company, joining the Territorials at Tamworth on 17 September 1909, and was wounded in the foot during the assault on the Hohenzollern Redoubt on 13 October 1915. As a result of his injury he was discharged as unfit for war service on 24 August 1916 and was later issued with a Silver War Badge. Cronise was presented with his Distinguished Conduct Medal at a ceremony held in October 1916, by which time he was employed at a hotel in Colchester.

One of the soldiers who died on 10 September was **3470 Private George Richardson**, of the 1/6th Battalion, The South Staffordshire Regiment (Territorial Force).

George Richardson was born at Rugeley in 1892 and had attested for the 6th South Staffords at Wolverhampton in October 1914. He was drafted to France on 28 June 1915 and was sent from Rouen to join the 1/6th South Staffords in Belgium a few days later. Having been employed at Holly Bank Colliery as a pit top coverer and banksman, Richardson was drafted to the Private Richardson was killed when the Germans exploded a camouflet, which collapsed the gallery he was working in underneath No. 37 Trench and released poisonous carbon-monoxide gas. His death was reported in The Walsall Observer on 12 February 1916:

"A Short Heath Territorial who made the great sacrifice while doing his duty for King and country in France is Private George Richardson, whose parents lived at 139, Coltham Road. For some time prior to the war he had served in the local Territorials, with whom he went to France early last year, and he is stated to have lost his life while on tunnelling work in the firing line. He is 22 years of age and unmarried, and formerly was employed as a banksman at the Holly Bank Colliery."

George Richardson has no known grave and is commemorated on the Ypres (Menin Gate) Memorial.

The 1ˢᵗ Australian Tunnelling Company Memorial

Zillebeke Hill 60. Memorial The Australian Tunneling Company.

The memorial to the 1ˢᵗ Australian Tunnelling Company commemorates the service of the sappers beneath the Hill 60 sector, and the soldiers of the Company who died. A memorial had first been erected in April 1919 by members of 1ˢᵗ Australian Tunnelling Company, but a more permanent structure was unveiled in 1923.

The original inscription on the 1923 Memorial had consisted of lead lettering set into the stone, but the following year alarming reports were received in Australian regarding its condition, as local people salvaging material on Hill 60 to sell as scrap had started to remove the valuable lead letters. A journalist of The Rockhampton Morning Bulletin in Queensland wrote an article regarding the vandalism, having recently returned from Belgium. His article was published on 24 December 1924:

HILL 60.

THROUGH AUSTRALIAN EYES.

"A member of the "Bulletin" staff, who not so long since visited Hill 60, writes:-

"In view of the recent cabled report of the dastardly desecration of the monument to the Australian Tunnellers at Hill 60, a short description of this historic spot, as it appears to-day, may be of interest. Those who do not know the nature of the country on the famous Ypres salient probably picture the ill-fated hill, which was such an important objective as to render an arduous engineering scheme and the explosion of a huge mine necessary to its capture, as a commanding eminence. In reality it is nothing more than a slight rise, and when my party inspected it, at 6 a.m. on September 3rd last, there was practically no indication of conflict in the surrounding district, save occasional huge masses of concrete gun emplacements or blockhouses, too heavy to be removed. The farm houses had been built up, most of them, we learned from our ex-soldier driver, on the original sites, and only a few shattered trees resisted the kindly efforts of nature and the dogged perseverance of man to efface all signs of war horror.

On the Hill itself, however, there was a marked difference. To approach the summit we had to scramble down a railway cutting and up a little path on the earthwork beyond, worn by the feet of countless tourists, or rather, perhaps, pilgrims. Light rain began to fall as we ascended the slope, and one soon began to realise what the place must have been like under war conditions, for with only one shower the greasy, clinging, clayey mud made movement difficult. The surface of the hill is all pitted and churned, where the natives of the locality have dug it over in search of bodies, for which a monetary reward is paid. Only a few days before our visit six had been disinterred, and we saw several crudely defined mounds, beneath which lay the bodies of some French poilus, awaiting transfer to a French war cemetery.

Clumps of coarse weed and grass are scattered over the hill and grow particularly thick around the huge crater mouth. The crater itself was practically filled with water, and presented an awe inspiring sight in the grey light of early morning. To attempt to visualise the scene when the huge mine was exploded was a veritable impossibility, for one could not conceive of those thousands of tons of earth thrown from their place by one vast upheaval. On the summit, towards the north-west, stands the simple granite memorial to the First Australian Tunnellers, who were in charge of the mining operations, which secured the hill for the Allies. The inscription, which has been defaced, is simply cut in the polished granite surface, and while it was easily legible at a considerable distance at the time of our visit, we were told that when the stone was dry it was necessary to approach very closely to distinguish it. The desecration of this monument is difficult to understand, for Colonial troops were universally popular in Belgium and

France, and, everywhere we met with courtesy and attention which, we were told, far exceeded that extended to English visitors."

The lettering was subsequently replaced by a solid bronze panel, bearing the "Rising Sun" badge of the Australian Imperial Force and the inscription:

IN MEMORIAM OF OFFICERS AND MEN OF THE 1ST AUSTRALIAN TUNNELLING COY. WHO GAVE THEIR LIVES IN THE MINING AND DEFENSIVE OPERATIONS OF HILL 60 1915-1918

THIS MONUMENT REPLACES THAT ORIGINALLY ERECTED IN APRIL 1919 BY THEIR COMRADES IN ARMS

1923

The 1ˣ Australian Tunnelling Company Memorial, April 1993

The 1ˢᵗ Australian Tunnelling Company Memorial
7 August 2018

It is possible to see the original carved lettering, from which the lead had been removed, by looking into the small gap between the replacement panel and the original memorial stone. The memorial sustained further damage during the Second World War when the panel was hit by bullets, probably during the fighting that took place in the area in May 1940 but other stories regarding how this happened also circulate. However, as "scars of war" the panel was not repaired and the bullet holes can still be seen today.

9 June 1917 – Rest Billets at Poperinghe

"In my last letter I told you that we expected to take part in what would probably be the "Greatest battle of the war," this has now begun and I am proud to say I belong to a Company which did every thing asked of them in this big offensive.

From the time this Company arrived in France they have been in the 3 most important parts of the Salient as far as mining operations are concerned and for the past 9 months we have been responsible for the holding of the biggest mines the world has known, 70 tons of aminol (sic), one pound of this explosive would be sufficient to destroy the Mansion House in London. In addition to holding these mines we have been on dugout work and the Company has to its credit one of the biggest and most successful systems in 2nd Army.

Our men worked their hardest right up to the time of the starting of the offensive and it is doubtful if any mines in Australia has the same class of men employed. Bad conditions, bad air, extra work (caused by the slackers staying home) and a very trying winter was what these men had to put up with and in addition they put most of this time in a section which is responsible for the loss of thousands of lives even in normal times, but the long line has turned; and to-day back in camp after the go ahead successes it is possible to have achieved the men are as proud as any men in the world. Tired and worn out they parade to-day to hear their O.C. read the telegram he received congratulating the Coy. This telegram came from the Army Commander General Plumer, through the controller of Mines and we know for certain they are delighted with our work. The O.C. said how pleased he was with officers, N.C. officers and men for the way they stuck to their work, every individual member was just as responsible as the other for the success we achieved. We have all had a long and exciting time sitting at our posts listening to the Hun working in the vicinity of the big mines and when occasion warranted it we blew him and I am pleased to say although we had to do this often we never did it until it was absolutely necessary and we are now certain with success of each occasion. We received back many blows and lost in all only 6 men underground through these blows. Many men were buried but we recovered them and on one occasion got 2 men out, one after 20 hours, and the other after 42 hours and both alive and well. In addition to this we repulsed a big raid on Easter Monday and received many decorations for same. For 3 weeks before the big blow we broke all records for gallery driving as I have already told you, the best being 41ft. 4ins. in a

6ft. by 3ft. 6ins. gallery in 24 hours with 8 men in the face and 6 men assisting to remove the spoil.

Now for an account of our actual work during the big offensive. Every man and officer had his work, some on roads, some on go on the top and inspect dugouts (Hun), some to construct trenches and of course the party to blow. I have a position (as the C.O. called it) of honour. I was with the C.O. and two other officers with the party detailed for the responsibility of blowing. I think a little consideration was shown to Queenslanders as our party consisted of the Major (Q'land) Captain Woodward M.C. (Q'land & N.S.W.) Lieut. Royle (Q'land & N.S.W.) and myself, the Section Sergt. Wilson also Q'land. We were responsible for keeping the whole dug-out system in repair as well as blowing and after the blow to repair the same in order to get the Brigade Head Quarters in their position which was our old dug-outs. Everything went great and luck stuck to us all through, we had the General and his staff in within 10 minutes of the blow, as all our work stood up well and my word he was pleased and told us so. He said it was the greatest sight and best bit of work he had seen since the war began. While we were doing this, others were repairing Hun dug outs captured for advance positions and other working trenches in "No Man's Land" (at one time) to connect us up to our new positions. Our casualties were light all through which of course was due to our dug out system.

Clinton was in charge of the trench party and made 360 yards of trench in 3¼ hours (easily a worlds record). Lieut. Hinder (N.S.W.) of football fame led the party to inspect Hun dug outs and from all accounts beat the Infantry and arrived first on Hill 60. Half an hour from the word go we had word back we had our objective. The Infantry with us were the Yorks and Northumberland men and they were great, they just went ahead as if on ordinary parade. The Artillery was perfect and the organisation generally marvellous. One signal runner had made 8 trips by 8 a.m. and the time of the blow (zero) was 3.10 a.m. I had the pleasure of visiting the taken positions with Major Henry C.O., and no wonder we had a rough time for the past 9 months. You can see everything from Hill 60 and one wonders how we hung out. The road party who did such great work was headed by Lieut. Carroll of Tasmania, his Father is well known in connection with Mt. Lyell Block, while Capt. McBride who represented us on the Corps is a Broken Hill man and he got his M.C. on Easter Monday. It is doubtful if he felt inclined, if there is a man in the front, who could write up the doings of the Coy. in a more serious and at the same time more humerous (sic) manner (let's hope he does so).

Other Officers who did great work are Lieut. Yates (M.C.) S. Australia, Lieut. Clayton, son of the Acct. of Commercial Bank, Sydney, and others who did just as much as anyone I have mentioned. Our big job is over but we are now at the disposal of the 2nd Army to do any thing required, which will consist of road building and dug outs and O. Pipes for Artillery. We are having a rest for a day, others get on with our work after which I believe we are to be given a spell after 14 months in the front line. I would like to mention the good work done by our second in command Capt. Anderson (Ballarat) and Lieut. Plummer (Tasmania), Adjutant, who kept the Transport up to us which is a very important part. The C.O. Major Henry was at the front the whole time and in thanking his men can speak from what he actually saw and is the proudest man on the front to-day. Everyone is in great spirits and I might mention every Coy. in the whole salient has done just as well as ourselves. Some well known names that will interest Ch. Towers[101] who are with us are Sappers Waldby, Featherstone, Anderson, Dubbo Davis, Millican, Sergt. Bradshaw (footballer) and many others."

A letter, written by **Lieutenant James Bowry, 1st Tunnelling Company, Royal Australian Engineers** to his parents, in which he described the part played by the unit at Hill 60 and the detonation of the two mines under Hill 60 and The Caterpillar on 7 June 1917. Lieutenant Bowry's letter was published in The Northern Miner, printed at Charters Towers in Queensland, on 21 August 1917.

Bowry retired with the rank of Captain and died in hospital at Perth on 9 March 1936, aged 54.

---

[101] Charters Towers, Queensland.

Messines

The village of Messines (now Mesen) has a history stretching back to Roman times and during October and November 1914 the ridge on which it stands was defended by dismounted British cavalrymen of the Cavalry Corps, reinforced by French troops, British and Indian infantry battalions and later by Territorials. Messines was captured by the 26. (1ˢᵗ Royal Württemberg) Division on 1 November and the British and French troops were pushed down the slopes into the valley below. With the taking of the Messines Ridge, the Germans had control of the high ground and this situation continued until the early hours of 7 June 1917.

Mining operations in the valley below Messines had commenced during the Spring of 1915, but by the middle of the year plans were being considered to utilise this type of warfare as a means of taking the ridge from the Germans. In January 1916 General Sir Douglas Haig, who had been appointed as Commander-in-Chief of the British Expeditionary Force on 10 December in place of Field Marshal Sir John French, directed the General Plumer, the commander of Second Army, to begin preparations to tunnel under the German lines. Plumer informed him that work had already commenced, and that 19 saps were being pushed towards enemy lines. By June 1917 there had been 21 mines completed and ready for detonation, in an arc stretching from Ploegsteert Wood in the south to Hill 60 in the north.

Nineteen of the charges, comprising some 933,200lbs of ammonal explosive, weighing 455 tons, were fired at 3.10 a.m. on 7 June 1917. Tremors resulting from the enormous explosions were reportedly felt in Belgium, France and on the Isle of Wight but the often-repeated story that the sound could be heard in London is a myth. The New Zealand Division were tasked with capturing Messines, and this was accomplished by the 2nd and 3rd (Rifle) Brigades by 7.00 a.m. **6/2133 Lance-Corporal Samuel Frickleton**, of the 3rd Battalion, New Zealand Rifle Brigade, was later awarded the Victoria Cross for his actions during the assault. During the period between 1 and 14 June, the New Zealand Division lost 4,978 killed, wounded and missing.

In the years following the Great War, the part played by the New Zealand Division in the capture of Messines on 7 June 1917 has been commemorated in many forms. The New Zealand Memorial Park is located on the site of Uhlan Trench, the German front line in 1917, and incorporates two concrete blockhouses that were stormed during the assault. A memorial, in the form of an obelisk, was erected on the site and unveiled by Albert I, King of the Belgians and Major-General Sir Alexander Hamilton Russell, who had commanded the New Zealand Division that day, on 1 August 1924.

The Messines Ridge (New Zealand) Memorial stands on the site of one of the buildings of the Moulin de l'Hospice that was captured by the New Zealand Division on 7 June 1917. The memorial, which is at the entrance to Messines Ridge British Cemetery, commemorates 828 New Zealanders who died while serving in the sector but have no known grave.

Another tribute to the battle was constructed near Brocton Camp on Cannock Chase in 1918, where the 5th (Reserve) Battalion of the New Zealand Rifle Brigade were quartered, when a relief model of the village and surrounding defences was built. Donated to the town of Stafford in 1919 when the battalion left for home, the model was run as a visitor attraction but eventually fell into disrepair and was claimed back by nature. The site was excavated by archaeologists in September 2013.

More recently a statue of a Sergeant of the New Zealand Rifle Brigade, representing Lance-Corporal Frickleton V.C., has been erected in the square at Messines, and close by the art installation "Victory Medal" by sculptor Helen Pollock was displayed during 2017 and 2018 before being moved to Le Quesnoy to commemorate the taking of the town by the New Zealand Division on 4 November 1918.

The church of St Nicholas is still a prominent landmark across the fields surrounding Messines, and was badly damaged by German artillery in October and November 1914. The building was constantly shelled in the intervening years and the church was rebuilt after the war. The crypt beneath the church was used as a shelter by the German troops between 1914 and 1917, including Adolf Hitler, who served here as a Corporal with the 16th Bavarian Reserve Infantry Regiment.

The Germans recaptured Messines, which was being held by the 19th (Western) Division, on 10 April 1918 and the town was not retaken until 28 September by 90th Brigade of 30th Division. By this time the Brigade comprised three battalions of the London Regiment that had been sent back to Europe after fighting in Palestine. Among these was the 2nd London Scottish, their 1st Battalion have fought its first action near Messines nearly four years before on 31 October 1914.

There is a Visitor Centre housed in the Tourist Office in the Market Square of Messines, in which there are multimedia displays and artefacts telling the story of the village during the Great War, and outside is a sculpture by Andrew Edwards entitled "All Together Now," which commemorates the Christmas Day truce of 1914.

The New Zealand Division Memorial
25 March 2018

The Messines Ridge (New Zealand) Memorial
February 1988.

Two "Dinks" of the 5th (Reserve) Battalion, The New Zealand Rifle Brigade, photographed at Brocton Camp on Cannock Chase in 1918.

Territorials at Messines - 1914

The 1/1st Oxfordshire Yeomanry (Queen's Own Oxfordshire Hussars) (Territorial Force) disembarked at Dunkirk on 22 September 1914, and had the distinction of being the first regiment of Yeomanry to be sent to France. Initially earmarked to act as Divisional Cavalry to the Royal Naval Division, the regiment was placed under the orders of General Headquarters and later moved to St Omer. On 30 October, the Oxfordshire Yeomanry received orders to march towards Messines to reinforce the Cavalry Corps, and came under the command of 2nd Cavalry Brigade on their arrival:

In a letter to his father in Oxford, **1853 Private Reginald Osborne Bolingbroke**, of the 1/1st Oxfordshire Yeomanry (Queen's Own Oxfordshire Hussars) (Territorial Force), described the march and the baptism of fire of the Yeomen:

"When we marched from our base on October 30th it was a jolly cold night, and rained on and off, and I was dead tired. I even went to sleep once or twice on my horse. We got our first taste shell fire when we were moved up with the King's Own Scottish Borderers... On the following day, under cover of the darkness, we relieved the 11th Hussars. A corporal and six men, of whom I was one, were pushed out ahead on outpost duty. I was on first shift and another shift. There was nothing between us and the German army, and our duty was to keep a sharp lookout in case of a German attack. I could see Germans everywhere – in fancy – and I nearly shot at some cows! It was a lively job and no mistake. We were relieved at dawn by another relief, and got back to the trenches. A battery of guns behind us commenced with a hearty 'good morning,' and then the fun began. We were shelled all day till dusk; a captive balloon directed the German fire. Several of our trenches were blown in, and the men had to be dug out. We were eventually relieved at night by the 4th Dragoon Guards after the worst 24 hours I have ever experienced. We occupied the post of honour in the centre, supported by the 9th Lancers and the 5th Dragoon Guards on our flanks. The German gunfire is very heavy and very accurate, but does little damage, and we were exceptionally lucky in coming out so well."[102]

2162 Private Claude Harry Daniell, who served with "A" Squadron, also recalled his entry into the battle:

---

[102] Banbury Advertiser, 26 November 1914.

"It was about seven o'clock that night when we set out and marched about 25 or 30 miles, being on the move all night. About half past nine in the morning we arrived at our destination. After handing over our horses we went straight into action somewhere between Ypres and Comines as emergency reinforcements. That day was fortunately for us a light one as far as we were concerned, and we didn't lose any men with the exception of one or two slightly wounded. We were not in the front trenches, however, but un support of the K.O.S.B.[103] and the Yorkshire Light Infantry[104] who lost, I believe, rather heavily. This was, of course, the first time we had really been under fire, and we got plenty of experience with 'Jack Johnsons' and shrapnel. We had to lie in ditches partly filled with water to get out of the way of the shells and rifle fire. We remained in that position all day, and then expected to advance, but had to retire as the troops we were supporting had lost rather heavily. After a few hours' sleep the lost trenches were re-taken however, and we were moved to a new position about five o'clock in the morning. On our fourth day in action we relieved the 16th Lancers and another cavalry regiment."[105]

Private Daniell was wounded on 3 November. Evacuated to England, he later recounted the circumstances in which he had been injured while being treated in hospital at Nottingham:

"On the Monday evening we went into the trenches again. I was one of a section sent out about a couple of hundred yards in front of the trenches on outpost duty early next morning. Just as it got light a shell came over and I suddenly had a smack on the leg. One of my comrades managed to bind up the wound, which was in the thigh, and then helped me back a short distance to a haystack between our trenches and the farm where we were posted. On the other side of the haystack there was a small dug-out, and there I lay from 6.30 in the morning till nightfall, with shells falling all round in an awful fashion. It was just like hell. The firing go so hot that my other comrades on outpost duty had to vacate their position and take shelter in the dug-out with me. There was room in that for about three men, and there were five of us wedged into it. Part of the time I had a man sitting on my head.

"At night a relief party came out and carried me back to the trenches. After being attended to by ambulance men I was moved to hospital at Boulogne, where I stayed till last Saturday night, and had the shell splinters taken out of my leg. About eight or nine hundred others came across with me in the

[103] 2nd Battalion, The King's Own Scottish Borderers.
[104] 2nd Battalion, The King's Own (Yorkshire Light Infantry).
[105] Nottingham Evening Post, 23 November 1914.

hospital ship. The doctor who attended me told me the regiment had done exceedingly well, and that General French was exceeding pleased with us, and had sent us his congratulations."[106]

Born in 1890, Claude Harry Daniell, who had employed as an accounts clerk before the war, had been drafted to France on 2 October 1914 with the First Reinforcement for the Oxfordshire Hussars. He was commissioned in The King's Own (Yorkshire Light Infantry) on 11 May 1917 and served with the 3rd (Special Reserve) Battalion. Daniell lived at "Oakdine" at Headington in Oxford after the war and died on 6 May 1957.

On 4 November, **1724 Private George Bennett** wrote to his father, James, who lived at 232 Iffley Road in Oxford, describing his experiences during the fighting near Messines:

"When I last wrote home I was on police duty at ----------.[107] We left there last Friday at midnight and marched with the regiment all night to the front in Belgium. The same morning at 10.30 we were under fire – quick work, wasn't it? Since then we have had four days of real soldiering – have earned splendid praise from the Regular troops with whom we have co-operated. Nearly the whole of the four days and nights we were in the trenches under tremendously heavy shell fire, and to-day while we rest we marvel that our losses were so small. For four days we have had to pass through as much as the finest troops in the world have had to pass through in this war, and we have only lost two men killed, and ten wounded. Captain Molloy,[108] in command of the Banbury Squadron, was killed, and Trooper Archer,[109] of the Oxford Squadron.

My squadron has only lost two men wounded, but there are lots of us who have had narrow escapes. I myself had a bullet pass through my haversack, without hurting me at all... The German shell fire is marvellous; their huge guns blow holes in the ground large enough to bury two or three horses, and the shrapnel is fired with marvellous precision. The ---------- infantry regiment of ----------,[110] which went in with us up to the firing line, have been badly cut up. I believe their casualties exceed 500.

---

[106] Nottingham Evening Post, 23 November 1914.
[107] St Omer.
[108] Captain Brian Charles Baskerville Molloy, who died on 1 November 1914 and is commemorated on Panel 5 of the Ypres (Menin Gate) Memorial.
[109] 1700 Private Harold Francis Archer was killed on 3 November 1914 and is also commemorated on Panel 5 of the Ypres (Menin Gate) Memorial.
[110] 1/14th Battalion, The London Regiment (London Scottish) (Territorial Force)

The 1/1ˢᵗ Queen's Own Oxfordshire Hussars leaving St Omer on 30 October 1914 to reinforce the Cavalry Corps fighting on the Messines Ridge.

This is all I have time to write now, except that I am in splendid health, and that we do not fear anything now that we have received our baptism of fire."[111]

Bennett was later promoted to the rank of Sergeant in the 1/1st Oxfordshire Hussars, before being commissioned as a Second-Lieutenant in the Royal Field Artillery.

1407 Corporal John Reynolds Ashford had been employed as an auctioneer's clerk for Simmons and Sons before the war. Born at Pinhoe in Devon in 1888, Ashford had attested on 31 October 1908 at Henley-on-Thames and served in "C" Squadron of the Queen's Own Oxfordshire Hussars. He had been promoted to Corporal shortly before the regiment embarked for Dunkirk and wrote his description of the impact of the fighting around Messines and Wulverghem on 10 November:

"We are almost used to "coal-boxes"; one exploded within 15 feet of some of us in a roadway. Fortunately, none of us got hit, although the cobbles flew all over the place... Without seeing, it is impossible to realise modern war – artillery all the time, with an occasional attack to make or repel. "Coal-boxes," unless they actually hit the spot, are not usually dangerous, except in the case of hitting the side of a trench, when they might bury two or three men. All the civilian population flee from the immediate vicinity of the battlefield, leaving everything as it falls from their hands. The German fire practically everything within range; farm stock wanders about untended until the cows' udders burst or they get hit with a stray shot. The poultry are generally "looked after" by the troops."[112]

---

[111] Reading Mercury, 14 November 1914.
[112] Glamorgan Gazette, 4 December 1914.

Ashford was appointed Lance-Sergeant on 17 March 1915 and advanced to Acting Sergeant on 30 May 1915, his rank being confirmed on 4 September. He was sent home and was discharged to a commission on 31 October 1915. Posted to the 6th Reserve Regiment of Cavalry, Ashford later joined the 1/1st Surrey Yeomanry, two squadrons of which served as part of XVI Corps Cavalry Regiment at Salonika, and was awarded the Military Cross in the King's Birthday Honours on 3 June 1919. The application for his 1914 Star was made on 8 April 1918, and Ashford applied for the clasp and roses, together with his British War Medal and Victory Medal, on 15 October 1919. He was sent the clasp and roses for the 1914 Star on 23 November 1922. John married Dorothy Mabel Newman on 12 July 1920 at St John's Church at Hampstead and died at Reading in 1966.

Writing to a friend, Mr T. E. Williams, who lived at 66 Stratford Street in Oxford, **1853 Private Reginald Osborne Bolingbroke** also recounted the events of the previous few days:

"I expect by the time you receive this letter you will already know in Oxford that we have been 'in amongst it.' We moved from the base on the evening of October 30th at a few hours' notice, and after marching all night we went straight into the firing line about 9 a.m. next morning. We were in action all one day; it was pretty lively, too, in parts. We had no proper trenches, but took shelter in a ditch. We were shelled all day, and it was pretty awful too – the Regulars we were with described it as 'perfect hell,' so you can imagine it seemed jolly bad to one who hadn't been under fire before. I expect you heard about the London Scottish; we were in action the same day. We have had two more days in the trenches since then, and had rather a rough day on November 3rd. We were in the front trenches, and there was absolutely nothing between us and the enemy.

We are attached to the 1st Cavalry Division, under General de Lisle. The general was very pleased with us, and told our colonel that in future he should not regard us as Territorials, but treat us exactly the same as his other regiments, which was the highest praise he could give us. The German shell fire is pretty awful, especially some of their shells which our men call 'coal boxes.' They do singularly little damage, however, especially if one keeps good fire, and we do this all right. We have only lost one officer and one trooper and several men wounded up to the present.

We are being used as infantry... and often don't see our horses for days at a time. We march up to the trenches under cover of darkness and relieve the troops therein, and are in turn relieved the next night after 24 hours in them. We then go back to the horses, have a days' rest, and then go up again, and so on, ad lib! We get plenty of food, even up in the firing line. We carry tinned rations, and sometimes we manage to get a 'dixie' of tea up. One day, while we were digging some support trenches in the rear, we were near a deserted farm house; we were in clover that day, for we obtained a large pan of the most excellent cream, a barrel of cider, dripping, &c. , and in the evening some of our fellows made a ripping stew out of bully beef and a miscellaneous collection of vegetables from the kitchen garden. It went down jolly topping. We are getting quite expert at digging trenches with nothing but a great coat, but we are very well hardened down now."[113]

Born at Beccles in Suffolk, Reginald Bolingbroke had been employed as a solicitor's clerk at Messrs Andrew Walsh, Grey, Rose and Co. at St Aldate's in Oxford and was a member of the Falcon Rowing Club before the war. Later Mentioned in Despatches and promoted to the rank of Corporal, he was severely wounded while serving in the trenches near Vermelles with the 4th Dismounted Battalion and died at No. 1 Casualty Clearing Station at Chocques on 27 January 1916.

On 16 September 1914, the 1/14th (County of London) Battalion, The London Regiment (London Scottish), disembarked at Le Havre, the first Territorial Force unit to set foot in France. Their departure for Southampton was reported in the Daily Record the same day:

LONDON SCOTTISH LEAVE.

"Amid great enthusiasm the London Scottish, who have been in camp at Garston, Hertfordshire, left Watford Junction yesterday for a destination unnamed. The whole stock of a tobacconists near the station was purchased by civilians and given to the soldiers."

---

[113] Banbury Advertiser, 26 November 1914.

"When we left Havre six signallers, of whom I was one, were detailed to go with three companies to a certain base which I may not name. We travelled in what we were told was fourth class – viz. covered – in horse boxes. We had over 40 in ours, and entrained about 7 p.m., reaching our destination the following morning at 10.30. It was by no means a fast journey, and although we were not too comfortable we managed to get some sleep. At the stations the natives very kindly supplied us with food, drink and fruit, which we were glad enough to have, for we had only some dog biscuit and bully with us.

At this place some of us slept in a chapel. It had a stone floor, and as we had no blankets we found it none too warm. Latterly we were shifted to the stage of a theatre – by the way it was not a London one – and laid hands on some carpets and scenery and made ourselves fairly comfortable.

Last Thursday we moved off, and came to another base just before noon, this time in an ordinary train, but it was just about as fast – I think 10 miles an hour is a good average. We got there shortly after midnight, and joined another party from the battalion which had come direct from London. We have a huge shed, quite clean, for quarters, and straw to lie on, so are much more comfortable. We lay down as soon as possible, and had the best night's rest we have had since we landed in France.

We are doing no signalling here. The men are taking turns as orderlies at the different offices, and the non-commissioned officers go on shell shifting – unloading and re-loading the trucks before they are sent up to the front. We are thinking of trying the London docks for jobs as navvies when we get back! I am going into the town now; we don't need passes here."[114]

1931 Private Charles Alexander Scott Dewar
1/14th (County of London) Battalion, The London Regiment (London Scottish) (Territorial Force)[115]

Born at Moulin, Alexander Dewar was the son of William Dewar, who lived at Tinghnalinne, near Pitlochry. He attested for the London Scottish at their headquarters at 59 Buckingham Gate on 1 November 1913. Stating that he was aged 20 years and one month, Alexander was employed as a stockbroker's clerk by Messrs Lyall Anderson and Co., and was lodging at 83 Milson Road in West Kensington.

Embodied on the outbreak of the war, Private Dewar signed the "Imperial Service Obligation," undertaking to serve overseas, on 12 September 1914 while billeted at St Alban's, and arrived at Le Havre with the London Scottish four days later. He was reported as wounded and missing following the fighting near Messines on the night of 31 October/1 November, but was later confirmed to have been taken prisoner. His capture was reported by The Dundee Courier on 28 November:

---

[114] Perthshire Advertiser, 7 October 1914.
[115] The writer of the letter is unidentified in the original article, but subsequent reports printed in local newspapers indicate that it was Private Dewar.

"Information has been received by Mr Wm. Dewar, Tinghnalinne, Pitlochry, that his son, Private C. A. Dewar, of the London Scottish, was wounded in one of the recent engagements in which the regiment took part in Flanders, and captured by the enemy, being now in hospital in Germany. The particulars of his wounds are not stated. The news was contained in a postcard written by Private Dewar himself to his sister."

Suffering from wounds to his abdomen and leg, Private Dewar was taken to a hospital at Lille by his German captors for treatment, and on being considered to be fit to travel was transported to the Prisoner of War Camp at Limberg on 14 May 1915. Dewar remained in captivity until after the Armistice and on his repatriation was posted on attachment to No. 55 Territorial Force Depot at 59 Buckingham Gate on New Years' Day 1919. He then returned home to Tingnalinne on two months' leave, granted to former prisoners of war on their return from Germany. On 9 February 1919, Dewar wrote to the Infantry Record Office at 4 London Wall Buildings E.C., requesting that he be demobilised on the termination of his leave. Alexander Dewar was eventually disembodied on 31 March 1919.

Alexander Dewar is recorded to have travelled to Singapore in August 1934, on board the M.V. Christiaan Huygens, and died in Surrey on 10 December 1936.

On 29 October, the battalion was despatched to Ypres on thirty-four London omnibuses, before they were rushed to Messines and placed under the command of the Cavalry Corps. On the night of 31 October the London Scottish took part in their first chaotic action.

1150 Private Norman Leslie McLennan was born at Croydon in 1893. He was employed as junior clerk when he had joined the London Scottish before the war and his parents lived at Kirkdale, 9 Mayfield Road South at Sanderstead in Surrey. Embodied on 5 August 1914, Private McLennan disembarked at Le Havre on 16 September.

Private McLennan later described his experiences during the fighting on Halloween night in a letter that was reproduced in The Croydon Advertiser on 21 November and The Cornishman on 3 December:

"Then suddenly bullets began to arrive from behind us as well as in front! Cheerful, wasn't it? We could hear the little beggars going "Phew-u! phew-u!" as Piper Latham[116] put it, exactly as if they were whispering "Cheero! Cheero!" in our ears... All this time the Germans were blowing the 'cease fire' on whistles in the hope of deluding us into stopping, and calling out: "Here you are, Scottish, over here." "Back to your trenches, Scottish," and "Scotland for ever," in a highly entertaining manner. I don't think they caught many people with their tricks though, except in one case which I heard of afterwards. Piper Latham heard a plaintive voice from the middle of a group of Germans saying, "No, I want the Scottish – I want the proper Scottish," and a small youth named Phelps[117] suddenly burst forth with two of the Germans after him trying to bayonet him. Latham stood up and shouted "Here you are, Latham, F Company!" and shot the leading Germans. Little Phelps rushed in, wounded in the arms, and gasped: "Good God, Latham, I

---

[116] 139 Lance-Corporal-Piper Harry Gould Latham, who is referred to by McLennan in his account, was killed on 16 November. He is commemorated on the Ypres (Menin Gate) Memorial.

[117] Born on 20 June 1893 at Kentish Town, 1661 Private Harold Charles Phelps had joined the London Scottish in 1912 and was taken prisoner at Messines, after having receiving gunshot and bayonet wounds to his right arm. For his services to his comrades while a captive, Phelps was awarded the Meritorious Service Medal, the award being published in The London Gazette on 30 January 1920. After being disembodied, Harold returned to work as a master butcher and on 25 April 1920 married Ivy May Nathan at St Paul's in Herne Hill. They lived at 11 Cathcart Hill in Highgate, and on 24 November 1920 Harold rejoined the London Scottish, stating that he was employed as a meat salesman, and was issued with the regimental number 6664823. He served for one year before being discharged at the termination of his period of engagement on 23 November 1921. By 1939 Harold and Ivy resided at 46 Grantham Road in Stockwell, and he was still employed as a wholesale meat salesman. Harold died in 1949.

am glad to see you!" and collapsed fainting in Latham's arms. Poor little chap."

McLennan was commissioned in the 4th Battalion, The Queen's (Royal West Surrey Regiment) (Territorial Force) on 11 June 1915 and attained the rank of Lieutenant. He was issued with clasp and roses for 1914 Star on 23 November 1921. Norman McLennan is recorded to have lived at 285 Kennington Road in 1932 and married Phyllis Marks at Croydon in 1937.

1303 Private Ralph Lovel Galt was born at Reading on 26 January 1887. He was living with his parents at 7 Twyford Crescent in Acton and was employed by his father, who was in business selling typewriters and office supplies, when he attested for the London Scottish at their Drill Hall at 59 Buckingham Gate on 30 May 1910, initially on a four year engagement. A member of "E" Company, he was still serving at the outbreak of the war and was embodied for service on 5 August 1914. Having volunteered to serve overseas while billeted at St Albans on 12 September, Private Galt landed at Le Havre with "D" Company of the 1/14th Londons on 16 September. He fought at Messines on the night of 31 October/1 November, and his account of his experiences during the action was reproduced in The People on 20 December:

"It was at night we first saw the Germans. The enemy was at the opposite side of a field behind a hedge. It was a terrible sight at night, with a farmhouse all alight and others at the side. We could hear the Germans yelling. A band was playing, and I heard afterwards that this was when the Kaiser came on the field. The enemy blew British whistles for the 'Cease fire!' and yelled it out. They also called out 'Scott-ee-sh!' One German actually walked across our trenches, but we yelled to a couple of fellows; they came back and shot him. One came up to my trench with his helmet under his arm and grass round his face, shouting 'Ind-ee-an!' But he got in the light of a burning building, and I saw the spike, so I shot him, and the fellow on my right put one in simultaneously."

Private Galt was admitted to No. 1 Stationary Hospital at Rouen on 3 December 1914, and was diagnosed as suffering from myalgia. He was evacuated to England on board the H.M.H.S. Asturias on 16 December, and was subsequently posted to the 2/14th Londons. Galt was serving with the 14th Reserve Battalion, The London Regiment (London Scottish) at Winchester when he was discharged at the termination of his period of engagement on 29 May 1916.

On his discharge from the Territorial Force, Ralph returned to work as a printer and stationer and lived at 27 Pennard Road in Shepherd's Bush. He married Ethel Ivy Woodyard at St Mary's Church in Ealing on 23 May 1917. They were living at 86 Bellevue Road in Ealing when Ralph was sent his 1914 Star by the Infantry Record Office at London Wall on 27 June 1919, and he is recorded in the 1939 Register as being employed in producing advertising, publicity and propaganda, residing at 15 Bleckynden Terrace in Southampton.

Ralph Lovel Galt died at Southampton in 1952.

1413 Private Frank Duncan Wyllie was born at South Hackney in 1893. He had attested for the East Anglian Division Transport and Supply Column, Army Service Corps (Territorial Force) at Ilford on 7 June 1910. On his enlistment, Frank was aged 17 years and ten months and was employed as a clerk by Messrs. J. Knight Ltd., living at 103 Warren Road in Leyton with his parents, John and Alice, and his siblings Ethel, Percy, Gladys and May. Driver Wyllie served with the Headquarters Company of the East Anglian Divisional A.S.C. until 13 February 1911, when he transferred to the 14ᵗʰ (County of London) Battalion, The London Regiment (London Scottish) (Territorial Force).

He attended the annual camps held at Dover (1911), Frith Hill (1912) and at Abergavenny (1913) with the London Scottish and on the declaration of war was embodied on 5 August 1914. Private Wyllie had signed the "Imperial Service Obligation," volunteering to serve overseas on active service, while billeted at St Alban's on 12 September and disembarked with the 1/14th Londons at Le Havre four days later.

Private Wyllie described his experiences at Messines in a letter to a workmate, who had sent him some cigarettes:

"They have not yet arrived – we get a few posts up here in the firing line – but please thank all who have so kindly contributed. By the time you receive this you will have read of the great 'Scottish; achievement, but no doubt you would like to hear the true details, as the newspapers get hold of a lot of rubbish.

On Oct. 31 we moved to action, in splendid formation, but under murderous artillery fire, which unfortunately 'laid out' a lot of our comrades. We were shelled all day with shrapnel and 'Black Marias.' Towards evening the artillery eased up a bit, and we guessed that something desperate was coming off. We were not kept waiting long, for the Germans hurled – (a number has been obliterated here) – Army Corps against us. Three times we repulsed them with great loss, and on several occasions they charged us with the bayonet, but we counter-charged them, and they turned and ran. During the night their great numbers told, and they began to get round us, but our chaps fought like fury, and towards morning we were forced to give a little ground, although we held on until reinforcements arrived. We were relieved after nearly 36 hours' continual fighting. It was a terrible sight from our trenches – the whole country was in flames behind the Huns, and we could hear a brass band playing the Austrian National Anthem. We hear from the staff that the Kaiser and Von Kluck themselves were in command of this great German effort."[118]

Private Wyllie remained with the 1/14th Londons throughout the Great War. In 1916, when his period of engagement was due to expire, he left the London Scottish on 26 May and arrived at No. 1 Infantry Base Depot the following day, in preparation to be sent home to be discharged. However, on 7 June he elected to continue to serve under the terms of the Military Service Act of 1916 and was rewarded with a bounty of £15. Wyllie was posted to the reinforcements for the battalion on 3 July and arrived back at

---

[118] Essex County Chronicle, 20 November 1914.

the battalion the following day in their trenches facing Gommecourt Park, the London Scottish having lost 590 all ranks killed, wounded and missing during their attack on 1 July. He went home on leave in November 1917 and again shortly after the Armistice in 1918, before embarking for England on 13 January 1919 to be demobilised. Wyllie was finally disembodied at No. 1 Dispersal Unit at Purfleet on 19 January.

Frank Wyllie died at his home at 169 Crossbrook Street in Cheshunt on 6 September 1948.

Born on 27 October 1892, **1591 Corporal Frank Cyril Hastwell** was the son of Benjamin Charles and Esther Hastwell, and was baptised at St Anne's Church in Lambeth on Christmas Day.

He was employed as an insurance clerk with the Sun Life Assurance Society, living with his parents at "Benesta," 35 Drewstead Road in Streatham, when he joined the London Scottish in 1911, and was embodied at the outbreak of the war. Hastwell disembarked at Le Havre on 16 September 1914 and took part in the fighting near Messines on the night of 31 October/1 November, being photographed at Wulverghem on the morning following the action.

Appointed a Lance-Sergeant, Hastwell was sent home on 22 May 1915 and on 9 June was commissioned as a Second-Lieutenant in the 3rd (Special Reserve) Battalion, The Dorsetshire Regiment, and returned to France with 46th Brigade Trench Mortar Battery. Later promoted to Lieutenant, Hastwell served on attachment with No. 4 Special Company, Royal Engineers from 1917.

Hastwell was issued with the clasp and roses for his 1914 Star on 16 April 1920 and was sent his British War Medal and Victory Medal on 23 February 1923. In the years following the war Frank became a restaurateur and worked as a singer, marrying Ada Louise McCallum in 1932. He is recorded in the 1939 Register as still residing at 35 Drewstead Road.

Frank Hastwell died on 29 June 1961 at St James's Hospital in Balham.

1591 Corporal Frank Cyril Hastwell, photographed at Wulverghem on
1 November 1914.

"After our first engagement we were kept in reserve for about two days, and then sent back for a week's rest. Then came another call for us to go into the firing line. It was a tight corner, where we were required, but it was a case of holding on to a part of the line where there were some excellent trenches and dug-outs. We crept down to our trenches in the night, and relieved another regiment who had had their spell. There was a bit of rifle fire, after we got in, but nothing exciting happened.

At dawn all was quiet except for one or two German snipers, who were hitting the trees (our line ran through some woods). We thought we were in for a soft time, and the C.O., Adjutant, Scout Officer and Scouts who were living in dug-outs, just behind the lines, started to wash and shave, but it was not long before the German shells started whistling round, and we had to get into our dug-outs with all haste. We spent the day reading and smoking until nightfall when the shelling ceased, and the scouts then got various errands to different parts of the line. My particular errand was to bring up a party of men to draw their rations. I had the company of another scot who had to go to the next company.

We started out, and as we did not know where they were we inquired of some engineers where the two companies of the 'Scottish' were. Following their directions we arrived at the trenches, and asked for the companies. My friend was directed further along the line, and I was pulled down into the trench. To my astonishment I had got 'A' Company, but not the right "Scottish," they were the K.O.S.B.'s, and seemed to treat me as a suspected spy. I had to undergo a long cross-examination, and I suppose my innocence persuaded them to let me go. They also directed me to the people I wanted, but my comrade did not have the same luck, and was kept as a prisoner till the morning, with the result that I had to take his message as well.

The following morning we started washing again, but the shells came over very early, and soon put a stop to that nonsense. They got nearer and nearer, until four 'Jack Johnsons' landed in amongst our dug-outs and buried the lot of us. We did not wait for any orders, but cleared ourselves of earth, branches, etc., and got to some fresh homes. Four scouts were wounded by this lot. The shells did not trouble us in our fresh homes, but came dangerously near several times. Anyhow, night put a stop to the shelling, and we found ourselves going on our nocturnal errands as before. Things went on in this manner all the time we were in the firing line – attacks by the Germans with rifles at night and shells in the day. Our day errands to Brigade Headquarters were the most dangerous, as the road all the way was shelled, and almost every other route. It was quite a science trying to dodge the shells and judge when the next one would land.

We were relieved in the end and went back as reserves for two days, after which we were sent right back for a rest, which we are thoroughly enjoying, as we have plenty of comforts just arrived from Headquarters – London papers, etc., so it is quite like a Christmas party."

A letter written while in rest billets at Pradelles by **1128 Private John Cherry Cree** to his father, who lived at 138 Station Road in Redhill. Private Cree served with the Scout Section of the 1/14th (County of London) Battalion, The London Regiment (London Scottish) (Territorial Force), and his letter was reproduced in The Dorking and Leatherhead Advertiser on 28 November 1914.

Born at Ipswich on 7 May 1890, John Cherry Cree was the son of Andrew and Agnes Cree and in civilian life was employed as an engineers' clerk by the National Telephone Company. Embodied following the outbreak of the war, Private Cree had landed at Le Havre with the London Scottish on 16 September 1914. On 3 December he returned home, on being recommended to receive a commission, and on 2 March 1915 became a Second-Lieutenant with the Royal Engineers Signal Service (Scottish Command). Cree attained the rank of Captain and in 1918 was serving with "L" Signal Battalion. He applied for his 1914 Star on 10 September 1919, and the medal was forwarded to him, care of the Golfers' Club at Whitehall Court. His British War Medal, Victory Medal and the clasp and roses for his 1914 Star were sent to him on 16 October 1920, by which time he was residing at his parents' home at 138 Station Road. He married Alice Rosenblatt in 1924, and in 1939 they are recorded as residing at 98 Whitchurch Lane in Edgware. At this time John was a civil servant with the Air Ministry, having previously been employed with the General Post Office. He was also serving on the Reserve of Officers, and held the rank of Captain with the Royal Corps of Signals. While employed as a civilian Staff Officer with the Air Ministry, Cree was appointed as an M.B.E. (Civil Division) in the King's Birthday Honours published in The London Gazette on 10 June 1944.

John Cherry Cree M.B.E. died at 98 Whitchurch Lane on 12 January 1959.

The Grave of D/3283 Private James Meston D.C.M.
at Delville Wood Cemetery
6 August 2018

D/3283 Private James Meston D.C.M., of the 6th Dragoon Guards
(Carabiniers), was awarded the Distinguished Conduct Medal for his actions
during the fighting at Messines on 31 October/1 November 1914.

He was presented with his medal by King George V the following month when he visited the front. Meston's gallantry was reported on in The Aberdeen Daily Journal on 22 December:

"During the recent visit of the King to France one of the soldiers upon whom his Majesty conferred the Distinguished Conduct Medal was an Aberdonian who performed a noteworthy feat of gallantry on the field of battle, and well merited his place in the roll of fame.

The medal was awarded to Private James Meston, of the 6th Dragoon Guards, for great gallantry near Messines, on October 31, when he went out repeatedly under heavy shell and machine gun fire, dressed the wounds of men of the London Scottish, and carried them out of action. At the same time, during the night attack which followed, he displayed the greatest gallantry, especially in walking up alone to the trenches and shooting five Germans.

Private Meston is a son of Mrs J. Meston, 50 Shiprow, Aberdeen. His brother, Private William Meston, of the 2nd Gordon Highlanders, was killed in action on October 28."

Born at Sunderland in 1889, Meston was also awarded the Order of St George, 3rd Class, by the Russians. He was killed on 26 August 1918 while advancing across the old Somme battlefield of 1916. His death was reported in The Aberdeen Evening Express on 21 September:

"Trooper (sic) James Meston D.C.M., Dragoon Guards, who was killed in action on 26th August, was the husband of Mrs Meston, 44 Blackfriars Street, Aberdeen. He was a regular soldier before the outbreak of war."

Private Meston was buried with six of his comrades who had also died during the operations on 26 August, but in 1921 his remained were exhumed and reburied at Plot V, Row M, Grave 10.

4323 Squadron Sergeant-Major Harry William Baker
11th (Prince Albert's Own) Hussars

Harry Baker had attested for the Hussars of the Line at Gosport on 6 November 1899 and at the time of his enlistment stated that he had been born at West Ham and was employed as a confectioner. He was stationed with the 11th Hussars at Marlborough Barracks in Dublin at the time of his marriage to Joan Mowat Breadalburn Sutherland Campbell at St John's Church in East Dulwich on 3 March 1908. Their entry in the marriage register states that Baker's father, Harry George William Baker, was deceased at the time of their wedding but had been an architect. Their daughter, Kathleen Joan Baker, had been born at Tunbridge Wells on 23 September 1907.[119]

At the declaration of the war, Baker held the rank of Squadron Sergeant-Major and disembarked with "B" Squadron from the S.S. Munificence at Le Havre on 16 August 1914.

Squadron Sergeant-Major Baker was killed on the morning of 31 October[120] when the 11th Hussars were fighting dismounted at Messines. The circumstances in which he had died were recounted in the regimental history published in 1936:

"At about 9 a.m. the squadron leader sent a report to the Colonel's shelter to say that the enemy could be seen advancing from the direction of Warneton. The adjutant was at once dispatched to Br Genl Briggs with this information. Shortly afterwards Squadron Sergeant Major Baker came to the headquarters dug-out to say that he had located two guns in action down by the Douve stream. He was desperately keen to point out their exact position to our gunners and although warned of the danger which he ran - for the shelling was now intense - he set off on his task; he had only gone a few yards from the trench when a heavy shell burst close to him and killed him."[121]

S.S.M. Baker's body was recovered and taken to Wulverghem, where he was buried in the churchyard.

---

[119] Kathleen died in Buckinghamshire in 1991.
[120] Some records state 1 November.
[121] Captain L. R. Lumley: History of the Eleventh Hussars (Prince Albert's Own) 1908-1934 (London, Royal United Services Institution, 1936), p.159.

Squadron Sergeant-Major Baker with his wife Joan and daughter Kathleen.

Some months following his death, his widow received the shocking news that S.S.M. Baker was a German by birth and had not been naturalised. A report published in The Surrey Mirror of 7 December 1915 records the story:

GERMAN-BRITISH SOLDIER.

HOW HIS WIFE LEARNED HIS NATIONALITY.

"After he had served 19 years in the British Army, and died on the field in France (sic), it was discovered that Squadron Sergeant-Major Harry William Baker, 11th Hussars, was a German. Recently, the Home Office granted a certificate of naturalisation to his widow, Mrs Joan Mowat Bredalbane Sutherland Baker, of The Bungalow, Peper Harow-road, Godalming, declaring her to be a British subject. Mrs Baker was born at Loch Fyne, in Argyllshire, but her marriage created her a German, and according to law an "enemy alien."

A remarkable fact is that although she had been happily married since March 1908, it was only a few months ago, after her husband had been dead eight months, that the discovery was made that he was a German. It became necessary for Mrs Baker to register under the Aliens Restriction Order, and she also for a time forfeted her pension. Now her nationality has been restored, together with her pension and the arrears which had accumulated during the suspension.

To an interviewer Mrs Baker said that in 1900 she was head nurse in the service of Mrs Webber, wife of Colonel Webber, Dublin Fusiliers, at 92, Elm Park-gardens, South Kensington. In that year Colonel Webber was detailed at Brookwood, and the soldier in charge of his escort was Acting-Sergeant Baker. For three years his regiment was abroad, but they corresponded, and on his return to England they became engaged, and the wedding took place at St John's Church, East Dulwich, on March 3rd, 1908.

"I never had the remotest idea that my husband was a German," said Mrs Baker. "In fact, he hated anything German. Before the war he never liked me to get any toys for our little girl that bore the words 'Made in Germany.' After my husband was killed at Messines, France (sic), on October 31st 1914, I received the official notification from the War Office. Eight months later I read in a paper that a Mrs Leibold, a German, had been prosecuted for failing to register.

In the report of the case it was stated that Mrs Leibold came to England from Germany 33 years ago, and that she had a son, a squadron sergeant-major in the British Army who, in the name of Baker, had served in the 11th Hussars and had been killed in action.

It startled me when I read it," continued Mrs Baker, "for I felt that there could only be one Squadron Sergeant-Major Baker in the 11th. The inquiries I made established beyond all doubt that it was my husband. I had understood from him that he was born in East Ham. It now appeared that he was born in Germany and that his mother brought him here when he was 2½ years old."

Baker's grave was destroyed during the war and he is commemorated by a Special Memorial erected at Wulvergem Churchyard in Plot B, Grave 2. The Commonwealth War Graves Commission state that he was killed on 30 October. The register for the cemetery records that he was the son of Harry George Baker, but no mention of his mother is present. His widow, Joan, lived at Springfield Gordale, at Halkirk in Caithness after the war, and she had the following inscription carved at the base of the headstone:

"God Be With You Till We Meet Again."

Harry's mother, Martina Leibold, died at 24 Lime Hill Road in Tunbridge Wells on 12 December 1929. Her funeral was reported by The Kent and Sussex Courier on 20 December:

"Mrs Leibold, of 24, Lime Hill-road, who passed away on Thursday week, was laid to rest at the Borough Cemetery on Monday. Floral tributes were sent by Mrs Baker and Grand-daughter; Mr and Mrs Berry; Mr and Mrs Clark; An Old Friend; Messrs Wood and Pannell; Mr and Mrs Hammond; A Friend; Miss Cole; Messrs Wood and Lowe; Mr and Mrs Smith; Miss Morgan. The funeral arrangements were carried out by Mr T. Potter, Southborough."

2048 Squadron Corporal-Major George Attenborough D.C.M.
1ˢᵗ Life Guards

Signallers of the 1ˢᵗ Life Guards Squadron, Household Cavalry Composite
Regiment, photographed on 15 August 1914 at Hyde Park Barracks as they
prepared to leave for France.

Born at Steeple in Essex in 1879, George Attenborough had attested for the
1ˢᵗ Life Guards on 20 April 1898 and joined the regiment three days later.
He embarked for active service in South Africa with the Household Cavalry
Composite Regiment on 29 November 1899 and served there for a year,
when the regiment returned home. He was awarded his first Good Conduct
badge on 20 April 1900, and for his service in the campaign was issued with
the Queen's South Africa Medal with clasps for Paardeberg, Dreifontein,
Johannesburg, Wittebergen, and the Relief of Kimberley. Attenborough was
appointed an Acting Corporal on 13 January 1902, received a second Good
Conduct badge on 20 April 1904 and was promoted to Corporal and
Corporal of Horse on 11 August 1905. While stationed at Windsor on 15
November 1909, Attenborough re-engaged to complete 21 years' service
with the Colours. He was posted to the 1ˢᵗ Life Guards Squadron of the
Household Cavalry Composite Regiment on its formation and disembarked
at Le Havre on 16 August.

On 31 October, the Household Cavalry Composite Regiment was holding trenches east of the village of Wytschaete and their positions were subjected to German artillery fire throughout the day. Corporal of Horse Attenborough described the fighting in a letter to his cousin written on 4 November:

"The night before last 64 of us (all 1ˢᵗ Life Guards) were lining about 400 yards of trenches near Ypres. About 11 o'clock we heard the Germans singing hymns, etc., so we knew they were about to make an attack. At 12.30 they made a terrific rush, giving a mighty cheer, and succeeded in getting into our trenches. We then went for them for all we were worth (64 against hundreds), and the result of it all was we lost 5 killed and 15 wounded, and I counted between 50 and 60 dead Germans in our trenches, besides taking 19 prisoners. There were dozens shot before they succeeded in getting in the trenches, and I heard that the Household Cavalry had killed between 500 and 600. You should have seen these German soldiers – some boys of 17, others elderly gents of 60. I never saw such a crowd, and they can't fight for nuts. Although we were outnumbered by probably ten to one, they made no fight at all when they saw we meant business. Some threw down their rifles and cried "Pity me! Pity me!" apparently the only English words they knew. What we can't make out is how the Germans manage to keep their numbers up, as their losses are enormous. They come in great hordes, their officers, in the rear, urging them on with revolvers, and woe betide the man who turns back. Of the 60 killed in our trenches there was not a single officer, and only one was made prisoner. The above is the best thing we have done during the war, as our own losses were so small in proportion to the enemy's."[122]

Corporal of Horse Attenborough was later awarded the Distinguished Conduct Medal for his actions during the fighting at Verloenhoek on 13 May, during the Second Battle of Ypres. By this time serving with "A" Squadron of the 1ˢᵗ Life Guards Attenborough, together with four troopers, remained in a shell hole after the rest of the squadron had withdrawn to the G.H.Q. Line. They remained holding the position until reached by a counter-attack mounted by the 10ᵗʰ Hussars, and then left the shell hole to join in the charge. The citation for his award read:

---

[122] Essex Newsman, 21 November 1914.

"For conspicuous gallantry and devotion to duty on the 13th May, 1915, near Ypres, when he remained in shell holes under a heavy fire during a retirement, and ultimately advanced with the 10th Hussars in a counter-attack."

The award was announced in The London Gazette on 3 August 1915. On 28 November 1915, Attenborough was appointed an Acting Squadron Corporal-Major to "D" Squadron, and was promoted to the substantive rank on 2 February 1917. He was also awarded the Long Service and Good Conduct Medal.

S.C.M. Attenborough was severely wounded on 19 May 1918 during a German air raid on Etaples and was evacuated to England, where he died of his wounds at 3rd London General Hospital on 1 July. Squadron Corporal-Major George Attenborough D.C.M. is buried at Burnham-on-Crouch Cemetery, Grave Reference: B. 24.

The clasp for his 1914 Star was issued to his widow, Jenny, on 17 December 1918. She and S.C.M. Attenborough had married on 18 February 1918 at the parish church in Witham, and she lived at 31 Mildmay Road in Burnham-on-Crouch after the war.

April 1915 - Wulverghem Sector

"It has come our turn for the trenches again, part of the companies going first, acting as rations and water parties for them. But the march we had in the dark was terrible, moving from one barn to another closer to the line. We were absolutely under rifle fire all the way, not knowing one second to another whether we should be shot, as bullets were whizzing high and low between us – the hottest time we've had yet. When we landed safely to our barn, we heard news of our mates being wounded. There doesn't have to be a finger tip shown about the parapet but that there is two or three bullets at it. You see, there is not much chance if you pop your head up. It means Red Cross at once. The barn where we are billeted has been shelled and stands in ruins, and all through the day the bullets keep whizzing past. We are not allowed out of the building at any time during the day, it is too dangerous. We are in it, right... We had a march under fire, going and coming from the trenches, while starlights and bullets were flying about. To-night I think we have to go in the trenches to take our turn of the fighting. This must be the hottest quarter there is. In places we are not fifty yards away.[123]

3768 Private Wilfrid Sheard
1/5th Battalion, The North Staffordshire Regiment (Territorial Force)

Wilfrid Sheard was born at Etruria in 1893, the son of Arthur and Lavinia Sheard, and was baptised on 14 April at St John The Evangelist at Hanley on 14 April. He lived with his seven brothers and sisters at 15 Cavour Street in Etruria, and studied at the Hanley School of Art. He was employed as a potter's flower painter when he attested for the 5th Battalion, The North Staffordshire Regiment (Territorial Force) at Stoke-on-Trent in October 1914, and on volunteering for "Imperial Service" was posted to No. 11 Platoon, "C" Company of the 1/5th Battalion. Private Sheard disembarked at Le Havre on 3 March 1915.

Private Sheard wrote another letter to his parents describing his life in the front line near Wulverghem and resting at "Aldershot Camp" at Neuve Eglise:

"Glad to say we arrived out safely. I am very well, considering what we have gone through. We have been paddling through the trenches. Now the wet weather has come for change. The water is anything from one to two feet.

---

[123] Staffordshire Weekly Sentinel. 14 April 1915.

We have plenty of fun, but it is rather risky work when one's legs are soaked. We do have to be careful. The ———— regimental band[124] came round our billets, and gave us a variable programme. I had the pleasure of playing one of the second cornets for a hymn tune, and one or two lively waltzes. One of them I couldn't quite catch. It was nearly all after beats, but I enjoyed it at the time.

Has ———— forgotten my weekly paper? We are absolutely barred from mentioning any military place. Don't forget "Weekly."[125]

During 1915, a number of sketches drawn by Private Sheard were published in The Staffordshire Weekly Sentinel.

This pen and ink drawing was originally published in the Sentinel on 18 December 1915. It shows members of the Signal Section of the 1/5th North Staffords playing cards in their billet. They are wearing goatskin jerkins to help ward off the cold. Also with them is a little stray dog, named "Belge", that had been adopted by one of the signallers on 30 June 1915. She was a great favourite, being described as; "one of the family", and would go with her master to repair broken telephone wires while in the line.

SOME NORTH STAFFORDS ENJOYING A LITTLE LEISURE

---

[124] 1/5th Battalion, The South Staffordshire Regiment. The battalion's band acted as musical support to the 1st Staffordshire (137th Brigade from 12 May 1915) Brigade throughout the war.
[125] Staffordshire Weekly Sentinel. 14 April 1915.

Private Sheard was posted to the 1/6th Battalion on 29 January 1918, on the transfer of the 1/5th North Staffords to 59th (North Midland) Division to amalgamate with the 2/5th Battalion. He remained with the 1/6th North Staffords throughout the rest of the battles of 1918, including the crossing of the St Quentin Canal at Bellenglise on 29 September, but on 9 November was sent home on leave and did not return to the 1/6th North Staffords until after the Armistice, on 23 November. Sheard was sent to England on 20 February 1919 and was disembodied on demobilisation on 23 March.

After the war Wilfrid married Gertrude Latham in 1920 and became a commercial illustrator, advertising his services in The Staffordshire Sentinel to local businesses. He also drew several caricatures of the players of Stoke City and Port Vale that were published in the same newspaper, and was one of the artists who painted the memorial canvas that was displayed at reunions of the 5th Battalion's Old Comrades' Association, part of which has recently been put on display in the Potteries Museum and Art Gallery at Hanley.

Wilfrid Sheard died in 1967, aged 73.

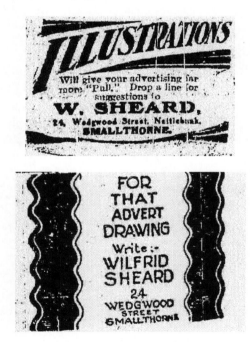

Advertisements for Wilfrid Sheard's work, which were published in
The Staffordshire Weekly Sentinel during 1925.

Douve Valley – November 1915

"We are beginning to feel the first edge of winter – rain, rain, rain! – and it is now that the Engineers' labours of the past few months are being put to the test. Communication trenches which in some cases twist and turn for a mile or more, and which in the dry weather were all that could be desired, are now beginning to fall in, but on the whole they have calculated very well.

The communication trench is the very life-blood to the battalion in the firing line. Along it plod the ration parties, the working parties, the stretcher-bearers with their wounded, a constant stream to and fro in broad daylight, quite secure from the enemy's fire. But with our dug-outs quite rain-proof, with ample rations, and with a nice little coke brazier burning inside, you need not worry very much about us out here – all is well on the British front in Flanders. Hostilities on both sides seem to have lessened considerably – by mutual consent, I suppose – for well do I remember when we entered the trenches last February for the first time. Trench warfare had practically just commenced, and the constant sniping that took place on both sides both day and night made it imperative to use the periscope, while if one dated to just poke one's head over the parapet in the daytime for a moment or two it meant certain death.

Yesterday I was lying with a powerful glass, partly concealed, observing for over half an hour from our front line. With my glass I followed every twist and turn, every sandbag, and every successive line of the enemy's barbed wire on the hill opposite, and not a shot came over. I could not see the least sign of life. There is a ruined village on the crest of the hill, and, study as I liked, I could not even detect a wreath of smoke to indicate that "Fritz" was at least cooking himself a meal. One felt a sporting desire to swarm over our parapets and investigate, but we know only too well that although the pace has slackened considerably since last winter, still "Mr Allemand" is not to be caught napping – he is a very cunning and clever adversary.

We are all following very closely events in the Balkans, and it would really amuse you to hear the arguments thrashed out night after night in our little wet homes in the trench. In a corps like ours we naturally have all sorts and conditions – native-born Canadians, who until now had never gone further than the elevators standing like sentinels on the horizon of their prairie homestead, a vast number of "the legion that never was listed," most delightful men to meet out here. They had been everywhere, seen everything up to a certain point, until that father of them all, "Old Man Booze," had called them imperatively to his fold, and they had all obeyed like naughty little children.

Only yesterday I was on guard with one man, a sometime naval officer. His voice and features are typical of his class. We passed a usually tiresome two hours most pleasantly. And so we have them all – ex-tea planters, ex-Indian civil servants, a sprinkling of the loud-talking Yank, men from the Klondike, men from the British Columbia backwoods, old sailors, old soldiers with a breast row of medals, Scotchmen, Englishmen, Irishmen, Welshmen. The whole lot of them could be picked out from one company of our battalion, and "Ours" is typical of a Colonial battalion. One could write a book about them all, while what an inspiration for an Empire poet! I remember one man telling me of how he enlisted. He was on a survey party away up in the Northern B.C., and one day an old Indian came along and explained in broken English. He said: "You know old Dutch? Well, old Dutch and Vancouver man they fight, but San Francisco man he no fight." And so they interpreted that Britain was at war with Germany, with the United States neutral. Without even waiting for verification, the whole survey threw up their work, and, getting into canoes, they paddled down over 500 miles, making for Vancouver, their only idea being to enlist. They were too late for the first contingent, and, in disguist, had to be content with following on with the second draft. And that was the way the call was answered at the outposts of Empire when Mother England called to arms.

In violent contrast we read in the daily papers of recruiting methods at home, touting from house to house like some importunate insurance agent. No, I must admit that, argue as we can, the Colonial has always the edge on us in that argument."[126]

28885 Private Noel de Purton MacRoberts
16th Battalion (The Canadian Scottish), Canadian Expeditionary Force

---

[126] Derby Daily Telegraph, 25 November 1915.

When McRoberts wrote his letter the Canadian Scottish were holding Trenches 139-142 in the Douve Valley, facing the Germans positioned on the high ground at Messines.

Noel MacRoberts had attested for the Canadian Expeditionary Force at Valcartier on 23 September 1914. Born at Newcastle, New South Wales, on 28 November 1890, he was married and was did not state an occupation on his attestation form. MacRoberts had previously served with The Royal Sussex Regiment for two years, and had been a member of the 72nd Regiment "Seaforth Highlanders of Canada" since the unit's formation on 24 November 1910 at Vancouver.

MacRoberts was commissioned as a Temporary Second-Lieutenant in The Royal Sussex Regiment on 15 December 1915 and was posted to the 13th (Service) Battalion (3rd South Down). He was reported as wounded in June 1916 and awarded the Military Cross, the citation for the decoration being published in The London Gazette on 27 July:

"For conspicuous gallantry. When two men of a wiring party fell wounded into the fire, 2nd Lt. MacRoberts immediately went out under heavy machine-gun fire to their assistance. With the aid of two men of the wiring party, he extricated the wounded men and finally got them into our trenches. It was a bright moonlight and machine-gun fire was continuous."

MacRoberts was awarded a Bar to his Military Cross weeks later, and the citation was printed in The London Gazette on 9 September 1916:

"For conspicuous gallantry. He reconnoitered and cut the enemy's wire, completing his work with a torpedo, under rifle and grenade fire. Later he led a successful raid into the enemy's trenches, and, though wounded, personally accounted for two of the enemy who opposed his advance. His coolness and personal gallantry were largely responsible for the success of the raid."

MacRoberts continued to serve with the 13th Royal Sussex and was awarded the Distinguished Service Order. He was appointed a Temporary Captain and became an Acting Major while serving as the Second-in-Command, on 20 February 1918. He later transferred to the 52nd (Graduated) Battalion which served with the Army of Occupation in Germany following the war before retiring with the rank of Major.

MacRoberts was commissioned as a Second-Lieutenant in the Infantry Branch (Supply and Transport Corps) of the Indian Army Reserve of Officers on 26 January 1920, with seniority from 15 December 1915. He was commissioned as a Lieutenant (Regular Forces) in The Royal Fusiliers on 25 February 1922, but relinquished the rank of Major that he had been granted on 15 September 1920. MacRoberts went on to serve with "Y" Company of the 2nd Battalion at Chanak in Turkey, before serving on attachment with the 3rd Battalion, The Nigeria Regiment. He returned home and retired on 21 June 1934.

MacRoberts was appointed as Recruiting Officer for The East Yorkshire Regiment, and joined the Hull and District Branch of the Regimental Association. On 24 September 1936 he was found guilty of four charges: Driving while under the influence of drink, dangerous driving, assaulting a police officer and resisting arrest; at Driffield Police Court. He was fined £43 and had his driving license suspended for five years. MacRoberts also served as an Air Raid Precautions officer for St Pancras area of London, and wrote an instructional pamphlet based on the effects of the bombing of Barcelona in March 1938. During the Second World War he was transferred to the Royal Pioneer Corps and served as Commandant at No. 544 Italian POW Camp at Cheltenham and No. 663 German POW Camp at Tidworth, before being retired having exceeded the age limit for service on 21 May 1947. In retirement he lived at 18 Montagu Square.

Noel de Purton MacRoberts D.S.O., M.C., died at 61 Inverness Terrace in London W2 on 9 October 1962.

First into Messines – 7 June 1917

26/284 Lance-Sergeant John English Thomson, who served with "C" Company of the 4th Battalion, 3rd New Zealand Rifle Brigade, was killed on 7 June 1917. It was reported by The Poverty Bay Herald on 28 September that he had the distinction of being the first of the "Dinks" to enter Messines. A comrade wrote:

"You know, of course, Jack Thomson has 'gone west,' but did you hear that he and another chap were recommended for the V.C.? He was the first New Zealander to get into Messines. He said he would be, and he was. They did some good work taking machine guns, but most unfortunately it cost them their lives. Both were very popular and will be much missed. You must give my sympathy to Mrs Thomson and family."

A notice was placed in the same newspaper on 10 June 1918 to mark the first anniversary of his death:

THOMSON. - In loving memory of (Jack) Sergeant J. E. Thomson, who was killed in action at Messines on June 7th, 1917.

He fought, but not for love of strife,
He fought, but to defend;
He stood for liberty and truth –
A soldier to the end.

Inserted by his loving aunt and uncle, Mr and Mrs J. English, Mangapapa."

Born at Blantyre in Lanarkshire on 28 November 1893, Jack was working as a bushman on a farm at Matawai when he attested for the New Zealand Expeditionary Force at Trentham Camp on 12 October 1915. At the time of his enlistment he was also serving with "A" Squadron of the 9th (Wellington East Coast) Mounted Rifles. He was posted to "C" Company of the 4th Battalion, 3rd New Zealand Rifle Brigade on 10 November embarked for service overseas on 5 February 1916. Rifleman Thomson fought on the Somme and was promoted to the rank of Corporal on 15 September 1916.

Thomson reported sick on 27 January 1917 and was admitted to No. 1 Australian Casualty Clearing Station before being evacuated to No. 2 Australian General Hospital at Boulogne, where he was diagnosed as suffering from influenza. On being discharged from hospital on 16 February he was posted to the New Zealand Base Depot, being appointed a Lance-Sergeant on 19 April, before returning to the 4th Battalion on 21 April.

Lance-Sergeant Thomson is commemorated on the The Messines Ridge (New Zealand) Memorial, and the register for the memorial records that his mother, Mrs Margaret Holloway (formerly Thomson), resided at 517 Gladstone Road in Gisborne.

The Ploegsteert Memorial

The Ploegsteert Memorial, taken on 11 November 1994.

The Ploegsteert Memorial records the names of 11,399 soldiers (11,386 British and thirteen South Africans)[127] from the British Expeditionary Force and South Africa who died in the south of Belgium, from Caestre-Dranoutre-Warneton to the north, to Haverskerque-Estaires-Fournes in France to the south, including the towns of Hazebrouck, Merville, Bailleul and Armentieres, the Forest of Nieppe, and Ploegsteert Wood. The memorial was inaugurated by the Duke of Brabant on 7 June 1931. Since 7 June 1999 the Last Post has been sounded at the Memorial at 7.00 p.m. on the first Friday of each month.

The earliest recorded fatality on the Memorial is **D/2700 Bandsman Ernest William Roake** of the 4th (Royal Irish) Dragoon Guards, who is stated to have been killed on 10 October 1914 but most likely died between 14 and 18 October. His name is carved on Panel 1.

---

[127] This total (which is provided by the Commonwealth War Graves Commission) may also include aliases.

Born in 1881, Private Roake came from Shepperton and had attested for the Hussars of the Line at Brighton on 29 August 1896, aged fifteen years and two months. At the time of his enlistment he stated that he was a "musician." Posted to the 20ᵗʰ Hussars, Boy Roake was issued with the regimental number 4098 and converted to adult service on reaching the age of eighteen on 28 June 1899. He was appointed as a Bandsman on 22 March 1901 and a Trumpeter on 10 September. Roake reverted to Private on 1 November 1905 and was discharged at the termination of his twelve years' period of engagement on 28 August 1908. During his service Roake had served in India, Egypt and in South Africa during the Boer War, being issued with the Queen's South Africa Medal with clasps for Cape Colony, Transvaal, Orange Free State, South Africa 1901 and South Africa 1902.

Shortly after his discharge, Roake re-enlisted for the Dragoons of the Line at Brighton on 25 November 1908 and was posted to the 4ᵗʰ Dragoon Guards. Roake was again appointed a Bandsman on 31 August 1909. He was stationed at Tidworth when war was declared and disembarked from the S.S. Winifredian at Boulogne on 16 August 1914. Bandsman Roake was reported as missing two months later and his death was presumed to have taken place on or around 10 October.[128]

Across the road from the Ploegsteert Memorial is Hyde Park Corner (Royal Berks) Cemetery, which was established in April 1915 by the 1/4ᵗʰ Battalion, The Royal Berkshire Regiment (Territorial Force) when 48ᵗʰ (South Midland) Division was serving in the area. The cemetery contains 87 burials, including four German soldiers, a Canadian and one Australian. The cemetery continued to be used for burials until November 1917.

The first burial made in the cemetery was that of **3053 Private William Giles** of the 1/4ᵗʰ Royal Berkshires, who was aged 17 when he was killed on 28 April 1915. From Reading, Private Giles was the son of James and Sarah Giles, who resided at 9 Hilcot Road and had attended Wilson School before being employed at Messrs. G. R. Jackson in the town. William enlisted in September 1914 and served alongside his brother Frank in the same company of the 1/4ᵗʰ Royal Berkshires.[129] His Platoon Sergeant wrote to William's parents and described the circumstances in which he had been killed and his burial:

---

[128] His rank is recorded as Private on the Memorial as Bandsman was an appointment.
[129] A notice recording his death was also placed in The Reading Observer of 8 May 1915 by his parents.

"He was struck through the head by a bullet from the German lines while waiting instructions for carrying out a fatigue for which he had volunteered. Although his death did not take place until about five hours afterwards, he did not suffer the slightest pain, for he was quite unconscious until the end. He was buried in a pleasant little wood in which grow primroses, cowslips and violets. His funeral was attended by his section, his Colonel, Adjutant, Company Officer, platoon officer and others. His grave is being tended by his comrades, who will plant primroses and other flowers thereon. A wooden cross, later to be replaced by an iron one, is fixed at the head, giving full particulars."[130]

Berks Cemetery Extension, where the Ploegsteert Memorial is sited, was opened in June 1916 and continued to be used up to September 1917. The original cemetery contained the graves of 295 British soldiers, 51 Australians, 45 New Zealanders and three Canadians.

Amongst the men buried in the original cemetery was **26068 Rifleman Ralph Joseph Dixon**, who served with the 4th Battalion, 3rd New Zealand Rifle Brigade, who was killed on 23 February 1917. His death was reported in The Poverty Bay Herald on 14 March:

"Rifleman Ralph Joseph Dixon, who was reported killed in action in France (sic), was the son of Mr J. S. Dixon, an employee of the Gear Company at Petone. Rifleman Dixon, who went away with the 17th Reinforcements, was for some time a guard on Somes Island. He had a bright disposition, and was a great favourite among his many friends."

The son of Joseph and Hebe Dixon, of Woolston near Christchurch, was aged 23 when he died and is buried in Plot I, Row L, Grave 19.

Further remains were concentrated at the cemetery in 1930 on the closure of Rosenburg Chateau Cemetery and Extension, and from smaller isolated burials and graves from the surrounding area. The cemetery then contained a total of 877 graves, the earliest dated burials being those of three soldiers of the 2nd Battalion, The Seaforth Highlanders who were killed on 30 November 1914 – St Andrew's Day – while holding positions near the Douve south of Messines. These men had originally been interred at Rosenburg Chateau Cemetery.

---

[130] Reading Observer, 8 May 1915.

On 25 November 1914 three soldiers of No. 1 Company of the 1/1ˢᵗ Battalion, The Honourable Artillery Company (Territorial Force), were killed while in the front line near Wulverghem undergoing "trench instruction" with 8ᵗʰ Brigade of 3ʳᵈ Division. Their deaths were reported in The Western Daily Press on 2 December:

"Official information has been received at the headquarters of the Honourable Artillery Company that No. 1 Company was in action on the 25ᵗʰ ult. and that three were killed. They were Sergt. A. E. Thomas, Pte. A. V. Jones, and Pte. C. A. Webster. There were no other casualties."

275 Sergeant Albert Edward Thomas was born at Gravesend in 1873 and was the son of George and Elizabeth Thomas, Albert had attested for Infantry of The Honourable Artillery Company at Armoury House on 14 December 1908, and at the time of his enlistment lived at 19 Prince of Wales Mansions in Battersea Park and held the post of Secretary at the Royal Free Hospital. Thomas was appointed a Lance-Corporal on 17 March 1910 and promoted Corporal and appointed Lance-Sergeant on 27 November 1911. He re-engaged, on the expiration of his four years' period of service, on 14 December 1912. Embodied at the outbreak of the war, Thomas at that time employed as Secretary to the Hampstead General Hospital. He was promoted to Sergeant on 12 August 1914 and signed the Imperial Service Obligation, volunteering to serve overseas, at Armoury House on 24 August. Sergeant Thomas disembarked at St Nazaire with the 1/1ˢᵗ H.A.C. on 20 September.

His personal effects were returned to his mother, who lived 30 Parliament Hill Mansions on Highgate Road, in 1915. These included her son's identity disc, a whistle, a glasses case, which contained his spectacles, a knife, letters, maps, news cuttings and a photograph, a dictionary, notebook and one unopened parcel. He also had a considerable amount of French currency in his possession, which amounted to 90 Francs in notes and gold, as well as coins valued at 7½d. Sergeant Thomas also had gold sovereigns to the value of £1.10.0d. with him at the time of his death.

Sergeant Thomas was originally buried at in the garden of a farmhouse - "Frenchman's Farm" - near Wulverghem. In October 1919, his remains were exhumed by men of 68ᵗʰ Labour Company and identified by his chevrons. He was reinterred at Wulverghem-Lindenhoek Road Military Cemetery: Plot V, Row E, Grave 28. On 23 January 1920, the Infantry Record Office at 4 London Wall Buildings E.C. sent notification that his remains had been reburied to his mother, Elizabeth.

The cemetery register records that his widowed mother later lived with his sister Marian at 16 Salcombe Gardens on Clapham Common.

1519 Private Albert Victor Jones was born at Minafon and both his late father and his mother, Jane Margaret Jones, were Justices of the Peace in Carnavon. He had been educated at The Leys School, where he served as a member of the Officer Training Corps, and King's College, Cambridge. Jones was aged 27 years and two months when he attested for the Honourable Artillery Company at Armoury House on 21 August 1914, and arrived in France with the 1/1ˢᵗ H.A.C. on 20 September.

An obituary for Private Jones was published in The Liverpool Daily Journal on 3 December 1914:

WELSH SOLICITOR KILLED IN ACTION.

CARNARVON FAMILY BEREAVED.

"Mrs Jones, of Minafon, Carnavon, yesterday received particulars of the death at the front of their youngest son, Mr Albert Victor Jones, who was serving with the Honourable Artillery Company. The news was contained in a letter sent by two of his companions, who said that Mr Jones was shot through the heart. He was buried where he fell.

Mr Jones was a solicitor by profession, and was with a firm of solicitors in London when he joined the Honourable Artillery Company as a private. An M.A. and LL.B. of Cambridge, he had a promising career ahead of him, and his untimely death at the age of twenty-seven has caused deep sorrow at Carnarvon, where his family are well known. He was the brother of Mr W. S. Jones, solicitor, and Mr E. W. Jones, of Carnarvon, both of whom are prominent figures in yachting circles. The late Mr John Jones, his father, was Mayor of the town in the Jubilee year, and was presented with a silver cradle to commemorate the birth of his youngest son, now deceased. As late as Monday Mrs Jones received a letter from her son describing how he had been twice in the trenches. That letter was written on the 23ʳᵈ ultimo, and the writer killed on the 25ᵗʰ."

Private Jones's remains were not identified after the war, although he too was probably buried at "Frenchman's Farm." He is commemorated on Panel 1 of the Ploegsteert Memorial, the only member of the Honourable Artillery Company to be commemorated there.

1253 Private Colin Ailesbury Webster was born at Bayswater on 13 May 1894 and was the only son of Mr Henry Webster and Mrs Kate Minnie Webster, who lived at 21 Kingsley Avenue in West Ealing. Baptised at All Saints' Church in Notting Hill on 1 July 1896, Colin attended Acton County School and on leaving was employed as a clerk by Messrs. Leeming Bros. at the Stock Exchange in London. He had joined the Honourable Artillery Company at Armoury House on 8 August 1914 and volunteered for "Imperial Service" on 22 August. Private Webster landed in France on 20 September.

A Sergeant of No. 1 Company later wrote to Private Webster's parents to express his condolences on their son's death:

"He had been a thoroughly good soldier throughout, and I can assure you we all (No. 1 Coy.) lament his loss."[131]

Private Webster's Princess Mary's Christmas Gift, which had been issued posthumously, was sent to his parents, and Colin's father wrote on 8 February 1915 to the Territorial Force Record Office at 4 London Wall to acknowledge that it had been received.

His personal effects were sent to his parents on 25 February 1915, and comprised: one tin opener, two spoons, one fork, one folding knife,fork and spoon, one jack knife, a cigarette case, a bracelet, a set of keys, one letter, a letter case which contained further correspondence and a diary, a copy of the Otter Swimming Club Year Book and Diary and his purse, which contained French and British currency to the value of £1.0.6d.

Private Webster was also originally buried at "Frenchman's Farm", and the wooden cross originally erected over his grave read:

"In Loving Memory of 1253 Pte. Colin Webster H.A.C., Killed in Action 25/11/14."

His father, Henry, was sent his son's 1914 Star on 27 October 1919, and the clasp was issued in March 1920. Webster's British War Medal and Victory Medal were received by him on 30 January 1922. The remains of Private Webster were also moved to Wulverghem-Lindenhoek Road Military Cemetery in October 1919 and reburied at Plot IV, Row F, Grave 4. The

---

[131] De Ruvigny's Roll of Honour, Volume 1 p.372.

register for the cemetery records that his parents lived at "The Dee," Palace Gardens in Clacton-on-Sea after the war.

1608 Private David Flockhart
6ᵗʰ Battalion attached 1/8ᵗʰ Battalion, The Royal Scots (Lothian Regiment) (Territorial Force)

Contrary to widely-held perceptions that an informal truce was universally observed along the Western Front on Christmas Day 1914, Private David Flockhart was one of the British soldiers who was killed that day and is commemorated on Panel 1 of the Ploegsteert Memorial.

Originally a member of the 6ᵗʰ Battalion, Private Flockhart had transferred to the 1/8ᵗʰ Battalion in order to bring that battalion up to strength prior to its departure for the front. The 1/8ᵗʰ Royal Scots had landed at Le Havre on 5 November 1914, and was place under the command of 22ⁿᵈ Brigade of 7ᵗʰ Division six days later. Private Flockhart's battalion had returned to the front at Touquet on Christmas Eve and on the following morning he was shot and killed by a German sniper.

His death was reported in The Edinburgh Evening News on 17 February 1915:

"Private David Flockhart, 6ᵗʰ Royal Scots, was killed in action on 25ᵗʰ December in France. He belonged to Gorebridge, and resided with his parents at 151 North High Street, Fisherrow, Musselburgh, and worked as a pony driver in No. 12 pit, Niddrie and Benhar Coal Company. He was 17 years of age."

David Flockhart is recorded by the Commonwealth War Graves Commission as being aged 18 when he was killed, and the register for the memorial states that he was the son of Mrs Eliza Flockhart, who lived at 69A Hercusloan in Musselburgh after the war.

18 September 1914 - "In a Cornfield Somewhere in Froggy-Land"

"Just to let you know I am quite well up to the present. I cannot tell you where we are, as I do not know, only that we are in a trench with a little time to ourselves, so had to take this opportunity to write. I must tell you we get plenty of food to fight on, not a six course dinner, but plenty of good, substantial food. We have only one thing that we grumble about. We cannot get a smoke of any kind, only tea leaves, so when you write you might put a few woodbines in the letter, you know, just to save the life of an old pal. I must tell you a big battle has been going on for six days now, and our boys are doing well. Cannot write more now as we are moving further up."[132]

L/7149 Private George Barranger
No. 6 Platoon, "B" Company, 1ˢᵗ Battalion, The Buffs
(East Kent Regiment)

George Barranger was born at Sittingbourne on 5 February 1884, the son of George and Emma Barranger, and attested for the Buffs at Canterbury on 5 February 1903, his 19th birthday. At the time of his enlistment he was employed as a butcher. On completing his training at the Regimental Depot, Private Barranger was posted to the 2nd Battalion on 22 May 1903 and while stationed at Dover was found drunk in town on the night of 5 February 1904 and was admonished by his platoon commander, Second-Lieutenant Crookenden. He was transferred to the Section B Army Reserve on 12 April 1906

George married Alice Mabel Allen in 1908 and their son, Leslie Norman George, was born on 18 September 1909. He is recorded in the 1911 Census as living with his wife, Alice, and their son at 25 Albert Road in Folkestone and employed as a barman. The Barrangers lived at 1 Garage Plain Road in Folkestone at the outbreak of the war, and he was mobilised from the Reserve and posted to the 1ˢᵗ Battalion, then stationed at Fermoy. Private Barranger disembarked at St Nazaire on 9 September and at the time he wrote his letter the 1ˢᵗ Buffs were moving up towards the front line on the Aisne.

---

[132] Folkestone, Hythe, Sandgate and Cheriton Herald, 10 October 1914. Private Barranger was writing to his sister, Mrs W. Burrows, who was married to an Inspector at the Central Station.

A month after he wrote the letter, Private Barranger was killed during the fighting at Radinghem. His death was reported in The Folkstone, Hythe, Sandgate and Cheriton Herald on 21 November 1914:

"Private G. Barranger, age 30, of the East Kent Regiment, "The Buffs," was killed in action in France on October 18th. When the war started he was timekeeper at the Grand, Folkestone. Formerly he assisted his sister (now Mrs Burrows, wife of Inspector J. M. Burrows, of the Central Station) at the Red Cow Inn. He leaves a wife and child, who live over the Grand garage on The Plain. It is stated in a letter conveying the King's sympathy that his grave is marked by a cross bearing his name and number. Pte. Barranger was know and esteemed by a large number of residents, particularly in the Foord district, and his death is keenly regretted. He had written home some cheery letters. In one he said: "The Germans are peppering us and we are peppering them. Soldiering is all right. I don't think I shall leave the Army again until I am compelled to."

Alice and Leslie Barranger were living at 15 Garden Road in Folkestone when his widow was awarded a pension of 15s. a week for herself and their son with effect of 17 May 1915. She later received the personal effects that were recovered from Private Barranger's body; letters, a photograph and an identity disc.

The location of Private Barranger's grave could not be found after the war and he is commemorated on Panel 2 of the Ploegsteert Memorial. The register for the memorial records that his widow, Alice, had remarried and lived at 25 Alma Road in Ramsgate after the war.

6920 Private James Nuttall
1ˢᵗ Battalion, The North Staffordshire Regiment

At 10.30 p.m. on 21 October 1914 a determined German assault managed to break through the 3ʳᵈ Battalion, The Rifle Brigade on the left flank of the 1ˢᵗ North Staffords, who were holding positions at Rue du Bois, dug in astride the road between Armentieres and Lille. "B" Company, commanded by Captain George Leman, also came into contact with a detachment of German infantry and both sides clashed. The enemy attack was beaten off after a fierce hand-to-hand fight with rifles, bayonets and boots being used vigorously.

An anonymous Non-Commissioned Officer who served with "D" Company of the 1ˢᵗ North Staffords recounted the fighting in his diary:

"Under shell fire the whole day, and our men's trenches and rifles blown to pieces several times. Good few casualties in the battalion. Germans broke through at one point, but were all killed, including two officers. A German officer in this break made a cut at one of our men with a sword, and the man countered with a bayonet. They were both picked up dead close together – a fatal blow on both sides. The sword, which is evidently an heirloom and encrusted with jewels, will grace our officers' mess some day."[133]

The soldier who was killed by the German officer was **6920 Private James Nuttall**, a Reservist from Uttoxeter. He was employed as a striker when he attested for The North Staffordshire Regiment at Uttoxeter on 10 June 1903, and had served in India with the 2ⁿᵈ Battalion. On his transfer to the Reserve, he returned to the town and lived with his sister in Eaton Street and was employed at the Leighton Iron Works. James also played football for several local sides, having previously been a member of the 2ⁿᵈ North Staffords' team while stationed in India.

The death of Private Nuttall was also mentioned by a comrade, **8290 Private James Joseph Dainty**, in an interview that he gave to the local press on returning home on leave after being wounded:

"Dainty had seen war before in India, but it was nothing to this. He said one of his chums in the regiment, who had been with him in India, was a man named Nuttall of Uttoxeter. One day, the Germans attacked and were driven back by a bayonet charge. Nuttall drove his bayonet into a German officer, who made a slashing cut with his sword and cut Nuttall's head in two. The two men fell dead together."[134]

The sword that had killed Nuttall was picked up from the battlefield, and was later put on display in the Officer's Mess of the 1ˢᵗ Battalion after the war. The following description was placed with the sword:

---

[133] Liverpool Daily Post, 17 December 1914.
[134] Staffordshire Weekly Sentinel, 5 December 1914. Born in 1882 at Stafford, James Dainty had served with the 2ⁿᵈ Battalion in India but his period of engagement had expired prior to the outbreak of the war. However, on 5 August 1914, he attested for the 3ʳᵈ (Special Reserve) Battalion and was posted to the 1ˢᵗ North Staffords, arriving in France on 12 September. Private Dainty was discharged on 17 January 1916 and was later issued with a Silver War Badge.

"This sword belonged to an officer of a Saxon Regiment, who was killed on 21ˢᵗ October, 1914, in front of Chapelle d'Armentieres, north of the Armentieres-Lille Road.

The trenches on our left had been lost, and, during the night our line was heavily attacked, and a considerable number of Germans working round our flanks attempted to surround the left sentry group of our outpost line. This was held by a section of "B" Company.

The men fought magnificently, and drove the enemy off, killing 14 of them, and the Saxon Officer who led the charge on the trench was bayoneted in the throat by No. 6920 Private Nuttall, but at the same time he cut down Private Nuttall with his sword. This is a very fine example of the excellent state of discipline in the Regiment, and the determination of all ranks to hold their positions at all costs."[135]

Private Nuttall's sister received a letter informing her that he had been buried close to where he was killed, but his remains were not located after the war. James Nuttall is therefore commemorated on Panel 8 of the Ploegsteert Memorial and is also remembered on the war memorial at Uttoxeter.

Commemorated on the same panel as Nuttall is **7032 Private Alfred Ward**, who was a 28 year-old reservist from Erdington in Birmingham. Ward had joined the North Staffords on 12 November 1903 and was working as a labourer at the time of his attestation. Mobilised on the declaration of war, he served with "D" Company of the 1ˢᵗ Battalion.

Before dawn of 13 October 1914, North Staffords received orders to advance towards Strazeele towards the Germans. Private Ward and the rest of "D" Company moved forward towards Merris, and soon came under fire. The unidentified Non-Commissioned Officer of "D" Company recalled the clash in his diary:

"We are advance guard company, and come under shell fire at 7.30 a.m. three miles out of Hazebrouck. Lost Private Ward about two yards in front of me – struck dead by a shell. He had just lighted a cigarette, and said it might be his last. The whole road was covered by shell fire."[136]

---

[135] The sword is now on display at The Staffordshire Regiment Museum at Whittington Barracks, near Lichfield.
[136] Liverpool Daily Post, 17 December 1914.

Soldiers of the 2ⁿᵈ Battalion, The Argyll and Sutherland Highlanders, photographed outside their billets at Boulogne shortly after disembarking in August 1914.

The fate of two soldiers who were serving with the 2nd Battalion, The Argyll and Sutherland Highlanders when they were reported as missing on 10 November 1914, following fighting between the eastern edge of Ploegsteert Wood and the St Yves-Le Gheer Road, was confirmed when their bodies were found on Christmas Day during the truce observed between British and German troops.

1174 Sergeant Alexander Park, who was aged 30 when he died, had served in India for nine years before the war and had taken part in the Abor Expedition in 1911. Park had only been transferred to the Reserve a matter of weeks when he was mobilised on the outbreak of the war, and embarked for France on 10 August 1914 among the first troops of the British Expeditionary Force to sail for the continent.

Confirmation that Sergeant Park had been killed on 10 November was reported in The Aberdeen Weekly Journal on 22 January 1915:

"Mr George Park, mason, Bridge Street, Strichen, received information yesterday that his son, Sergeant Alexander Park, Argyll and Sutherland Highlanders, had been killed in action, and had been buried on Christmas Day. Beyond those facts no information was vouchsafed as to when or where he met his death. Early in December, Sergeant Park was reported by the War Office as wounded and missing, and nothing further had been heard of him until yesterday, when a post-card conveying the intelligence of his death was received from the captain of his company.

His death is rendered all the more pathetic from the fact that after spending several years on service in India, he had been home for only some four weeks when he was recalled to the colours, and set out with the Expeditionary Force for France. Mr and Mrs Park and family will have the sympathy of the community in the loss they have sustained, coming as it has done after a long spell of anxiety as to Sergeant Park's welfare."

The clasp for Sergeant Park's 1914 Star was issued to his next-of-kin on 17 November 1920.

9475 Private James Struthers was also a Reservist and had sailed for France on 10 August 1914. His body was recovered on Christmas Day and the circumstances of its discovery were recounted in an article published in The Scotsman on 5 January 1915:

"Mr and Mrs William Struthers, 7 Thimble Street, Renton, have received news of the death of their son, Private James Struthers, of the 2nd Argyll and Sutherland Highlanders. Private Struthers, who was a Reservist, was posted as missing by the War Office authorities on 10th November last. The last letter received from him by his parents was dated the 31st October. Information had been received from other sources from the front that he had been killed, but definite news has now been received by his parents. The letter was sent from Corporal R. Hanks, of the 1st Somerset Light Infantry, who stated that as they were burying the dead on Christmas Day, they found a postcard addressed to Mr William Struthers, 7 Thimble Street, Renton, on the body of one of the Highlanders they interred on the battlefield. As the postcard was addressed and ready for posting he thought it his duty to forward the same to Struthers' parents, so that their minds could be set to rest regarding their son."

The clasp for Private Struthers' 1914 Star was issued to his parents on 6 December 1920.

The remains of Sergeant Park and Private Struthers were not identified after the war and they are both commemorated on the Ploegsteert Memorial, Park on Panel 9 and Struthers on Panel 10.

Just above the carved name of Private Struthers is that of **9080 Private John Reilly**, who was also killed on 10 November 1914. Born at Kells in County Meath, he was living in Glasgow when he joined the Argylls at Paisley in December 1902. Reilly embarked for France with the 2nd Battalion on 10 August 1914 and landed at Boulogne. In a letter written to a friend at Lurgan in County Armagh he described his experiences during the Battle of Le Cateau on 26 August:

"I suppose you have read all about it – Le Cateau. When I saw all the troops, besides cavalry and artillery, I thought to myself, "It's victory for us this morning," but when we got split up you could only see your own brigade, then only your own regiment, and down till it came to companies. We then advanced in artillery formation to what proved a death trap, the Germans shelling us for all they were worth. We broke up into sections and advanced, five paces distant at the double, in short rushes. I had got down after one of the rushes, and as three men of the Welsh Fusiliers passed about five yards from me with a machine gun on a cart drawn by two horses, as shell came along and, striking our embankment, killed one of the horses. We still kept advancing till we came into their rifle and machine gun range. They were dropping on the right, left, front, and back of me. I have got a bullet which lodged in my pack, and which I did not find till two days after. I am keeping it as a souvenir. We lost seven officers and about 350 men in that battle. Of course, as you are aware, our army had to retire – we were outnumbered by thousands."[187]

---

[187] Belfast Newsletter, 2 November 1914.

23 December 1914

"Fancy, only two days to Christmas. We should not know much about it but for the parcels of nice things we are getting from our loved ones at home. The mail bags are full every day, and there is quite a lot of excitement when the contents are distributed. Last Saturday, Dec. 19th, we made an attack on the Germans, and drove them out of their forward trenches. I think we must have driven them back 300 yards. Of course, that is a lot now, as the ground is in such an awful state, up to your knees in mud. The Germans must have lost heavily, as our artillery gave them a good doing before we advanced. They never showed much resistance. They have left a terrible lot of dead lying about. One German came in and gave himself up, bringing in one of our wounded. I think he deserves the Iron Cross. I shall have to speak to the Kaiser about him. What do you think of soldiers' wives having to be put under police supervision? I don't think much of it, nor does any married man out here."[138]

7553 Rifleman Arthur Arnold
1ˢ Battalion, The Rifle Brigade

---

[138] Cambridge Independent Press, 8 January 1915. Rifleman Arnold had arrived in France with his battalion on 26 August 1914. He was issued with the clasp and roses for his 1914 Star on 17 December 1920.

A Reservist serving with the 1ˢᵗ Battalion, Rifleman Arnold wrote to his wife in Royston and described the aftermath of his battalion's attack on the eastern edge of Ploegsteert Wood four days previously.

On 19 December 1914, 11ᵗʰ Brigade of 4ᵗʰ Division made an attack on a German position known as The Birdcage. After a preliminary bombardment, the assault began at 2.30 in the afternoon. The first objective of the 1ˢᵗ Battalion, The Rifle Brigade was to capture "German House", which was achieved relatively quickly, and troops of "I" Company reached their second target, "Second House." However, supporting troops were unable to reach the forward company due to being hit by friendly fire from their own artillery. The surviving Riflemen withdrew but German House was held and occupied. The 1ˢᵗ Battalion, The Rifle Brigade lost five Officers and 65 Other Ranks killed, wounded and missing.

Among those Riflemen killed during the attack was **292 Rifleman David Jones**. The circumstances in which he died, and an extract from a letter recovered from his body during the brief truce on Christmas Day, were reported in The Western Mail on 28 December 1914:

"Intimation has been received at Carmarthen that Corporal (sic) David Jones, of the 1ˢᵗ Rifle Brigade, son of Mr John Jones, blacksmith at the Towyn Works, Carmarthen, has been killed in action in France (sic). No official notification has yet been received from the War Office, but the news of Corporal Jones's death was conveyed to the Rev. Griffith Thomas, vicar of St David's Carmarthen, in a communication from Quartermaster-sergeant A. Clifford, of the 1ˢᵗ Rifle Brigade, who enclosed an uncompleted letter addressed to the vicar which was found in one of Corporal Jones's pockets. "Corporal Jones," says the quartermaster-sergeant, "was killed on the 19ᵗʰ inst. He died bravely fighting the enemy."

The unfinished missive, dated December 17, which was found on Corporal Jones, reads as follows:-

"Reverend sir, – Just a few words to let you know that I am getting along all right and in good health. I often wish I was back in the old place again, but before we can return we have some work to do – " Here the letter ends abruptly."

Aged 29 when he died, Rifleman Jones was the son of John and Frances Jones, who lived at 18 Magazine Row in Carmarthen. He is buried at Rifle House Cemetery: Plot IV, Row G. Grave 9.

The death of **2961 Serjeant Douglas James Muddle** was reported in The Sussex Agricultural Express on New Years' Day 1915:

BUXTED SOLDIERS DIES AT HIS POST.

"War, in its deadly toll of human lives, has claimed yet another young, promising and efficient soldier from the Uckfield district, one whose future, had he not met with an untimely end, would, without doubt, have been for the weal of himself and fellow men.

It was on Tuesday that the news of the death of Sergeant D. J. Muddle was received by his parents, Mr and Mrs C. Muddle, of The Ramblers, Buxted, and caused desolation in their family circle, as well as a feeling of sorrow, deep and profound in the district where the family have for many years resided.

Sergt. Muddle was born in the parish and received the early part of his education at the Buxted schools, where, as the result of that industry and attention to duty that characterised his after life, he won a scholarship at the Uckfield Grammar School, where he completed his scholastic studies.

On leaving school he took up the duties of rural postman, which he faithfully performed up to the time of his entering the army, a little over seven years ago, when he joined the Rifle Brigade. As those who knew him had expected he applied himself closely to his duties and gradually rose in position, being made a sergeant about two years ago. Mr Muddle, senior, is a local preacher in the Wesleyan connection, and the home influence was so borne on the young man that he, like his father, took an active interest in supporting the cause. He had even passed one of the exams necessary to qualify him to become a local preacher, the examiner being the Rev. J. Burrows, who was at the time superintendent of the Lewes circuit.

Whenever he could do so, whilst quartered at Colchester Barracks, he walked 2½ miles on Sundays to help in the Sunday School of a small and struggling chapel. He was the third son of Mr and Mrs Muddle, and was 24 years of age; he was engaged to be married to Miss Mina Mason, of Dublin, and it was from his fiancee that the sad news was sent to Buxted, she having received it from a friend of the dead soldier. He had been expecting to be home for 10 days about Christmas time, but this leave was postponed until the end of January.

COMRADES' APPRECIATION.

In a letter which Q.M. Sergt. Sherwood wrote to Miss Mason, he said that Sergt. Muddle was killed in action on the 19th December, and in expressing his persinal regret at his loss, said that he had always found him very straightforward, living a righteous life: he was quite satisfied by years of experience of him that he had never done any man in the army any injury.

HIS LAST LETTER.

It was in December that Sergt. Muddle wrote what proved to be his last letter to his parents. He wrote quite cheerfully and said he had a splendid Christmas mail, which included quite a lot of parcels, and Christmas puddings, etc. He asked that his thanks might be conveyed to all who had thought of him. He said that they were then billeted in a school, where they stayed three days at a time. "It is nice to be where it is warm and to get a wash and brush up," he said, "the wet and cold make the trenches not too desirable. There is nothing doing where we are, but on the left they are a bit busy."

Two days later he died a soldier's death."

Serjeant Muddle's body was recovered from the battlefield by his comrades and he is buried at Rifle House Cemetery: Plot IV, Row H, Grave 2.

The death in action of **5449 Rifleman William Charles Hewitt** was reported in The Leamington Spa Courier on 8 January 1915:

"News was received on Saturday that Private William Hewitt, son of Mr and Mrs H. Hewitt, of Mill End, had been killed in action. The deceased was only 19 years of age, and enlisted in the 1ˢᵗ Battalion Rifle Brigade in March, 1914 (after a years' service in the Territorials), as his particular friend, Harry Cox, of Henry Street – also an ex-Territorial – was already in that Battalion. Cox has now bee promoted corporal, and he it was who sent the sad news to Private Hewitt's parents. Deceased went to the Front early in October, and was in the same company as Corporal Cox, so that although official notice has not yet been received, there appears, unfortunately, no possibility of better news. Private Hewitt had written home on Christmas Eve, when he said:-

"I am going on well, and am hoping to come home for good, for I don't think the war will last long. The weather has been terrible; hardly a day passes but what it rains. By what I hear and from the way the Germans have been beaten around here I do not think the war can last long."

Deceased often referred to the pleasure he had experienced in having another Kenilworth man in his Company, and also in finding that Pte. Arthur Drane and Pte. Fred Puffett belonging to the Rifle Brigade, although he had only occasionally met these latter soldiers."

Another report regarding the death of Rifleman Hewitt was printed in The Coventry Herald, also on 8 January 1915:

"The parents of Rifleman W. Hewitt, of Kenilworth, have just learned that he has been killed in action. A friend of Rifleman Hewitt – Corporal Harry Cox – wrote home to his own mother asking her to inform Mr and Mrs Hewitt that their son had lost his life in an action in which both were taking part. Beyond that no news has been received, and, of course, it is some time before the official notification comes through the War Office.

Rifleman Hewitt was only nineteen years old, and was well-known locally, being a native of Kenilworth. For many years he worked in the town as an errand boy, but the last place at which he was employed was the Dunlop Company at Coventry. He was a member of the Rifle Brigade when war was declared, having joined that branch of the Service in March. For twelve months previous to that he was attached to the Territorials.

The letters he sent home contained very little news relating to the war. He did not even let his parents know he was in the trenches until late in November, whereas he had gone into them at the very beginning of October. Some time ago, however, he expressed a desire that the war would soon end so that he could come home again."

The son of Harry and Sarah Georgina Hewitt, who lived at 23 Hyde Road in Kenilworth after the war, William Hewitt is commemorated on Panel 10 of the Ploegsteert Memorial. He is recorded by the Commonwealth War Graves Commission as being aged 18 when he was killed.

Ploegsteert Wood – December 1914

"We are right in it – right in the thick of it! No longer are the L.R.B.s "Saturday-Night Soldiers," nor are they the spick-and-span Battalion known in London. You ought to see us – muddy from head to heel, dirty, unshaven faces, grimy hands, rusty rifles (barring the action and bore), shruken and torn equipment, rusty swords, very weary at times, yet hard and hungry men, tried and found fit. That's the L.R.B.! My first experience of war was rather a trying one. Half our Battalion was ordered to go up and relieve some of the Somerset Light Infantry, who had been having a rotten time. We crept to our trenches under screen of darkness, with beating hearts. There was no need to tell the boys to keep down, as the German snipers were sending their whistling birds flying about us. We all reached our places quite safely, however, and flung ourselves down on the straw in the trench. This was on the night of November 20th-21st. The ground was hard with frost, and covered with snow. When morning broke and I could look round, I found I was in a shallow trench, with two others sharing a "booby-hutch."

We soon (had) a fire going, made tea, and fried some bacon, and then we made a discovery. We were less than 200 yards from the German trenches. Swish! Down went my head under cover. During Saturday things were fairly quiet, and we had a good time sniping at the enemy. That evening our party was swelled by a special reserve man of the S.L.I. Poor chap! He didn't stay long! While we were having breakfast the next morning, Sunday, we had four doses of shrapnel right over our "hutch." The first three upset my nerves a bit, and the fourth killed one of "ours" on my right, and mortally wounded the S.L.I. on my left. He was leaning on my legs, and got it in the shoulder. I was very glad to be relieved that night. The trench was enfiladed from the left and was fired on from front and rear. We spent the next night in reserve trenches in a wood; and that same wood has been the scene of many hours work. The next three nights we spent in a ruined village, the cloak room floor of the school being my bed, but more of this anon. On Thursday night we returned to the same trench, but it was different then, and the frost had gone, and there were about 18 inches of water in the bottom. In this some enterprising soldier had placed some wooden boxes with straw wattles over them. Everywhere was mud, and fires were impossible, so we had cold water and cold "grub." Things were fairly quiet, but for sniping in our immediate neighbourhood for a while, but got lively later on, and we "stood to" with swords fixed for a while, but nothing happened. That's wrong. The rain happened, and the tide in the trench rose, and we lay in muddy water for 36 hours. Get rid of it we couldn't, because the head cover we had didn't stop the bullets. As soon as we were given some sand bags to make head cover, we went out to the back of the trench and got them filled safely, and put the bags in place. About 10.30 the bank fell in, and nearly buried some of us, and it was all slimy and sticky in the water. We did our best with it, but I was not sorry to return to ‑‑‑‑‑‑‑‑ that night.

Three days in the trenches on end is quite enough at a time. We crawled back through about ten inches of mud, very weary and tired, to the best billet I, personally, have struck up to now. We sleep comfortable, although we are well within shell fire range. A few minutes spent here would show you the horrors of war which no words of mine can describe. Only those who have seen it can realise the desolation of a town after a bombardment, or what war means to the country people. Opposite here is what was once a beautiful church. Now there is no porch or doorway, very little roof, and perforated walls with gaping holes. A shell has smashed the clock in the tower. The interior is chaos. Only the chancel has escaped. Money will never restore this poor country to its condition in July last. A soldier should not think of these things, I suppose, but then I'm not a professional soldier, so perhaps I may be excused. The people are already returning here to their ruined homes, although we may receive a shell at any moment. A few people still work in the fields in a half-hearted way. Conditions of life here, as far as we are concerned, are rather strange. Very rarely are we able to take our boots off or get a good wash. The C.O. got the engine of the brewery (almost a ruin) going this week, and most of us got a bath. That was the first time I had my clothes off since leaving Crowborough. I also put on clean clothes, and am trying to get the others washed. I hope we don't move off before they come back, as I should not like to lose them, even though the extra weight tells. We are all being issued with fur coats, which are of various hues, and are worn under the overcoat. They will be a "welcome nuisance," I expect, for it is cold here at times. I got my feet numbed with cold over a week ago, and they are still very painful. I expect I have developed chilblains on my toes. If I write much more, the Censor may get tired of the letter, and destroy it!

Best wishes to all."

A photograph of the brewery at Ploegsteert, taken in January 1915, where the brewing vats were used as rudimentary baths by the troops.

The unidentified writer of the letter served with the 1/5th (City of London) Battalion, The London Regiment (London Rifle Brigade) (Territorial Force), which had arrived at Le Havre on 5 November 1914. On 17 November, the L.R.B. came under the command of 11th Brigade of 4th Division, and served in positions in Ploegsteert Wood. The letter was published in The Sussex Express, Surrey Standard and Kent Mail on 8 January 1915.

The reference made to "swords" instead of bayonets in the letter is a peculiarity of Rifle regiments. This dates from the Napoleonic period, when Rifle Corps, such as the 95th Rifles and 5th Battalion, 60th (Royal American) Regiment of Foot were issued with sword-bayonets for their Baker and Brunswick Rifles. This tradition continues in the modern regiment – The Rifles. It was also at this time that the London Rifle Brigade gained the nicknames, such as "London Fatigue Party" or "Fatigue Fifth," based on their work on the positions in Ploegsteert Wood.

Steenwerck - 11 April 1915

"Well, at last we have been in the trenches and had our baptism of fire. We came out of action last night at 9 o'clock and went in at 7 o'clock on Friday night. I have read all about the fighting in the war and life in the trenches, its dangers, etc., but now I have seen and realised it. I have had 24 hours of it, and seen so much of what we heard about. We advanced up to the trenches just as it was getting dusk, and the nearer we got the more bullets came whistling over. It was very dangerous work getting into the trenches. Our platoon was put into a trench with some Somerset Light Infantry – Regulars, of course, but fine fellows, Britons every one. Our trench was in one place only 85 yards from the German line, and at the most 250 yards. It is most exciting, and you have got to be on the qui vive all the time. All our company came through safely as far as I know at present. So far there has been two casualties in the Battalion – two fellows in C Company being wounded. My word you have got to keep your head down. People say the Germans are bad shots, but let them come out and see for themselves. They do not miss anything; just put anything on top of the trench and there is a bullet ploughing its way over in no time. There is hardly any sleep to be obtained, and during our stay in the trenches it rained smartly at times. You would be surprised how much fighting is done at night than in the day. I am glad to say I came through it quite safely. I had a good many shots at the Germans... My idea of trench life is not so bad. Of course it isn't very pleasant when the Germans start dropping shells into your line and the shrapnel begins to fly. At first we all felt a bit nervy, but after the first half hour I got quite used to it."[189]

2653 Private Ernest Watts
"D" Company of the 1/5th Battalion, The Gloucestershire Regiment (Territorial Force)

Private Watts was describing to his parents, who lived at 11 Dean's Walk in Gloucester, his first experience of trench warfare under the supervision of soldiers of the 1st Somersetshire Light Infantry in their positions at Ploegsteert Wood. Watts had disembarked at Boulogne with the 1/5th Glosters on 29 March 1915 and by the end of the war had been appointed a Lance-Corporal. He was disembodied on 29 April 1919 on his demobilisation.

---

[189] Gloucester Journal, 17 April 1915.

Ploegsteert Wood – August 1915

"I am quite well at present, but have just had a very narrow escape from death by the bursting of a shell. It happened on Wednesday morning, we had just come out of the trenches the day before and were returning from the baths, which are about three miles distant, when our artillery opened fire at the enemy. The Huns replied, but the noise of our artillery deadened the sound of their guns, or we could have been down and probably should have avoided the full force of the shells. There were ten of us in the section returning from the baths, and as luck would have it I was a few yards in front of my comrades. The shell was a high explosive one, and out of the ten of us one was killed outright, three died soon afterwards, and now two of the other poor fellows have got to have their legs taken off, as they were smashed to pieces, and I am afraid the other four will never be able to come out here again. My poor mate was one of those who died shortly after being hit, and I shall miss him terribly, as we used to work together, and enlisted together, and have been comrades out here. I shall never forget the sight after the shell had hit our men, to stand and see it was awful, and I was the only one who escaped being hit.

It is very hot in the trenches now, we seem to get scarcely a breath of air at times, and we are practically fighting for our lives nearly every minute. It is not so nearly so rough for us when the Saxons are in the enemy trenches as when the Prussian Guards (sic) are there. We can tell when they change them. I was out on listening post the other night. We have to get about 25 yards in front of our trenches and we could hear them laughing and singing, then shortly afterwards we were blazing away at them and they at us. It does seem so funny. The way we get about here is really wonderful. There are so many different trenches, all leading in different directions that it is more like London for roads.

While fetching water this morning I came across a chap in the Norfolks, who told me he has seen Archie's grave, it is about ten minutes walk from here and when I come off sentry duty I shall try and find it. I shall have to go by way of the trenches as it would be unsafe to attempt it by road. It is most difficult to find the names of places here now, as there is not a single house standing anywhere near, and everywhere we go there are many graves.

We had a fine sight yesterday when five of our aeroplanes were up over the lines for nearly two hours, and the Huns were firing at them at least 1,000 rounds of ammunition at them and the way our airmen dodged the shells was marvellous. It seemed as though they must be hit, but not one of them were brought down. I think this is all now and if I have good luck I hope to see you all in September.

With love to all.

I remain, your loving son."[140]

12312 Private Fred Fisher
"B" Company, 7ᵗʰ (Service) Battalion, The Suffolk Regiment

Private Fisher had disembarked at Boulogne on 30 May 1915 and was writing his letter to his parents, Clarence Sidney and Rosa Fisher, who lived on High Street in Henlow. Fisher was later transferred to the Machine Gun Corps and was transferred to the Class Z Army Reserve on 25 June 1919.

The "Archie" mentioned in Private Fisher's letter was his brother, **5505 Rifleman Archie Sidney Fisher**, who served with "C" Company of the 1ˢᵗ Battalion, The Rifle Brigade.

Archie was reported to have been killed on 15 November 1914 (the Commonwealth War Graves Commission records the date 16 November), and his parents received notification from his company commander, Captain F. Blacker, that he had been buried with a number of other soldiers from the battalion at St Yves and their graves had been marked with engraved crosses. He had been drafted to France from the 5ᵗʰ (Special Reserve) Battalion on 9 October 1914.

Rifleman Fisher's grave was not located after the war and he is commemorated on Panel 10 of the Ploegsteert Memorial. The register for the memorial records that his parents later resided at Hungerfields, at Hurstpierpoint in Sussex.

---

[140] Biggleswade Chronicle, 3 September 1915.

Berks Cemetery Extension, 11 November 1994.

2059 Private Frederick George Cooper
1/6th Battalion, The Royal Warwickshire Regiment (Territorial Force)

George Cooper came from Birmingham and was the son of Arthur Cooper, who lived at 127 Holloway Head, and had joined the 6th Battalion, The Royal Warwickshire Regiment, at their Drill Hall at Thorp Street shortly before the war. In peacetime George was employed at Messrs. Hope Cementers in Lionel Street.

Having volunteered for service overseas, Cooper was posted to the 1/6th Battalion and arrived at Le Havre on 22 March 1915. He had been on active service barely a month when he was shot in the head by a sniper and killed on 21 April while on sentry duty in the line in the Douve Valley.

Aged 19 when he died, Private Cooper was originally buried at Rosenburg Chateau Cemetery: Plot III, Row A, Grave 6, but his body was moved in 1930 and reinterred in Berks Cemetery Extension at Ploegsteert: Plot III, Row C, Grave 15.

The grave of 1934 Private John Wilfred Huggonson,
1/4th Battalion, The Oxfordshire and Buckinghamshire Light Infantry (Territorial Force), taken in April 1993.

1934 Private John Wilfred Huggonson
1/4ᵗʰ Battalion, The Oxfordshire and Buckinghamshire Light Infantry (Territorial Force)

John Huggonson was born on 26 May 1892 and was the son of George and Isabella Huggonson, of Coulterthwaite at Leck, in Lancashire. He attended Queen Elizabeth Grammar School, was a member of the church choir at Leck and played cricket for the local team in Kirby Lonsdale. Huggonson later attended the Stoney Institute in Lancaster, where he studied manual teaching, before taking a post in Grantham. At the outbreak of the war he was attending Culham College in Oxford, where he was undergoing teacher training. John Huggonson had enlisted in the 4ᵗʰ Ox and Bucks shortly before the war and in August 1914 was embodied for service.

He volunteered for service overseas and was posted to "B" Company of the 1/4ᵗʰ Battalion, arriving at Boulogne with the battalion on 29 March 1915. Private Huggonson was shot and killed by a sniper on 18 June 1915 while serving in the line at Le Gheer, in front of Ploegsteert Wood. His platoon commander, Lieutenant Hugh Deacon, wrote to John's father shortly afterwards:

"Your son was shot just half-an-hour ago. He could have suffered no pain. We did everything that was possible and the doctor was there a few minutes after he was shot, but he never regained consciousness. I feel his loss doubly, as I always considered him one of the best men in my platoon."

Private Huggonson is buried in Hyde Park Corner (Royal Berks) Cemetery: Row B, Grave 15.

655 Bugler Steven William Smith, of the 1/4ᵗʰ Battalion, The Oxfordshire and Buckinghamshire Light Infantry (Territorial Force), came from Witney and was killed in action on 17 June 1915. The circumstances of his death were recorded in the battalion's War Diary:

"1 man was killed by a stray shot in the Subsidiary Line."

Aged 32 when he was killed, Bugler Smith was the son of Stephen and Sarah Smith and his widow, Gertrude Alice Smith, lived at 6 Corn Street in Witney. He is buried at Hyde Park Corner (Royal Berks) Cemetery: Row B, Grave 14.

The grave of 655 Bugler Steven William Smith,
1/4th Battalion, The Oxfordshire and Buckinghamshire Light Infantry (Territorial
Force), taken in April 1993.

The British Legion Great Pilgrimage - 90 Years On

V.C.s IN PILGRIMAGE TO BATTLEFIELDS.

Members of the British Legion, who are taking part in the great pilgrimage to the battlefield, at Victoria Station, London, yesterday. Left to right: Corporal Hutt, V.C., R.Q.M.S. Scott, Colonel J. Brown (Chairman of the Legion), Lady Edward Spencer-Churchill, and Corporal A. Wilcox, V.C.

The Royal British Legion's Great Pilgrimage 90, which took place between 5 and 9 August 2018, commemorated the ninetieth anniversary of the Great Pilgrimage undertaken between 5 and 9 August 1928.

The idea for the 1928 Pilgrimage had been conceived following the success of a smaller visit undertaken by 150 members of the British Legion in June 1927, during which the contingent had visited Ostend and Zeebrugge and had been present at the dedication of the Tyne Cot Memorial. The National Committee appointed a Pilgrimage Committee to undertake the planning and execution of the 1928 event and approached the President of the British Legion, Earl Haig, for his approval and support. Haig was initially wary that the proposal should not be for a "joy ride" across the old battlefields but that the event should be a meaningful pilgrimage. He also suggested that the 8 August should be the key date for commemoration, as it would mark the tenth anniversary of commencement of the Battle of Amiens, when the British Expeditionary Force, together with the Canadian Corps, Australian Corps and French troops, began their advance that would lead to the

Germans suing for peace in November. Britain and her Empire had declared war on Germany on 4 August 1914, so this too was considered in the planning. Earl Haig had intended to lead the British Legion as the Pilgrims marched through Ypres to the Ypres (Menin Gate) Memorial, but his death on 29 January 1928 meant that this did not happen. However his widow Lady Haig took a full part during the Pilgrimage in August.

Accommodation was sourced in towns and cities across France and Belgium, by liaising with the local authorities and ex-serviceman's groups, and the Félix Potin food distribution company was contracted by the Legion to provide 98,000 picnic boxes to feed the Pilgrims during the course of the Pilgrimage. Barracks, schools and even private houses would be used as billets for the Pilgrims, and the cost of the Pilgrimage was set at £4/5s per person, which equates to around £250 ninety years later. This sum was beyond the means of some of those whom the British Legion wished to see attend the Pilgrimage, and financial support was provided by donors to enable widows, mothers who had lost sons and disabled ex-servicemen to be able to participate. The itinerary was also set, with locations on the Somme, Vimy Ridge and Ypres being decided upon.

Registration for the Pilgrimage was opened in February 1928 and it was hoped that each branch of the British Legion could guarantee at least one or more Pilgrims would take part. The closing date was set at 1 March. When registration was completed some 11,000 people had registered to take part in the Pilgrimage, above the expectations of the organisers. It was also confirmed that H.R.H. The Prince of Wales would attend the Pilgrimage and take the salute when the British Legion marched through Ypres on 8 August.

In May, the Pilgrims who had registered received their travel documents, including a combined railway ticket and special passport, and a booklet which provided them with information regarding on the Pilgrimage and helpful advice. The section entitled "The Pilgrim Abroad" included the following hints:

"FRENCH MONEY for spending in FRANCE and BELGIAN MONEY for spending in BELGIUM."

"It is customary to bring soap with you. It will not normally be provided."

"The foreign police regard the preservation of order as their primary duty. It is not their function to assist all and sundry as in England. They should be treated with the greatest politeness and obeyed immediately."

"Cigars, cigarettes, tobacco, etc. of very good continental brands are cheap. English brands are seldom obtainable and very expensive."

The booklet also included the arrangements to transport 11,000 Pilgrims to their ports of embarkation for the continent. The Pilgrims would be divided into 22 Train Parties, each given a letter between "A" and "T", and were divided into geographical areas from all over Britain. The British Empire League contingent provided "A" Train Party, the British Legion Pilgrims travelling from the Irish Free State formed "H" Party, and three of the train parties were composed solely of ex-servicewomen and the Women's Section of the British Legion. Every Pilgrim was also issued with a badge bearing the letter of their train party, which was to be worn at all times. The booklet also recorded that each train party was allocated a town in France or Belgium that would serve as their base for the entirety of the Pilgrimage.

Typical of the contingents was that drawn from East Anglia, which formed Train Party "S" and consisted of 417 Pilgrims. The party was organised on military lines as follows:

In Command:　　　　　　Major H. Hussey M.B.E.
　　　　　　　　　　　　Secretary, East Anglia Area of the British Legion
　　　　　　　　　　　　Wilton House, 19 Christchurch Street, Ipswich

Headquarters Staff: Mr H. F. Curran, Mr H. J. Betts

No. 1 Company (Essex): Col. M. P. Hancock D.S.O, Mr A. Cowell, Mr H. A. Beatt.

No. 2 Company (Cambridge): Mr W. A. Diver, Mr H. P. Hodges, Mr J. Stimpson.

No. 3 Company (Suffolk): Major T. H. Bryan M.B.E., Captain C. H. O. French, Mr A. P. May.

No. 4 Company (Norfolk) Mr C. W. Jex, Mr H. L. Bond, Mr J. H. P. Lloyd.

Also included with the East Anglian Party were a Mr and Mrs Page, who had travelled from Australia to take part. Despite the formality of the arrangements, one Pilgrim reported that:

"We were all friends, and everything was everybody's. Class distinction – if one can describe it as such – fell away, and we are all 'pals' just as in the old days."[141]

The contingent assembled on 4 August at Parkeston, but the Party and Company Accommodation Officers had gone ahead to France in order to prepare for their arrival. The Pilgrims sailed from Harwich on board the L.N.E.R. Steamer "King George," but the crossing was rough and they were glad to reach the Mole at Zeebrugge the following morning. On their arrival the Pilgrims were greeted by an officer from the Belgian Army, and then disembarked and were served breakfast. After a guided tour of the Mole and the scene of the raid made on 23 April 1918 by the Royal Navy and Royal Marines, the Pilgrims then visited the Museum before the majority boarded a special train to take them to their billets at Armentieres. A contingent from the East Anglian party also made a visit to Bruges, where they represented the British Legion at the annual service in memory of Captain Charles Fryatt, a Merchant Navy Captain who had been executed by the Germans on 27 July 1916.

On arriving at Armentieres the Pilgrims were greeted by the Maire and representatives from the local ex-servicemen's organisations, before marching to the town's war memorial to lay a wreath in honour of French soldiers killed during the Great War. The Pilgrims were then treated to a banquet at the Salle de Fetes and, after some of the ex-servicemen visited the local estaminet for their "Vin-Blanc" or beer, retired to their billets for the night.

Archie Candler, who had served with the 2nd Battalion, The Suffolk Regiment during the war and was with No. 3 (Suffolk) Company, recalled that:

"We went to the town hall, and they gave us a wonderful reception, and we had a fine lunch. A siren was blown when it was time to get up, and again when it was time to catch the train. The train stopped, and we got out just like we used to during the war. We had community singing while we waited

---

[141] British Legion: *The Battlefields Pilgrimage*, (Letchworth, The Garden City Press, 1928), p.65.

- "Mademoiselle from Armentieres" and other favourite songs - and the fellows called out just as they did in the war: "Wait a minute guv'nor; we want to run to the engine to get some hot water and drum up."[142]

On 6 August the East Anglians entrained at Armentieres, destined for Beaucourt on the Somme. On their journey they passed through the mining district around Loos-en-Gohelle and Lens, and then passed Arras. On reaching Beaucourt the Pilgrims were issued with their packed lunches and individuals boarded taxis and char-a-bancs to take them across the battlefields to visit the graves of loved ones or old comrades they had left behind in France. The majority of the party visited Newfoundland Park, the preserved battlefield near Beaumont-Hamel where the 1ˢᵗ Battalion, The Essex Regiment had fought on 1 July 1916. **Mrs Flora Sharpe**, whose husband had died serving with the 7ᵗʰ Suffolks in 1915, remembered that:

"It was very difficult to travel as you were liable to fall into a shell hole which had been overgrown."[143]

After a picnic tea the party boarded the train back to Armentieres.

The destination for the Pilgrims on 7 August was Vimy Ridge, and again the East Anglian Party took the train to Vimy Station before visiting the preserved trenches on the ridge and the French National Memorial on the Notre Dame de Lorette. On their return from Vimy the party made a visit to one of the British cemeteries at Armentieres, where they laid a wreath, before they entertained their French hosts at a dinner held at the Cafe de l'Harmonie. The evening continued with a band concert held in Victor Hugo Square and one of the disabled Pilgrims took over the baton from the bandleader to much acclaim. He was reported to have enjoyed the evening so much that he nearly missed the train to Ypres the following morning!

The main event of the Pilgrimage took place on 8 August at Ypres, and the East Anglian Pilgrims were awoken by Reveille at 5.30 a.m. and entrained from Armentieres for the last time. Pilgrims from the other parties billeted across France and Belgium converged on Ypres and after breakfast at the Ecole Moyen the wreath bearers, the County Sign Bearers who carried banners depicting the Divisional Signs for the 12ᵗʰ (Eastern), 28ᵗʰ, 32ⁿᵈ and 54ᵗʰ (East Anglian) Divisions and the Branch Standard Bearers were organised in readiness to march to the Ypres (Menin Gate) Memorial. The column

---

[142] Bury Free Press, 11 August 1928.
[143] Ibid.

marched through the Lille Gate and into the city on its approach to the memorial, where a Service of Remembrance was conducted by the Archbishop of York, accompanied by the British Legion Military Band. On the conclusion of the service and the sounding of Last Post and Revielle, the Pilgrims, with their standards and banners, marched past the Prince of Wales and Prince Charles of the Belgians, who stood on a dias in the Grand Place together with the President of the British Legion, Earl Jellicoe, and General Weygand, who deputised for Marshal Foch. "Reflex," a columnist writing for The Essex Newsman, reported on the scene:

"There have been moving scenes at the great Battlefield Pilgrimage which ended on Wednesday, when the Prince of Wales led the 11,000 pilgrims in a Service of Remembrance at the Menin Gate, Ypres. Later the Prince took the salute at a march-past of this army in mufti – men and women who had served in the war or had given their dear ones in the Service. One touching incident was when the Prince, observing Lady Haig marching in the ranks, had her called out to a place on the platform."[144]

Following the climax of the Pilgrimage, the East Anglians boarded their train at Ypres Railway Station for Zeebrugge, and sailed back to England on the St George and landed at Harwich on the morning of 9 August. After bidding their good-byes to their comrades at Parkeston, the Pilgrims dispersed to their homes.

East Anglian Pilgrims at Vimy Station on 7 August 1928.

[144] Essex Newsman, 11 August 1928.

The return of one contingent of the Pilgrims to their village in Suffolk was reported by The Bury Free Press on 18 August 1928:

"BRITISH LEGION PILGRIMAGE – The following members from Isleham attended the Pilgrimage to the battlefields: H. P. Hodges, S. W. Rice, J. H. Talbot, E. Brown, V. Bugg, E. Waters, A. Fenn, B. Collen, and A. B. Frost. All speak of the wonderful receptions from the Belgian and French comrades. Leaving Isleham station by the 5.37 p.m. train, the party arrived at Parkeston Quay and joined the other Pilgrims on board the L. and N.E.R. turbine steamer, King George. At Zeebrugge the party was conducted over the historic Mole, and then went on to Armentieres. The battlefields of the Somme were visited, also those around Vimy Ridge, whilst the party went also to Ypres for the ceremony at the Menin Gate. The cemeteries are a credit to the nation, and the relatives were pleased to find such careful attention to the graves."

Captain Arthur George Cleale, who was a member of the Chelmsford Branch of the British Legion and had travelled with No. 1 (Essex) Company of "S" Train Party, summed up the Pilgrimage thus:

"To put it into a few words, I have never had such a four days in all my life. Everything was done that could be done, both by the headquarters organisation and the municipal authorities, and the solemnity of the occasion was the dominant note. The Mayors of the different places extended both hands of welcome and friendship, and public buildings were thrown open to us. There was a magnificent reception wherever we went. At Armentieres we laid a wreath on the War Memorial. Our visit to Vimy Ridge impressed us all. There were still signs of the war to remind us of what those sleeping in the cemeteries and their comrades went through. At Ypres the great service of remembrance was most touching. Many of the war-stricken villages have made wonderful recoveries, but the people in them still remember Tommy for what he was in the war and opened their doors in welcome."[145]

Born on 8 February 1873, Arthur Cleale had been in business as a cycle agent and ironmonger prior to the Great War, and later as a garage proprietor. During the war he had served with the 1/2nd Battalion, The Essex Volunteer Regiment and "C" Company, 2nd Volunteer Battalion, The Essex Regiment, being commissioned as a Temporary Lieutenant on 7 September 1916, and a Temporary Captain on 10 March 1917.[146] As well as being

---

[145] Essex Newsman, 11 August 1928.
[146] London Gazette, 3 July 1917, 1 October 1917 & 8 December 1917.

involved in the activities of the Chelmsford Branch of the British Legion, Captain Cleale served as Chairman of the Chelmsford Volunteers' Association and as a Director of the West Essex Permanent Building Society. Arthur Cleale died at St John's Hospital at Chelmsford on 5 July 1957.

A representative of another group of Pilgrims wrote to the Editor of The Yorkshire Post to express her and her companions' gratitude to their fellow travellers:

"Sir, - On behalf of the twelve Newcastle-on-Tyne Legionaries (women's section) I should like to thank the party leaders and members (T Party) of the British Legion Pilgrimage for their courtesy and consideration towards us during our journey, from joining them at Doncaster until our return there.

They were really splendid. No words of mine can express the gratitude we feel towards them, and we one and all of us will ever keep a warm corner in our hearts for the Yorkshire people. – Yours, etc.

(Mrs.) S. MAULE.
21, Elswick Street, Newcastle-on-Tyne, Aug. 14."[147]

Charles James Mullett, who was on the 1928 Great Pilgrimage representing the Ramsgate Branch of the British Legion, reflected on his experiences while visiting the former battlefields of France and Flanders:

"In the past week on this pilgrimage I have rubbed shoulders with members of the Legion from all parts of the country, men broken in limb and health but not in spirit for the defence of what they believed to be the right, men who have missed death and disaster miraculously, and thank God for it; men who have touched the border-line of eternity and, in their own phrase, "got away with it."[148]

---

[147] Yorkshire Post, 16 August 1928:
[148] Thanet Advertiser, 10 August 1928.

Packed Lunches

August 1928:

Charles James Mullett, a journalist who worked for The Thanet Advertiser who was representing the Ramsgate Branch of the British Legion on the Pilgrimage, recalled the packed lunch he was issued with on arriving at Beaucourt on 6 August:

"Each ration was enclosed in a neatly-tied cardboard box. The contents consisted of a freshly-cut slice of ham, a large cut of delectable sausage, a French roll, a hard-boiled egg, a section of cream cheese, a papier-mache plate and "glass," a knife and fork, a miniature salt castor, a large tomato, and a bottle of beer. Something like rations!

The cartons containing beer bore a yellow label. Those with lemonade carried a blue label. Most of the old soldiers voted yellow."[149]

John Thomas Gammon M.B.E. from Exeter, who had been awarded his honour for his bravery during the explosion at Halifax Harbour in Nova Scotia on 6 December 1917, also reported on his packed lunch that he was issued with on 7 August:

"On our arrival at Vimy Station each Pilgrim was given a lunch box containing lunch roll, ham and brawn, boiled egg, tomato, banana, knife and fork, piece of cheese, packet of salt, papier mache cup, bottle of beer, or mineral water..."[150]

August 2018:

The 2018 version of the packed lunch issued to Pilgrims on GP90 consisted of:

Two rolls: one ham, one cheese
One packet of crisps
Fruit
One sugar waffle
One bottle of water

---

[149] Thanet Advertiser, 10 August 1928.
[150] Western Times, 18 August 1928.

Pilgrims on the British Legion Great Pilgrimage assembled for the Service of Remembrance at the Ypres (Menin Gate) Memorial on 8 August 1928.

The culmination of both the original Great Pilgrimage of August 1928 and the Royal British Legion GP90 commemoration was a Service of Remembrance at the Ypres (Menin Gate) Memorial. Both were held on 8 August.

An unidentified Pilgrim from Thame in Oxfordshire, who was a member of "B" Train Party of the British Legion Great Pilgrimage in 1928, later recounted his experiences of the ceremony held at the Ypres (Menin Gate) Memorial on 8 August:

"As we stood in that great hall with the names of tens of thousands of those of our comrades who had no known burial place inscribed on its panelled walls I saw nearby some of our women-folk with the tears gently rolling down their faces and a brave smile come stealing forth, I wondered whether the sacrifice had been worth it, whether the League of Nations and the Pact to outlaw war would bear fruit or whether our sons and daughters would be plunged into a struggle with which our own great war would fade into insignificance.

As the smile came and as later in the ceremony the sun came forth in all its glory so the hope of the former came in full strength, and we marched past our Prince with the consciousness that we had done our best and, come what may, posterity could point no finger of scorn at the present generation."[151]

A journalist of The Nottingham Journal who accompanied the Pilgrims also described the scene:

"Strong men who spent years in the turmoil of the trenches sobbed under the strain of the occasion. Bravely they stood in silence for two minutes with their womenfolk, almost overpowered by an onrush of memories."[152]

Ninety years later the scene was repeated by the Pilgrims on GP90. Representing 1,100 Branches of the Royal British Legion from all over the British Isles and across the globe, including the Falkland Islands and Hong Kong, some 2,200 people travelled to France and Flanders by coach and spent two days being guided around sites on the former battlefields of the Somme, Arras, Vimy Ridge and Ypres. The heat during the 6 and 7 August

---

[151] Thame Gazette, 21 August 1928.
[152] Nottingham Journal, 9 August 1928.

2018 was intense, with temperatures reaching 100ºC, so hot that the road surface near the Vimy Memorial melted.

Fortunately the weather had cooled by the time the Pilgrims arrived at Ypres on 8 August. Assembling at the marshalling area in Minneplein, they then marched to the forming-up point in Elverdingestraat and presented an impressive sight for those who witnessed them.

Headed by the Band of Her Majesty's Royal Marines Scotland, the huge column in ranks four abreast was led by 1,100 Branch Standards and followed by the same number of wreath bearers, carrying their own tributes to be placed at the Ypres (Menin Gate) Memorial. The procession then marched past the Cloth Hall and up the Menenstraat.

On reaching the Menin Gate, as had been done ninety years before, an Act of Remembrance was held beneath the memorial conducted by the Archbishop of York, Dr John Sentamu. At the conclusion of the ceremony the Standard Bearers and the other Branch Representatives marched back to Elverdingestraat, and on passing the Cloth Hall some spontaneously started to sing "It's a Long Way to Tipperary."

On being dismissed the Pilgrims returned to Minneplein after what had been a long parade. Some of the Standard Bearers from Yorkshire again began to sing as they marched in formation towards their coaches. For those who took part in the GP90, either as participants or as guides on the battlefield tour, the experience was something that would never be forgotten.

The Pilgrims of 1928

Born on 7 January 1889, **Archibald Candler**, better known as Archie, attested for the Coldstream Guards at Bury St Edmunds on 15 August 1905, stating his profession as musician. Issued with the regimental number 6301, he was posted to the 2nd Battalion and appointed as a Drummer. In 1908 Candler, who had already earned his first Good Conduct badge, transferred to The Suffolk Regiment and was issued with the regimental number 7715. He served with the 2nd Battalion and was on the Permanent Staff at the Regimental Depot when war was declared, playing regularly for the Depot football team. Drummer Candler rejoined the 2nd Battalion at the Curragh and sailed from Dublin for France, disembarking at Le Havre on 14 August 1914. Promoted to Corporal while on active service, Candler was severely wounded in the leg at Sanctuary Wood on 25 September 1915 and was discharged as physically unfit for service due to his wounds on 25 May 1916 while on the strength of the Regimental Depot. Archie was subsequently issued with a Silver War Badge.

In the years following the war Archie was employed at Robert Boby Ltd. in Bury St Edmunds, where he worked as an engineer's bookkeeper. He married Olive Ruby Lilian Game in 1922, and also joined the Royal Ancient Order of Buffalos and the British Legion branch in the town.

In August 1928, Archie revisited the battlefields as a member of No. 3 (Suffolk) Company of "S" Train Party. On his return to his home at 40 Guildhall Street in Bury St Edmunds, Candler was interviewed by a journalist of The Bury Free Press and gave his impressions of what he had seen while on the pilgrimage:

"It is marvellous how they have cultivated the land around. There are big shell holes that have never been filled up, and in the middle of the wheat fields you can see these big, cement redoubts, built by the Germans; gun emplacements, and so on, which are so substantial – nearly a yard thick – that they will never be able to shift them. The people there are rebuilding their own houses at night-time, after they have done their day's work. Some are living in the front and the backs are all blown out. The majority are in our Army huts and corrugated iron built up for shelter till they are in a position to build proper houses. Barbed wire is still about and some of the women tore their stockings and skirts on it."[153]

---

[153] Bury Free Press, 11 August 1928.

Among the places Archie visited was Vimy Ridge:
"We went all round the ridge and through the trenches, and here and there dud shells were sticking up, and there were a few rifles lying about. In the evening we were entertained to an open-air concert, with bands. We visited some of the cafes, and in a body like that, of 450, there was not a man the worse for drink. The way it was conducted and the way the people behaved themselves was splendid."[154]

Archie also saw the names of comrades from the 2nd Suffolks commemorated on the Ypres (Menin Gate) Memorial, and brought back two souvenir ashtrays, one from Hill 60 with bullets for legs, and another of the Menin Gate.

Archie was elected as Chairman of the Bury St Edmunds branch of the British Legion in 1935 and on 26 October 1955 was presented with his gold badge, to mark his twenty years of service in the role.[155]

Archie Candler died at his home at 40 Guildhall Street on 4 April 1960.

---

[154] Ibid.
[155] Bury Free Press, 28 October 1955.

Mrs Clara Bearman travelled on the Great Pilgrimage as a member of No. 1 (Essex) Company of "S" Train Party, and was able to visit the grave of her late husband, **72352 Private Augustus Stanley Bearman**, who had served with the 15th (Service) Battalion, The Sherwood Foresters (Nottinghamshire and Derbyshire Regiment) (Nottingham), and had died on 27 February 1918.

Born at Bocking in 1885, he was the eldest son of Harry and Ellen Bearman, who lived on Market Place in Braintree, and married to Clara Stone at St Matthew's Church in West Kensington on 11 September 1911. Their son, Bargrave Stanley Bearman, was born on 18 March 1913 and was baptised at Holy Trinity Church in Upper Tooting on 27 April. Augustus lived with his family at 70 Boundaries Road in Balham.

Augustus was employed as a drapers' assistant when he attested for the Royal Flying Corps at Battersea on 8 December 1915, having previously been rejected for service by another Recruiting Office for showing symptoms of heart disease. Issued with the service number 38956, Private Bearman was drafted to France on 27 August 1916 and posted to No. 13 Balloon Company R.F.C. On 7 May 1917 he was awarded seven days' Field Punishment No. 2 for "neglect of duty." On 1 September he was drafted to the 63rd (Royal Naval) Division Infantry Base Depot to be trained as an infantryman, and on 24 September was transferred to The Sherwood Foresters, being posted to the 15th (Service) Battalion.

Private Bearman was killed as a result of an accidental explosion while unload Stokes Mortar bombs from a G.S. Wagon while working at the 35th Division Salvage Depot at Kempton Park Camp, south of St Julien. The Salvage Officer of 35th Division later wrote to Private Bearman's father:

"The men of the Salvage Corps join with me in offering our deepest sympathy to you. It must be some consolation to you to know that Pt. Bearman died in faithful exercise of his duty, and gave his life for his country. We had learned to appreciate his soldierly qualities."[156]

News of his death at the front was reported in The Essex Newsman on 9 March:

---

[156] Essex Newsman, 23 March 1918.

"On Thursday Mr Harry Bearman, Market Place, Braintree, received official intimation that his eldest son, Augustus Stanley Bearman, 32, formerly R.F.C., latterly Notts and Derby Regt., was killed in action by an explosion in France on Monday. Before the war the deceased was engaged in the drapery business of Messrs. Harper Bros. at Balham. He was married and leaves a widow and little son. He was one of the choristers at St Peter's, Bocking, when that church was opened, and sang there for several years. He was educated at Braintree College House School under Dr Amott, and was well-known and esteemed. Mr and Mrs Bearman have two other sons serving in the Army."

Following the explosion, Private Bearman's body was placed in a Nissen Hut at Kempton Park Camp before being buried at No Man's Cot Cemetery, where his grave can be found at Row B, Grave 29.

On 18 May No. 6 Infantry Record Office at Lichfield sent Clara her late husband's personal effects consisting of letters, photographs, cards, photo case, his mirror, wallet and pocket book. Probate was granted to his widow on 24 July, his effects being valued at £451 9s. 2d., and she was also awarded a weekly Widow's Pension of 20/5d, effective from 16 September 1918.

On 5 December 1920, and memorial tablet was unveiled at St Peter's Church in Bocking by Mrs Hills, the wife of the churchwarden, to his memorial. The inscription reads:

"To the glory of God, and in memory of Augustus Stanley Bearman, late of the Sherwood Foresters, beloved husband of Clara Bearman, and eldest son of Harry and Ellen Bearman, of this town, killed in action in France (sic), February 27, 1918, aged 32 years. Many years a chorister of this church. His life for his country, his soul to God."[157]

Clara Bearman was able to find Augustus's grave while on the Great Pilgrimage, and her visit was reported by The Essex Newsman on 18 August 1928:

[157] Essex Newsman, 11 December 1920.

"WAR GRAVE FOUND. – A party of 30 from Braintree took part in the British Legion pilgrimage to the battlefield scenes in France, among them being the widow and brother of the late Mr A. S. Bearman, who fell in action, and to whom there is a memorial tablet in St Peter's Church. The pilgrims were able to locate the grave, upon which they found the inscription of which they had been previously notified."

When Clara Bearman visited her husband's grave she found that the last sentence of the inscription that had been included on his memorial tablet at Bocking had also been carved at the base of his headstone. Clara never remarried and later lived at Bagshot in Surrey. She died in 1973 while a resident in the Home of Compassion Nursing Home at 58 High Street in Thames Ditton, aged 88, and was buried in the churchyard of St Peter's in West Molesey on 5 October.

An unidentified Pilgrim, who wore six sets of war medals while visiting the battlefields of France and Flanders in August 1928.

Mrs Flora Sharpe, who lived at 77 Queen's Road in Bury St Edmunds, also took part in the Pilgrimage and was a member of No. 3 (Suffolk) Company of "S" Train Party. She had the opportunity to visit the grave of her husband, **3/9607 Company Sergeant-Major Charles Sharpe**, who had served with the 7th (Service) Battalion, The Suffolk Regiment and died of wounds on 20 October 1915 after being admitted to the West Riding Casualty Clearing Station at Lillers.[158]

C.S.M. Sharpe had served for 23 years with The Suffolk Regiment, enlisting at Aldershot in 1888, seen service in South Africa with the 1st Battalion and 8th Battalion, Mounted Infantry (he was Mentioned in Despatches) and was awarded the Long Service and Good Conduct Medal in 1907. He was discharged in 1911 and worked went to work in Bury St Edmunds. He joined the 3rd (Special Reserve) Battalion shortly after the outbreak of the war and landed in France with the 7th Suffolks on 30 May 1915. C.S.M. Sharpe was mortally wounded during the fighting for the Hairpin near Hulluch on 13 October 1915, and he is buried at Lillers Communal Cemetery: Plot IV, Row D, Grave 10.

Flora was interviewed by a journalist from The Bury Free Press following her return from the Great Pilgrimage, and said:

"I have come back with more content now that I have seen my husband's grave, and if it is any comfort to other mothers that I have seen the graves of their sons – it would be to me – they can rest assured that every cemetery I saw is well kept and it is like entering a pretty English garden."[159]

Flora Sharpe died at Bury St Edmunds in 1962, aged 83.

[158] Bury Free Press, 30 October 1915.
[159] Bury Free Press, 11 August 1928.

THE BATTLEFIELDS REVISITED.

WHERE LOVED ONES FOUGHT AND FELL

WORTHING PILGRIMS AT YPRES AND VIMY RIDGE

Worthing pilgrims— part of the 11,000 who visited the battlefields of France and Flanders last week under British Legion auspices—entering preserved front line German trenches at Vimy Ridge.

Mrs Gertrude Bowley, who lived at 6 Warwick Place in Worthing, was one of the widows who took part in the British Legion Great Pilgrimage in August 1928. Her late husband, **M2/269520 Private Frank Bowley**, who worked as a milk carrier before the war, had served with 594th Mechanical Transport Company, Army Service Corps, attached to X Corps Heavy Artillery. He had died of wounds after being admitted to 105th Field Ambulance R.A.M.C. on 28 July 1918, aged 34, and is buried at Lijssenthoek Military Cemetery: Plot XXVIII, Row G, Grave 18A.

Two photographs taken by Mrs Bowley, one in the preserved trenches on Vimy Ridge and another taken beneath the Ypres (Menin Gate) Memorial, were reproduced in The Worthing Gazette on 15 August 1928.

Born on 2 August 1884, Gertrude Bowley never remarried and died at Worthing in 1969, two months before her 85th birthday.

Mrs Mary Ann O'Connor (left), who lived at 31 Acorn Street in the Netherthorpe district of Sheffield, was a member of "T" Party of the British Legion Great Pilgrimage in August 1928. She wore the medals issued to three of her sons who had died during the Great War:

10389 Lance-Corporal John Francis O'Connor, who was killed on 18 November 1914 while serving with the 2nd Battalion, The King's Own (Yorkshire Light Infantry). He is commemorated on Panel 47 of the Ypres (Menin Gate) Memorial.

14296 Driver Michael O'Connor, who served with 112th Battery, XXIV Brigade, Royal Field Artillery and died of wounds on 20 July 1915. He is buried at Hop Store Cemetery: Plot I, Row C, Grave 24.

201267 Private Thomas O'Connor, who was killed in Italy on 15 June 1918 while serving with the 9th (Service) Battalion, The York and Lancaster Regiment. He is buried Granezza British Cemetery: Plot I, Row D, Grave 1.

All three of Mrs O'Connor's sons were also commemorated on the Roll of Honour inside St Vincent's Catholic Church on Solly Street in Sheffield.

Mrs O'Connor carried the Sheffield Branch Standard during the ceremony held at the Ypres (Menin Gate) Memorial, in place of ex-Sergeant Bernard Birch, who was ill and could not attend the Pilgrimage.[160]

Mary, who was born in County Mayo on 9 July 1867, later lived at 28 Moorfield Flats in Shalesmoor and died in 1945, aged 78.

---

[160] Sheffield Independent, 6 August 1928.

"We joined the big pilgrimage to France in August. I would not have missed it for anything. It will live in my memory as long as I live. About 11,000 people made the pilgrimage – every class and creed – some of the highest and some of the lowest in the land, all there to visit the battlefields and the graves of their dead. It made one realise the war brought everyone level – all suffered alike.

The organisation was wonderful; special trains were waiting at London, where we all had our different parties, numbered "A" to "W." Each member wore a badge, with the letter of his party attached. Special boats took the pilgrims to France, where a hot meal was provided on arrival at Calais. I belonged to the overseas party "A", which was billeted at Amiens, and visited the battlefields from there each day. We visited Beaucourt Hamel, (sic) in the Somme Valley. All along the route were objects of interest – stumps of trees, an old tank, a cemetery, etc. – and on arrival there we found that a section of the Somme is being cared for by Newfoundland. The trenches are left in their war-time condition, the old duck-boards are still down, although now broken and rotting; dug-outs are intact; and the trenches wind in out of each other for miles. The ground around about is strewn with relics of old rifles, shoes, dixies, water-bottles, barbed-wire, etc., and one can see the broken remains of a machine gun, and beside it a helmet, rifle, and water-bottle of the gunner – telling all plainly that he died at his post. A beautiful monument is built there to the Scottish Highlanders, and Lady Haig, who was there as a pilgrim, was visiting it at the same time as we were. We all stood motionless as a Scottish piper, with his bagpipes, struck up a "Scottish Lament."

We also visited the famous Vimy Ridge, the scene of such fierce fighting. The Germans held the Ridge right up to 1917. It is a long range of hills. One can easily see why the enemy fought so hard for it, as it commands miles of country. The movement of troops for miles around could be seen from the Ridge. It is simply honeycombed with trenches. One can walk through them for miles. Their construction is wonderful; the dug-outs etc., are specially built, and a great under-ground tunnel connects with the front line. Men, munitions, and supplies were all brought into the line in this way. "No Man's Land," in between the trenches, is ploughed up by shell-fire. There are holes everywhere, and one can hardly take a step between. We thought the enemy fire was bad enough; but our own fire must have been hell! I remember how we used to shell it for days without a break. A beautiful monument is being built on top of the Ridge, in memory of the Canadians who eventually captured it. A monument, also, is being built on the left of the Ridge to the Frenchmen who took that portion of the line. It is a nice idea – a big column, with a beaconlight always burning at the top which never goes out. It stands as a silent reminder of those sleeping beneath. Thousands and thousands of our men and Frenchmen fell at Vimy.

We went over to Arras, Albert, Poperinghe, etc., and Ypres Salient (where I received my wounds). Ypres Salient is now a cemetery. The cemeteries are beautifully kept; every grave is marked by a white stone, as the wooden crosses at first used rotted very quickly. Every stone is exactly alike, row after row. On many stones are the name and rank of the soldier; but on many others no name appears – just the simple words, "A British Soldier: Known Unto God." The main gate, built at the entrance to Ypres, is a monument to the boys who were missing and have no known graves. It has 60,000 names on its panels, and on one panel – No. 23 – is devoted to the Australian boys. I found the name of my cousin – Claude Bower. He was reported missing after a big battle at Ypres.

It was at the Menin Gate that the big ceremony was held in honour of our dead. The Prince of Wales, King and Prince of the Belgians, Marshal Foch, Admiral Jellicoe, etc., were present, and 11,000 pilgrims. There was no hitch of any kind. Each party was allotted a place and marched to it. Our party was on the right side of the Gate. It was a most impressive sight. Flags of every Division and country which took part in the war were flying from the ramparts. After the service there was a march past – women first. It was splendid to see them trying to keep in step to the band – old and young women, mothers and widows; many wearing rows of medals. Then came the men; every man with his medals up, swinging along, shoulder to shoulder, as in the old days. The Prince of Wales, King of the Belgians, and all the Royal party stood on a raised dais, on the right of (the) Menin Gate, and the Prince took the salute.

The towns in the war area are now re-built, and a good proportion of the battlefields are cultivated and growing crops. Wild flowers and scarlet poppies are growing on every side. Roads have been re-made, and everything looks prosperous. No mud to be seen anywhere, as you go through the trenches – so different to the grim days of conflict!

The French people turned out in thousands to give us a welcome. They cheered, waved, and gesticulated, and when a little rank of blinded men from "St Dunstan's" marched by, arm-in-arm, the roar that went up could be heard for miles."[161]

Selby Garfield Bower
Formerly 1504 Lance-Sergeant, 2nd Battalion, Australian Imperial Force

Born at Armidale, Selby Bower was aged twenty-three years and seven months and stated that he was employed as a grazier when he attested for the Australian Imperial Force at Sydney on 17 November 1914. He sailed from Australia with the 3rd Reinforcements for the 2nd Battalion on 10 February 1915 and was promoted to Corporal on 11 February.

After training in Egypt he was posted to the 2nd Battalion on the Gallipoli Peninsula, joining the battalion at Anzac Cove on 5 May. Bower was appointed a Lance-Sergeant on 22 June, but on 25 August was admitted to 3rd Australian Field Ambulance suffering from influenza. Evacuated to Mudros, Bower was admitted to No. 1 Australian Casualty Clearing Station before sailing for Malta on 31 August and being sent to St Patrick's Hospital for treatment. On 10 September he embarked on the H.T. Scotian for England, and on his arrival was admitted to the London War Hospital at Epsom on 18 September. While being treated in hospital at Epsom Lance-Sergeant Bower met Lydia Mary Jones, a nurse at the London War Hospital, and they married in 1916.

Following his discharge from hospital and convalescence at Weymouth, Lance-Sergeant Bower was posted to the 1st Training Battalion A.I.F. at Perham Down on 6 July 1916 and was drafted to France on 31 July. He joined 1st Australian Infantry Base Depot at Etaples on 1 August and was sent back to the 2nd Battalion, rejoining the unit on 10 August at their billets in Pernois. On 12 September, while serving in the front line near Zillebeke, Lance-Sergeant Bower received severe wounds to his left leg and foot, fracturing his fibula and tibia, from a German minenwerfer shell burst. He was admitted to 1st Australian Field Ambulance before being evacuated to No. 17 Casualty Clearing Station at Remy Siding. From there he was sent to Boulogne and was admitted to No. 3 Canadian General Hospital on 18 September before sailing on board the H.M.H.S. St David for England. Bower arrived at the Queen Mary Military Hospital at Whalley on 19 September where he remained until 13 March 1917 when he was transferred to the 3rd Australian Auxillary Hospital at Dartford. On his

---

[161] Selby Bower wrote his letter to Mr H. E. Williams, of Armidale, New South Wales, and it was reproduced in The Armidale Chronicle on 12 January 1929.

discharge from hospital, Bower was posted to No. 2 Command Depot A.I.F. at Weymouth on 26 April. Unfit for further service at the front, Bower embarked on board the Hospital Ship A.14 on 21 July, and arrived back in Australia on the H.M.A.T. Euripides on 19 September. His arrival back home was reported by The Armidale Advertiser on 25 September:

"By Saturday morning's mail there returned to Armidale Sergt. Selby Bower, a son of Mr Geo. Bower, the well-known Armidale wool-buyer. Three years ago this month the gallant Sergt. answered the call of King and country, being among the first to do so from this district. He returns with a badly injured foot and leg, but with the knowledge of a duty worthily discharged. He was always a popular young fellow, and his wide circle of friends have given him a very hearty welcome home. Sergt. Bower was attached to the 2ⁿᵈ Battalion and saw practically the whole of the Gallipoli campaign up to shortly before the memorable evacuation. He participated in the famous Lone Pine charge, and passed through the whole campaign scathless except for slight illness. Afterwards he went to France, and survived the multitudinous dangers at Pozieres and on the Somme until finally, at Ypres, a 12-inch German minenwerfer shell burst near where he and nine of his comrades were standing. All the rest were killed, the Sergt. alone escaping, though with a sadly damaged foot. This occurred at night time, and the Sergt. had been dodging these little German favours all day. Though at first his recovery was despaired of, six months in hospital made a very big difference, especially the devoted care and attention of one excellent English nurse, who subsequently became Mrs Bower. It was indeed a romantic love affair. Mrs Bower is due in Australia by the next mail boat.

The Sergt.'s leg is some three inches short at present, and he is to undergo an operation at Randwick to have the bones reset and lengthened. Despite his many stirring experiences the young soldier looks exceedingly well, though he cannot walk without crutches. As to the war generally he says there is much yet to be done, and every man possible is needed, chiefly to bring the battalions up to their proper strength and give the boys so long out there a decent rest. He says the German organisation is wonderful, but their soldiers are long-distance fighters only. Never did he have a chance to get into a hand-to-hand contest – they always either ran or threw up their hands."

Lance-Sergeant Bower was discharged as physically unfit for service, as a consequence of his wounds, on 14 March 1918, and received his war medals at a ceremony held at the Town Hall in Armidale on 3 September 1921.[162] Selby worked as a butcher after the war, but he and Lydia left Armidale in 1923 when he purchased the Coliseum Picture Theatre at Lithgow. They lost everything when the building was destroyed in a fire during the early hours of 31 August 1924.[163]

On 12 May 1928, the Bowers sailed for England on board the S.S. Koln, and during their trip stayed with Lydia's mother.[164] It was during this visit that Selby went to France and Flanders as part of the British Legion's Great Pilgrimage.

Mentioned in Selby's letter was his cousin, **6 Private Claude Bower**, who served with "A" Company of the 33rd Battalion, Australian Imperial Force and who is commemorated on the Ypres (Menin Gate) Memorial. Claude had attested at Armidale on 11 August 1915 and at the time of his enlistment was aged eighteen and employed as a groom. He embarked from Sydney on 4 May 1916 and landed at Southampton on 9 July. Private Bower was drafted to France on 21 November 1916 and was killed on 14 October 1917.

Claude's brother, **7213 Private William Eric Bower**, enlisted for the Australian Imperial Force at Armidale on 31 December 1916. Aged eighteen and seven months, he was employed as a car driver when he attested and left Sydney with the 24th Reinforcement for the 13th Battalion on 7 February 1917. Arriving at Devonport on 11 April, Eric Bower joined the 4th Training Battalion at Codford Camp and was drafted to France on 18 October, being taken onto the strength of the 13th Battalion six days later. Eric was severely wounded in the abdomen on 8 August 1918 and died of his wounds at 11.10 a.m. the following morning after being admitted to No. 61 Casualty Clearing Station. He is buried at Vignacourt British Cemetery: Plot VI, Row A, Grave 13, and the following inscription is carved at the base of his headstone:

In Loving Memory of the Noble Son of Mr & Mrs Bower
Age 19. (R.I.P.)

---

[162] Armidale Chronicle, 27 August 1921.
[163] Armidale Chronicle, 9 June 1923, Sydney Sun, 1 September 1924 & Armidale Express, 9 September 1924.
[164] Armidale Chronicle, 18 April 1928.

William Hartley Barnes M.S.M., who lived at 20 Grove Lane in Padiham, near Burnley in Lancashire, travelled with "T" Train Party from Yorkshire to take part in the Great Pilgrimage.

Born on 24 November 1884, William was employed as a carpenter when he attested for the Royal Engineers at Burnley on 7 April 1915, being issued with the service number 89430. On the outbreak of the war Barnes was a member of the National Reserve, having previously served with the 5th Battalion, The East Lancashire Regiment (Territorial Force). He embarked for Egypt on 14 June and was posted to 71st Field Company, which formed part of 13th (Western) Division. After serving at Suvla, Barnes was appointed a paid Lance-Corporal on 8 December and promoted to 2nd Corporal on 5 February 1916. He went on to serve in Mesopotamia and was promoted to Corporal on 13 May, and advanced to Sergeant on 3 July. He spent one month in India on leave the following year, and was admitted to hospital on 15 October 1918 suffering from malaria. Embarking for home on Boxing Day, Sergeant Barnes was posted to the Royal Engineers Depot at Chatham on 19 February 1919 and was transferred to the Class Z Army Reserve when he was demobilised on 25 March. He was awarded the Meritorious Service Medal on 22 September 1919.

One of three men from Burnley who went on the Pilgrimage in 1928, William was interviewed when he returned by a journalist of The Burnley Express regarding his experiences. For him, the pilgrimage was personal as he went to visit the area where his brother, 8393 Sergeant John Barnes, who served with "D" Company of the 1st Battalion, The East Lancashire Regiment, had been killed on 7 November 1914 during an attack mounted through Ploegsteert Wood to Le Gheer. After laying a wreath, William visited a cemetery where many of his brother's comrades were buried:

"Close by is a cottage known as the "Lancashire Cottage," which, during the war, was the headquarters of the East Lancashire Regiment. The man who tenanted the cottage during the war is still in occupation, and he told Mr Barnes that he would always remember the lads from Lancashire. If any visited the spot where he lived he would always welcome them." [165]

William Hartley Barnes M.S.M. died at Burnley in 1978, aged 93.

---

[165] Burnley Express, 15 August 1928.

Arthur Oswald Brown was one of the members of the Biggleswade Branch of the British Legion who went to France and Belgium on the Great Pilgrimage in August 1928. Born at Langford in on 28 February 1881, Arthur had been employed as a coach painter and, although he had attested under the Derby Scheme did not see service overseas. He later became the licensee of The Lion Inn on Caldecote Road in Biggleswade.

Arthur sailed for France with "B" Train Party and on arriving at Amiens complained that he was suffering from pains in his stomach. A French doctor was called, and it was determined that Mr Brown was suffering from colic. Told to rest, Arthur did not take part in the excursions of Beaucourt and Vimy Ridge, but was determined to be present at Ypres on 8 August for the service at the Ypres (Menin Gate) Memorial. This he did, and he also took part in the march- past of the British Legion pilgrims that followed.

On returning to London Arthur went to visit his daughter at Highbury and he was taken ill at her house. Admitted to Middlesex Hospital on 10 August, it was discovered that he was suffering from acute appendicitis and was operated on immediately. A further operation took place the following day but Arthur died that same evening, 11 August, at the age of 47. His funeral took place at Biggleswade on 16 August.[166]

[166] Biggleswade Chronicle, 17 August 1928.

"Dear Brownie and comrades at Geelong,

I promised to write and tell you something of the British Legion Pilgrimage to the battlefields of France, so here goes.

Saturday, August 4th, was a very wet day in London and promised anything but fine for our trip. At Victoria Station I met two members of the Geelong branch, E. A. Alsop and W. J. F. Butterworth. They were very well and asked to be remembered in me letter to all "digger" cobbers in Geelong. They also joined the Pilgrimage as did many Australians from all parts of the Commonwealth.

The trip across the Channel was very rough, and hundreds failed to appear at the dinner table. Arriving at Calais we had tea and supper there and entrained for Amiens, arriving there about 2 a.m. Sunday, where we were all sent to our billets (just like old times) and Sunday being a free day we were at liberty to go where we liked so three others and myself got a taxi and visited "Villers Bret," Corbie, passing through Hamel to Sailly Laurette, then to Cressy and Chipilly where we inspected "Big Bertha" the great gun that fired upon Paris 75 miles away and eventually captured by the Australian Third Division. Then on through Fay and back another route, so we saw a good deal of the country through which we passed in 1918.

There is not a sign of a trench, or a dug-out, (except, of course, where they are preserved) and in their place miles and miles of splendid crops of all sorts; one can hardly credit that the people who cleared away all signs of devastation, and are building up new villages in places where the old ones were destroyed, building is going on everywhere.

Monday we visited Beaumont Hamel, and the Newfoundland Park where fine monuments have been erected, trenches preserved, duckboards and all. The Ulster Cemetery is close by, and in company with several others I also paid a visit. These cemeteries are kept beautifully and made one almost wish that he were one of the "Glorious Dead."

Tuesday we visited Vimy where the Canadians are building a wonderful monument which I should like to see when finished. The tunnels and trenches are concreted, and lighted with electricity, and should last for all time.

Wednesday we went to Ypres. This, of course, was the crowning day of the whole tour. The people are re-erecting a beautiful city, though there are still evidences of the ruthless destruction, particularly to the great Cloth Hall, part of which is being left in its original condition as a monument. The early morning was damp, but when we got out of the train the rain stopped and the day turned out full of sunshine. The Menin Gate Memorial is a beautiful thing, where are engraved the names of over 35,000 (sic) soldiers who have no known grave. The Prince of Wales and the Crown Prince of Belgium were there among the thousands of people, and the march past of 11,000 pilgrims was a great sight.

On Thursday I visited the cemetery at Sailly Laurette, where I found the graves of four of my old comrades who were killed in the battle of Bray on August 22, 1918. They were buried side by side, and Les Parrott, of Geelong, will remember them well – Lieut. J. McConnell, Sergt. M. H. Lewis, D. G. Bethune, and C. E. Marriott, all of the 3rd Pioneer Battalion. I am sorry that I did not get the names and where buried of some more Geelong boys. There must be hundreds lying at peace in the many cemeteries that I visited.

The whole Pilgrimage was wonderfully organised, and everyone concerned deserves the greatest credit. We arrived in Paris yesterday evening and I have been very busy sight-seeing ever since. Paris is a fine city with its crowded streets with the taxis flying around like flies.

To-day I visited the Arch de Triomphe (sic), where the French Unknown Soldier is buried, and also the Perpetual Flame which is most unique. I also visited the Effel (sic) Tower and went to the top from where a wonderful view of Paris and the surrounding landscape for miles can be obtained. The trip is nearing the end, and I hope to get back to London on the 13th.

I hope you have not fallen asleep while reading this – or perhaps you were like Jack Brownlee – had some refreshments half way through. Anyhow I trust that this letter finds all the Geelong boys well, including yourself, and with best wishes from yours in comradeship,

A. J. Williams."[167]

[167] Geelong Advertiser (Victoria), 23 October 1928.

Arthur John Williams was a member of the Geelong Branch of The Returned Sailors and Soldiers Imperial League of Australia and had travelled to England in order to take part in the Great Pilgrimage.

Formerly 3615 Private A. J. Williams, 3rd Pioneer Battalion, Australian Imperial Force (8th Reinforcements), Arthur was employed as a blacksmith when he attested for the Australian Imperial Force at Geelong on 7 August 1917. After training at Broadmeadows Camp, Private Williams embarked for Egypt on 21 November, arriving at Suez on 15 December. He sailed for Port Said on 9 January 1918 and, after brief stops at Taranto and Cherbourg, arrived at Southampton on 2 February. Posted to Sutton Veny, Williams was not drafted to France until 17 June, and joined the 3rd Pioneer Battalion on 24 June. He was wounded during a German bombardment on 24 August and evacuated to England, being admitted to the Princess Christian Military Hospital at Englefield Green three days later. Private Williams was repatriated to Australia on 19 October, having been diagnosed as suffering from "physical asthma."

The graves of the four members of the 3rd Pioneer Battalion that Arthur visited on the 1928 pilgrimage are at Beacon Cemetery near Sailly-Laurette on the Somme. The men are buried next to each other in Plot V, Row J of the cemetery: **Lieutenant James McConnell** is buried in Grave 1; **1504 Private David Gordon Bethune** in Grave 2; **3323 Private Charles Edward Marriott at Grave 3** and **247 Sergeant Michael Herman Lewis** is interred in Grave 4.

Among the Standard-Bearers on the Great Pilgrimage was **William Arthur Carr M.M. and Bar**, representing the Nutley Branch of the British Legion. He was accompanied by his wife Alice.

Born at Maresfield on 11 May 1872, G/874 Private William Arthur Carr had served with the 7th (Service) Battalion, The Royal Sussex Regiment during the Great War. He disembarked at Boulogne on 1 June 1915 and was awarded the Military Medal and Bar for gallantry, notification of his first award was published in The London Gazette on 18 July 1917, and the award of the Bar to the decoration gazetted on 17 June 1919. Private Carr was transferred to the Class Z Army Reserve when he was demobilised on 26 March 1919.

William and Alice lived at Rose Bungalow, on Dodd's Bank in Nutley, and he worked as a builder's labourer. His part in the Great Pilgrimage was reported by The Sevenoaks Chronicle and Kentish Advertiser on 10 August 1928:

"BRITISH LEGION. – Conveying with him the blue and gold silk standard belonging to the branch, Mr W. A. Carr, M.M. (sic), represented the Nutley branch of the British Legion in the British Legion Pilgrimage to Flanders. Mr Carr was accompanied by Mrs Carr."

Hendon and Finchley Times – 17 August 1928:

THE BRITISH LEGION.

Golders Green and District Branch in Battlefield Pilgrimage.

"The London contingent of the Battlefields Pilgrimage, which was over 500 strong, and which included prominent members of the Golders Green and District Branch, left Victoria at 11.59 a.m. on Sunday, August 5th, for Henin Lietard, which was to be their home in France for three days. The route was via Dover and Calais, and the crossing was enjoyed by all. A British Legion band on board played lively tunes. The party disembarked at Calais to the strains of the French National Anthem, and a hearty welcome was accorded them by both French and English people who had gathered on the quayside.

After a pleasant journey through parts of France known to most of the pilgrims, the destination was eventually reached at 7.25. On detraining, the people of Henin Lietard headed by the French Old Comrades' Association, gave the party a wonderful welcome, which was followed by a civic reception by the Lord Mayor at the Town Hall. After this, the party dispersed and went to their temporary homes, where they were one and all enthusiastically received. Henin Lietard is a small town which was badly damaged in the war, but has made a wonderful recovery in the past ten years, all the damage having been made good, and is now a very flourishing and prosperous coal-mining town, with a population of approximately 24,000. On Monday the day was spent roaming the devastated area round Beaucourt Hamel, and on Tuesday a similar day was spent at Vimy Ridge. On both days special trips were arranged for those of the pilgrims who wished to visit the cemeteries where our less fortunate comrades had found a peaceful resting place.

On Wednesday, as is well known, a most beautiful and impressive ceremony was held around the Menin Gate at Ypres. After this, the rest of the day was spent in exploring the town until 7.30 in the evening, when the party left Ypres for their return to London. The return journey was made through many well-known places on the western front where history was made during the Great War, but where now new towns have sprung up and fields where once death stalked are now being extensively cultivated. The party crossed from Calais to Dover at night, and all enjoyed a glorious moonlit voyage, arriving at Dover at 1 o'clock. The party eventually reached Victoria at 5.30 a.m. on Thursday, August 9th, tired, but very happy."

Armistice Day 1936 Reflections of an Old Contemptible

"To most people November 11 conveys the fact that on that date in 1918 came the Armistice, and with it a cessation of the slaughter of the Great War of 1914-1918 – and of a feeling of relief the world over.

We remember all those of our kith and kin, who gave their lives for the Allied Cause, and for the final subjugation of the German and their Allied armies. We remember some relative, friend or comrade, as the case may be, as the clock strikes the eleventh hour, and personally I hope that remembrance may never cease.

But there was another November 11, and once which was the most vital in the history of both this nation and the Allies. That was November 11, 1914. On that date there stood around Ypres the battered remnants of the British Army, that "Contemptible" Little British Army, so designated by the ex-Kaiser. That small and very much harassed Army, which did not exceed 150,000 men, was on that morning subjected to what was probably one of the most murderous artillery bombardments of the war, considering the small artillery with the British and the shortage of shells, rendering it almost impossible to counter the heavier guns of the Germans, and the fact that there were no elaborate trenches, in most cases each man scooped out a "hole" for himself, and it must always be to those who took part in this battle a miracle that there were any who survived.

THE GERMAN ARMY'S ATTACK.

At 9-30 on that morning, amidst a storm of wind and rain the German Army attacked. That Army consisted of a total of close on 600,000 troops and amongst them were over 13,000 of the crack Prussian Guards, 1st and 2nd: the Kaiser Franz Grenadiers No. 2, the Koningin Augusta Grenadiers No. 4, and the battalion of the Garde Jager, these were the elite of the German Army. The Kaiser's order was "Victory or Death," and the goal was Calais and the other Channel ports.

The heavy shells of the German artillery had in many cases buried alive many British, and the enemy came on in massed formation. All day long the murderous and unequal struggle continued, and despite the odds against them in men and guns the little British Army held on.

Darkness came and with it no cessation of the attack. Our men were almost exhausted, and the losses had been terrible. Of the 1st Brigade less than four officers and 400 men were surviving. They had lost their Brigade commander, General FitzClarence V.C., and the same could be said of the losses of the other brigades in the line. Despite all the line was held. It is true that the enemy did gain about 500 yards of ground in the battle, but a shorter line was at once dug, organised and manned, and the barrier to Ypres and the Channel ports was as strong as ever. The American correspondent said of the British troops on that day – "They were like wild beasts, fierce and undaunted. They had, it seemed, given their all, almost their humanity, to save Britain, and may the day never come when Britain will refuse to save them."

GERMAN BID FOR YPRES.

This attack of November 11 represented the high water mark of the German efforts to capture Ypres and the road to the Channel ports, and as a result of the sacrifice of the little British Army the ebb was a rapid one. The losses of the British were considerable, as can be expected under such odds, but the losses of the Germans on this date were even more so. The figures given were 50,000: the Prussian Guard alone lost 1,200 killed, 4,000 wounded and 1,719 missing. The fact that the enemy did not recoil has obscured the completeness of the great victory, but one judges victory or defeat by the question as to whether an army has or has not reached its objective. The salient fact remains that the Germans did not advance five miles in the whole month of the fighting around Ypres, and in that month's fighting they lost not less than 150,000 men, without any military advantage whatever, gaining only the villages of Gheluvelt, Wytschaete and Messines, of little advantage to them from the military point of view.

HELD THEIR GROUND.

And amidst the many memories which so very naturally return to the minds of survivors of that little British Army of August-November, 1914, on this date each year, none can ever be more memorable than the date which proved to be very significant to the history of the Allied cause.

Had the German Army broken through the thin khaki line around Ypres and passed on to the possession of the Channel ports what would have been the history of the world to-day? There were no reserves, no supports, behind that British Force that stood at bay on that date. Had they failed the road to the Channel was open, but they held their ground.

One can see to-day the tablet erected on the ruins of the Cloth Hall. Ypres, the words – "On this day, November 11, 1914, the attack of the Prussian Guards was shattered by the little British Army at Ypres, and the road to the Channel Ports was barred."

This, then, is the other commemoration which is so deeply remembered by the survivors of the "Contemptible" Little British Army of 1914, when this solemn anniversary in remembrance of all those who gave their lives for their King, Empire and humanity comes to us each year, and we remember the sacrifice of our kith and kin and of our Allies.

JAMES RITCHIE,

Hon. Secretary
The Old Contemptibles Association.
Northern Ireland."[168] [1]

Chum James Ritchie was a founder member of the Belfast Branch of the Old Contemptibles Association of Northern Ireland and acted as Standard Bearer of the Branch's King's Colour.

8689 Lance-Sergeant James Ritchie served with the 2nd Battalion, Scots Guards and disembarked at Zeebrugge, as a Lance-Corporal, on 7 October 1914. He had joined the Scots Guards on 3 September 1913 and was discharged on 17 August 1917 due to sickness, being issued with a Silver War Badge. Ritchie was sent his 1914 Star by post on 13 January 1919 and issued with the clasp and roses on 20 February 1920.

The following year he, together his fellow Chums of the Old Contemptibles Association of Northern Ireland, made a pilgrimage to the former battlefields of France and Belgium, with Chum Ritchie carrying the King's Colour at a ceremony held at the Ypres (Menin Gate) Memorial on 26 August 1937.[169]

---

[168] Larne Times, 14 November 1936.
[169] Belfast News-Letter, 7 September 1937.

Chum James Ritchie at Mons on 23 August 1937
(Courtesy of Melville Patterson)

In August 1939, The Old Contemptibles Association of Northern Ireland made their fourth annual pilgrimage to the former battlefields of the Great War in France and Flanders. On his return, Chum James Ritchie described his impressions of the trip and his feelings as war clouds again gathered over Europe:

"In all our wanderings, we were deeply impressed by the calmness of the Belgian and French peoples in (the) face of threatening war clouds. Here and there in the little villages of Belgium one could see an anxious mother with tears in her eyes as the gendarmes passed from house to house issuing the calling-up papers for three classes, and those of us who had served during the Great War knew that the mothers remembered the holocaust the Belgian nation endured in those early days of 1914.

As one wanders over the lands of France and Belgium, fertile and well-filled, one often wonders are the stones of the war cemeteries not a noble memorial to the insane uselessness of war. Is it again to be that at the bidding of one man, one German, or by his actions, that land must again be wrecked by shells and drenched with pitiless poison gas? Must the cemeteries, British, Belgian, French, and German, large as they are, be made more full still, and beautiful towns, cities, and homes destroyed? It is a crude interpretation of civilisation to think that at the dictates of one man this should ever happen again."[170]

---

[170] Ibid, 2 September 1939.

37970755R00177

Printed in Great Britain
by Amazon